Mary's
Voyage

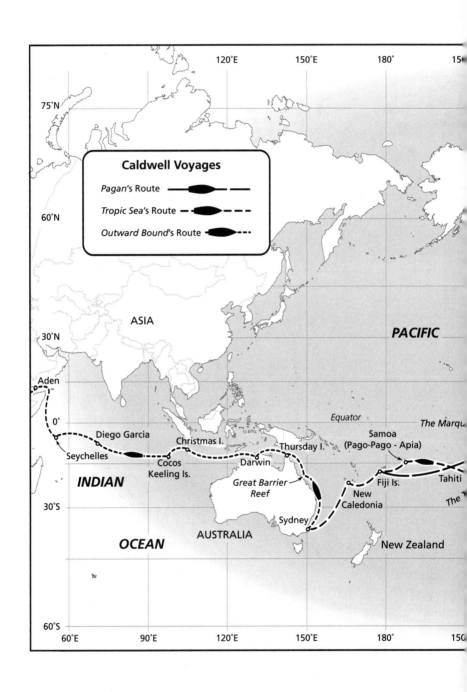

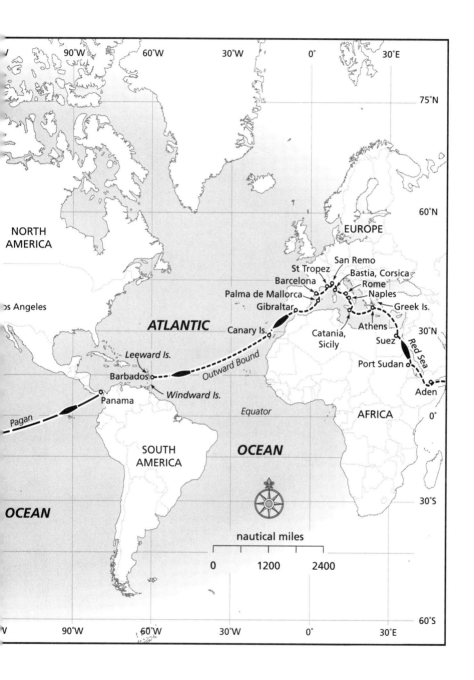

90°W 60°W 30°W 0° 30°E

75°N

60°N

NORTH
AMERICA

EUROPE

San Remo
St Tropez   Bastia, Corsica
Barcelona   Rome
Palma de Mallorca   Naples
Gibraltar   Greek Is.
os Angeles

ATLANTIC

Canary Is.   Athens   30°N
Catania,
Sicily   Suez
Leeward Is.   Port Sudan   Red Sea
Barbados   Aden
Panama   Windward Is.   *Outward Bound*

Pagan

Equator   AFRICA   0°

SOUTH
AMERICA   *OCEAN*

OCEAN   30°S

nautical miles

0   1200   2400

60°S

90°W 60°W 30°W 0° 30°E

copyright@mitroart.com

Mary's Voyage

MARY CALDWELL
and
MATTHEW M. DOUGLAS

SHERIDAN HOUSE

First published 2008 by
Sheridan House Inc.
145 Palisade Street
Dobbs Ferry, NY 10522
www.sheridanhouse.com

Library of Congress Cataloging-in-Publication Data
Caldwell, Mary
    Mary's voyage / Mary Caldwell and Matthew M. Douglas.
        p. cm.
    ISBN 978-1-57409-267-7 (pbk. : alk. paper)
    1. Caldwell, Mary—Travel. 2. Caldwell, John—Travel. 3. Ocean travel.
4. Sailing. 5. Voyages around the world. 6. Oceania—Description and
travel. 7. Caribbean Area—Description and travel. 8. Grenadines (Saint
Vincent and the Grenadines and Grenada)—Description and travel.
9. Palm Island Resort—History. I. Douglas, Matthew M. II. Title.
G540.C25 2008
910.4'5—dc22   2008022959

ISBN 978 1 57409 267 7

Printed in the United States of America

Contents

Acknowledgements

Mary Caldwell and I would like to thank the members of her family who have directly contributed in historical and memorial ways to the writing of this book. We would also like to thank Diane Herbruck for reading a number of early drafts as well as for her fine editorial skills, comments, and suggestions. Credit is also due Jennifer Kaufman for her support and assistance in gathering and organization information for *Mary's Voyage*. Finally, we would like to thank Lothar and Jeannine Simon for their assistance in publishing this memoir of *Family at Sea* and unpublished notes and manuscripts by Mary's deceased husband, John Caldwell.

Dr. Matthew M. Douglas

Foreword

For anyone who's ever had a serious case of wanderlust, *Mary's Voyage* is the ultimate vicarious adventure. Every time I read drafts of this work, I had the itch to sell all my belongings, stow my family and their gear, and take off for parts unknown. What a hearty, adventuresome soul Mary Caldwell was and continues to be!

To think Mary had the gumption to nearly raise her family on board a 35-ft boat! Now that's a woman I'd like to meet! And in some ways, I feel I know her, through this poignant—and often funny—story of her life from California, then sailing the long way around the world, and finally creating the family resort of Palm Island.

I've known Dr. Matthew (Matt) Douglas for twenty five years; for a very good portion of those years, I've "traveled" with him as he's unfolded the Caldwell family stories, both when he created a screenplay adaptation of John's *Desperate Voyage*, and then again as he interviewed Mary and made her story come alive on the page. I continually consulted my atlas, and had to substitute the well-crafted narrative in places I couldn't find on my maps. Through her story, one can see how the fascinating, kind and helpful people she and her family met across the globe truly shaped their world.

I know you'll enjoy this armchair adventure; it should inspire you to consider living a life quite different from the one you now plod through.

Smooth sailing!

Diane Wendover Herbruck, MA
President,
The Wordsmiths, Inc.
Grand Rapids, MI

April 2008

I

The Lure of the Sea

"*E*veryone thinks we're raving lunatics," I complained to John one night as I wrestled to feed our son Johnnie at the dinner table.

"No guts no glory," came the curt response. John shoved more beef into his mouth and chewed thoughtfully. The steely muscles of his arms tightened, reflecting years of sinewy effort spent trimming sails and weighing anchors.

"So *are* we crazy?" I queried again, stuffing more peas into little Johnnie's mouth.

"Of course we are!" he muffled excitedly between bites. He raised a fork and poked it in the air to dramatize his argument: "But look at it this way. The rest of the world is even crazier. It's all about greed and screwing your neighbor and smiling while you do it. So why would anyone in his right mind follow the dumb ass rules set up by the worst of our society? Now, that's sheer lunacy!"

"Yeah, I suppose," I sighed. I had heard similar sermons many times before and I was hopeful John's mood would quickly pass. But it was too late: I had already turned on the spigot to his familiar diatribe. John put down his fork and took the napkin off his lap, folding it neatly on the table. He opened his hands like Buddha.

"Everyone in the States is trapped by his own tiny little brain, his pathetic job, and the need to be safe. Mary, I can't be that way anymore. We need to really *live*! We need *adventure*! What could be better for the entire family?"

He stood up and pointed his finger at his captive audience.

"I have a vision for our whole family—a dream of sailing

around the world! Just think—we'll be the *first family* to ever attempt to do that—now that's *living!*"

Johnnie, then sixteen months, stared appreciatively at his father, who slowly sat down and stabbed his fork into another piece of meat.

"I'd rather die at sea than be buried in California after thirty years of mindless government routine and a gold watch. God save me! Take me out to the backyard and shoot me!"

"Yes," I said, convinced once more. "You're absolutely right."

Looking back after all these years, I realize now that I just wanted to be reassured. I was pregnant and expecting our second child in December of that year. But pregnancy is mundane at best. The lure for both of us was the mystery of the open sea; the feeling that anyone could break away from the drudgeries of everyday life and escape from the stifling cage of civilization. The lure of untold adventure was tempting to the point of obsession. For years we had imagined being pushed by the trade winds, setting anchor in lush tropical bays, and swimming in coral-filled lagoons. A pipe dream? Yes, but one that had possessed both of us since 1949, when we began to save money in earnest for the purchase of a boat.

After that watershed conversation, John and I talked excitedly about our trip virtually every night. We had a first destination on our world adventure: Sydney, Australia, but that was it. There would be no itinerary, no departure date, and no timetable. Our voyage would be up to the fate of the gods and the vagaries of the winds and currents. John was fearless. And because John had no fear I also had no fear.

"I'm no Limey and I've had plenty of experience," he would say with confidence.

And indeed he had! John had learned about the sea the hard way: he had previously attempted a voyage from Panama to Australia aboard the twenty-nine-foot cutter PAGAN to be reunited with me, his Aussie bride, after World War II. Now, that *was* a crazy trip—John had no sailing experience prior to sailing out of Panama. His nearly tragic solo voyage ended on a small island near Fiji, after PAGAN floundered and was smashed on a coral ridge. In the process of failing, however, he learned the brooding ways of the seas and the caprices of a small boat sailing upon it.

Our first job was to find a solid, seafaring boat. I accompanied John on many excursions to boatyards and marinas, searching for just the right vessel. We sized up uncountable masts, hulls, sterns, deck plans, rigs, interior layouts, and power installations in our search for the perfect boat. Then, almost miraculously, we spotted a picture of TROPIC SEAS in a newspaper advertisement. She looked beautiful—decks of Honduras mahogany, a spacious cockpit, and a full six feet of head room for comfortable passage below. Created by the world-renowned boat designer, John Hanna, TROPIC SEAS was geared especially for the treacheries of the South Pacific. But she was so small, just 36 feet—barely the length of a modest family room—what chance could it have against the unpredictable whims of the open ocean? TROPIC SEAS drew only five feet of water (important for navigating through shallow coral-encrusted lagoons) and she was rigged with short masts to prevent breakage during gales when winds could exceed one hundred miles per hour. Best of all, her hull had bent frames of white oak three inches thick, with three remarkable fir strings bracing her from stem to stern. It would take a mighty storm to dismantle this boat!

Of course, I was particularly interested in the comforts provided below decks. After all, if we were going to spend months on the open seas, we needed creature comforts to get us through it all, especially for our overactive Johnnie. I descended below decks and it was love at first sight.

"John!" I shouted. "It's gorgeous down here!"

He scrambled down to join me. His eyes lit up. The small galley had an all-inclusive compactness just within the main hatch. It had wood and kerosene stoves, an icebox, sink, dish lockers, and storage bins. There were transom seats with single bunks above them. A roomy head was at one bunk end and a hanging locker at the other. In mid-cabin was a spacious drop-leaf table to feed my growing crew. Forward of the galley was a second cabin with a double bunk and an incredibly soft sponge-rubber mattress. There was also a hanging locker and more storage space on the starboard side.

"So, you like it?" he asked cautiously.

"It's beautiful!"

I could instantly see the relief spread across his face. TROPIC SEAS was a sailor's dream: It had a forty-horse Gray Marine engine and water tanks with two hundred gallons storage. A full hundred gallons of fuel could be tucked away in tanks beneath the cockpit seats, providing us with a comfortable supply in case we needed fuel to traverse the doldrums. The deck was watertight from hull to hull. TROPIC SEAS was not your typical Los Angeles boat, built to look at and not to sail. She would not be a speed craft, but there was enough room, comfort, and strength to provide faithful service on the greatest of earth's oceans.

"This baby will get us to Australia—hell, it'll take us any-where!" John announced. I clapped with joy and Johnnie followed, not having a clue as to why.

We put our earnest money down and TROPIC SEAS was ours. We moved out of our apartment and aboard the next day. To pay for our "house boat" John took a job as a social worker administering to the welfare of destitute children within Los Angeles County. The job paid poorly as most jobs do that are connected with the general welfare of the community, but extra income from lecture fees and writing allowed us to pay one hundred and twenty-five dollars a month on TROPIC SEAS. Everyday, John would bring home the tra-vails and frustrations of his office: mothers deserted by husbands, women with illegitimate children, women in social turmoil. This was, of course, awful to listen to, but it impressed upon John the weariness and woes of mistreated women in our society. It taught him to be sensitive to women and their special plight in this world.

"There is absolutely nothing I can do for any of them," he complained nightly. "An uncaring society has left them all behind."

Thoughts and intimate talks of adventures on distant seas often rescued us from the mental trauma of dealing with John's constant world of trouble.

"Come on, honey," I would say, "let's go check on our plans." His eyes would brighten and with Johnnie in my lap we would pore over maps of distant islands.

Life on the boat was unique. We lived aboard in the Watchorn Basin of San Pedro's harbor along with the guttural growl of the lighthouse, the blasts and snorts of freighters from around the world, and the chugging of fishing boats and tugs. By night we worked and planned, constantly changing lists of things that had to be purchased and things that had to be done. Our to-do lists seemed interminable. But we always kept the vision alive: once we were done with the preparations and on our way we knew the wind would be free. And we would be free as well.

"Smell that air!" John gushed one night after Johnnie was tucked into bed. I played into his mood.

"It smells like the tropics of northern Australia!"

"Yeah, the tropics! Nothing beats the doldrums of life like the tropics." Of course, it really smelled like the bowels of San Pedro harbor, but it scarcely mattered. Our imaginations had become our reality.

2

Practice Makes Perfect

We would take our home out often, learning firsthand about the prevailing winds and ocean currents throughout the year. We quickly discovered that high winds could swoop down quite unexpectedly over California's costal waters. It happened the second day we sailed. I remember watching the filmy horsetail-like clouds moving quickly across the sky as the wind stiffened. We were flying over the waves when a huge rolling swell suddenly drew us shoreward toward the hills of Santa Barbara. The wind began to whine in the rigging and the rolling of the boat made me dizzy and queasy. Then seasickness swept over us. I held Johnnie in front of me with my arms slung under his stomach as he vomited like water from a fireman's hose across the deck.

"Mommy!" he cried. "I so sick!" He grabbed his little potbelly.

"We'll make it stop," I gasped.

It was not an honest promise. I remember being unable to walk and like Johnnie I began to vomit and continued to heave until I could retch no more. Finally, John grew sick just watching us but somehow he managed to stagger around and was not completely overwhelmed by the growling swells beneath us. He crawled to the engine and tried to start it to no avail. Years of lack of use had fouled it. I clambered below with little Johnnie, holding him tight and reassuring him that everything would be fine, but my stomach still contracted violently and the room spun out of control.

I secured Johnnie in his crib and ventured up to the deck and saw John furiously working on the engine. He cussed profusely. Nothing.

He hunched and panted like a Tasmanian devil over its kill, pulling this, shaking that. Then there was a sputter, followed by another, and in a moment the reticent engine smoked to a clanging life.

"Get the tiller down!" he shouted to me over the deafening sound of the gale.

"Yes *sir!*" I shouted back with a weak hand salute. He smiled.

While John worked the engine I shoved the tiller down and TROPIC SEAS slammed headlong into the pitching swells. The breaking water and sea froth boiled over the deck, drenching us to the bone and making our footing precarious. We clung to our posts, not speaking, concentrating on the storm around us. After an hour or so we had made some progress away from the treacherous coast, but the most demanding period was yet to come. We fought the rising seas all night, taking turns at the tiller, two hours on, two hours off: John sick but seaworthy, me sick and not so seaworthy, with a vomit basin my constant companion. A day later, totally exhausted, we pulled into harbor. Of five massive storms that battered the California coast that winter, we rode out three on the high seas, getting used to seasickness and vomit. To our total surprise Johnnie quickly became immune to seasickness.

We saved like monks to pay off the boat: no dining out, no movies, no new clothes, and no repairs on our car—which disintegrated at an exponential rate every time we started the engine. Unexpected royalties from John's *Desperate Voyage* often buoyed us and kept us just a few days away from bankruptcy. And sometimes a fee from one of John's *Desperate Voyage* lectures bought food for a week. A year later we had half of TROPIC SEAS paid off and added a new member, Stevie, to the family in December 1950. He became a crewmember at the age of three days. He was such a precious baby. By twenty-one days Stevie had a solid sea stomach and sported a devil-may-care jack-tar grin.

We rode out several other storms that year with Stevie packed between pillows on the cabin floor and Johnnie wrapped in blankets under the main cabin table. The fight for control in the many storms we encountered seemed never-ending. I became a veteran at the tiller, holding the boat to course even in the roughest and

wickedest of oceans. Although I tried not to show it, I constantly
worried about the children below decks, wrapped up and immobile.
I would crane my neck to listen for the smallest whine but miraculously it never came. Mothers know the different cries of their babies. They can distinguish a cry of panic from a cry of pain, a cry of
hunger from a cry of discomfort; and mothers can also hear their
children cry even over the seemingly deafening sound of a gale.
When Stevie did cry it was always because of hunger, not fear, and I
would have to leave my post at the tiller to breast-feed, and then
John would do double-duty on deck. By the end of the next year we
were a fearless team, a crew that toiled calmly and logically even in
the height of adversity. We were ready to face the Pacific!

When 1952 came we were still in San Pedro with just a few jobs
remaining on our to-do list.

"How does June 1st sound?" asked John one night at the dinner
table.

"To . . . ?"

"To leave, of course . . . to set off for Australia!"

"Oh my God," I responded. "That sounds perfect! Do you think
we can be ready?"

"Absolutely."

Those months were full of anxious dreams. The hours dragged
on in John's choking office, and at dinner he would gaze off into
space a good deal of time. Each free moment I had from the children was spent mulling over plans and preparations. I needed to
coordinate food supplies, medical supplies, and think of indestructible games and toys that would last aboard our home. John surrounded himself with sailor friends, one of whom had twice
girdled the globe in an engineless thirty-foot yawl. At the tender
age of 75 he finally "broke down" as he described it and married a
much younger woman. Then he set out to circumnavigate the
world again with his new bride. His yawl floundered in a hurricane
in the New Hebrides, but he came back to California at 81 and built
another boat. John's friends were very much like him: independent,
daring, confident, and full of free spirit. It was only natural that I
developed a similar personality; the ordinary fears of life became

quite trivial for me and adventure became the bedrock upon which my soul existed.

Then suddenly an event arose that threatened to destroy our sandcastle dreams: I was pregnant again. We were at once excited and dismayed, confused and uncertain. We wanted both our trip and our baby, but how could we have both? What woman in her right mind would sail pregnant halfway around the world with no doctor for prenatal care, no doctor to help deliver the baby, not to mention a firm destination for delivery? This dilemma stretched even my adventuresome spirit. We discussed the situation fervently, quietly at night, as if someone might eavesdrop and chastise us for even thinking such foolishness.

"I don't know if I can do this," I confided in John one evening.

"Baby, don't worry . . . I'll be there to help you! We're a team!"

"But what about storms and hurricanes? What if we're off course and stuck in the doldrums for a month or more? What will we do if *you* have to deliver our baby on the high seas? Worse, what happens if there's trouble with the pregnancy?"

"I'll do whatever I've got to do to make this work," he said emphatically. "Don't forget, I've been through far worse! I've eaten shoe leather, drunk motor oil, and eaten seabirds alive just trying to survive long enough to see you once again in Australia! Nothing would stop me on this adventure. Nothing. I'd deliver triplets if I had to and grow another nipple to nurse them!" I laughed and choked back the tears. Being pregnant was hard on the bladder.

"OK," was all I could muster.

John exuded supreme confidence and our spirit of adventure prevailed. With good passage John thought we could manage to have the baby in Tahiti. What craziness! Most women were planning on which *hospital* to have their baby. We were planning which *island* we'd have the baby, assuming of course that we lived in a perfect world, that everything would go as planned, and that we would even be close to Tahiti near delivery day (which as every woman knows is never when the doctors say).

Now, John was an avid student of the great modern philosophers. Descartes said that life cries to be lived and Camus said to live to the point of tears. According to John, most people do neither and instead live prison-like lives of desperation and sameness. John was very persuasive to the point where I felt I had become John's student (although not a perfect one because he often scolded me for reading trashy novels instead of quality philosophical treatises). In the end we agreed to go with our dreams but we decided to tell no one of my pregnancy. We did not want to listen to admonishments from our friends, and besides, what baby would prefer the smog and rush of Los Angeles to the peace and purity of a tropical island? Yes, we would have another baby and a fantastic family voyage. We *could* and *would* do both!

As if a sign from above, the next day a big check came in from a translation of John's book, *Desperate Voyage*, and we knew in a moment of imagined divine revelation that our long fight with indecision was over. We would go. There was an ecstatic scramble aboard TROPIC SEAS. Store lists, job lists, and gear lists were finalized and completed. All was omitted but what was of the absolute essence for health and for the morale of our crew at sea. As the old whaler men put it, "No more cats than can catch mice."

3

~~~~~~~~~~~~~~~~~~

The Dream Begins

On May 8, 1952, John walked away from his office a free man—free from traffic, free from phones, free from a society of abused women and their unsolvable problems. Somehow word leaked out that our leaving was imminent and over the next few weeks a stream of visitors entertained us: people who had always dreamed of doing what we were about to do. We left at twelve sharp on departure day. John cut the mooring lines so there could be no turning back. People packed the wharves to wave us off. I tended to the children, holding both of them up to wave to the crowd.

"Hey babe!" he shouted at me from his perch in the mainsail, "We're on our way!"

I remember tears of excitement and trepidation filling my heart. We were really going to sail to Australia—my homeland! John came down, gave me a huge bear hug and then scrambled back up on the sails.

We had a smooth passage out of the harbor to Avalon where we stopped for a week to ready our ship. In Avalon Johnnie and I found a whimpering kitten cowering behind a wall. John said it reminded him of the kittens on PAGAN that provided company, entertainment, and solace during his long solo voyage. We rowed the kitten out to TROPIC SEAS and signed him on as crew.

"He's adorable! What should we name him?" I asked Johnnie.

"Fraidy Cat!" came the immediate reply.

"OK, Fraidy the Cat it is!"

"No," he admonished, *"Fraidy Cat!"*

"Oh . . . *Fraidy Cat!*"

"Yeah, 'cause he's 'fraid of the water!"

There was no immediate reason to leave Avalon (after all, we agreed there would be no itinerary except for a birth in Tahiti). One day John and I were tied two-to-two in canasta. He hated losing to anyone, but especially to me. Suddenly he felt the "urge" (as he put it) to set sail just before the fifth game. He knew I was going to win that fifth game and that was the immediate stimulus that provoked us to truly depart from California. I would remind John of this incident many times over the years. Of course, he conveniently forgot the conditions under which he felt the need to set sail. So much for the frail male ego!

We sailed through the decaying battlements of World War II, among bustling naval monsters, past an island crammed with fighter aviation. It was a dour sight for the first leg of our tropical adventure. No matter, we were finally on our way. We both felt a bit jittery upon departure, but our spirits were buoyed by a huzzah of foghorns, catcalls, and tossed leis from nearby craft. Everyone seemed so excited for our adventure. I remember the sky was cerulean blue and the heat of the sun seemed to draw us out of the channel. I had washed Stevie's diapers before we sailed and John hung them to fly and dry cheerily in the windward rigging for all to see. (Diapers dried this way were always fluffy soft; I recommend it to every housewife.)

We were a gay and carefree little world unto ourselves, buzzing merrily along under full sail, past the hungry eyes of regimented American men yearning for freedom. I held fast to the tiller; Johnnie and Stevie waved to passing boats. John unfurled Old Glory across the stern. We ran for the close-lying Coronados group, sixteen miles to the south of Point Loma. We dropped a starboard anchor in fifty feet of water and were treated as rank intruders by a shimmering school of seals that barked and wailed at us from their rocky haven. I went below to cook dinner while John and Johnnie readied the decks and gear, securing everything just in case the weather changed. I served my first hearty sea meal in a glowing cabin of warmth. Afterwards, we bedded our sons in the snug forecabin and then turned to reading relaxation as the boat swayed softly like a crib in a tree. In the morning we would be on the first great leg of our trip; it would be over three thousand miles before the Marquesas exposed their tropical shores to us.

That night we talked about John's voyage on the PAGAN, as we often did. He never told me everything, but he always expressed how much he missed me and how he would have done anything and everything (and he did) to be reunited with me after World War II.

"I would have walked across a thousand miles of hot Fijian coals to be reunited with you, Mary," he said softly, gently kissing my face and neck. We were steering together into the starlit night and he hugged me closely, running his hand up and down my waist.

"I was so worried!" I stammered. "I heard nothing for months! Not even a sign that someone had spotted you!"

"And I remember when I was dying from starvation, your image kept me going. After I shipwrecked I knew I was drowning. Hell, I weighed just eighty pounds! But I saw images of you. I couldn't have done it without you even though you weren't there."

"Oh, I was there, all right, I was there," I said softly, kissing him on the tip of his nose. I placed his hand on my bosom. "I'll always be there for you." He leaned his head on mine and stayed like that without speaking for a very long time. Then the memories of that awful voyage returned, as they often did when he slept.

John reflected on the brutality he experienced from the Pacific on that trip. His memories created a frightening conversation about our current trip. Was there a reef, a sea monster, or a freak happenstance waiting to take our lives? Perhaps a fire would start by spontaneous combustion or one of us would have an unexpected appendicitis attack, or worst of all, perhaps I would suffer a miscarriage or early birth. What would we do? If there was to be a turning back, it would have to be now.

John and I looked around the cabin and we both smiled at each other. No, there would be no turning back. Our boat was fit and so were we.

The next morning we sailed for Guadalupe, a high, solitary rocky island jutting up from the ocean floor, about 150 miles off the Mexican coast.

The sea was not terribly rough during this passage, but because of morning sickness I preferred to stay on deck and tend the steering rather than face the lurching galley below. I actually would get sicker breathing in the stale cabin air when the motion of the boat grew lively. So it fell to John to change Stevie's diapers, feed him his baby food, make up his bottles, cook our meals, and wrestle with the dishes in the bouncing galley. It was my job to make the bunks, bathe the kids, sweep and swab below, and keep the cabin shipshape. This plan worked well for the ensuing days: I manned the tiller and John became the housewife (which was unheard of sixty years ago). I steered the tiller by choice and for the sheer love of it. I enjoyed every zephyr of wind coming my way and the freedom it brought to my senses.

A few days later we were steering into a westerly, damp and penetrating, bringing our crew gray seas and skies. Blankets were moist and when John changed Stevie he remarked that the baby had the sniffles. We worried about Stevie's health constantly because a California doctor had told us before the voyage that our baby was born with a defective immune system and would have serious developmental problems. But worrying never accomplishes anything constructive. Another bleak day came out of the east and there was the damnable gray world of continuing wet and cold. Stevie's sniffles had worsened to a congested head and throat and Johnnie was also coming on with a cold. With the extra care for the children some of our obligatory chores fell behind and we soon fell into a day-and-night sea routine that targeted us for fatigue. We floundered near Guadalupe, but could not see it because of the weather. John listened intently for the sound of waves breaking on a rocky shoreline. Nothing. He turned to me:

"What'd you think, Mary? Should we try to find land or make a run for the South Seas?" I could tell from the tone of his voice that he was unsure.

"You can't see anything out here . . . what if we crash on the rocks at night?" I responded. He stiffened.

"I'm *sure* I could hear a rocky shore if we were close. I think we should keep our southerly course and bypass Guadalupe."

"Well, OK," I said, just to be agreeable, but I was certainly not convinced. I could tell John was not convinced either.

Then a cold dark sea closed in and John could see the despair setting in my face. I turned and went below decks.

"OK, that does it," he said flatly. "You've left me with no choice." He turned to Johnnie: "C'mon, son, we've got business to do!"

With that pronouncement he followed me below decks with Johnnie. Down in the bowels of our boat they mixed up a greasy and fishy-smelling sandwich from salad dressing, margarine, catsup, tomatoes, onions, canned fish, and pork and beans. They proceeded to down this gruesome hash with great noisy gusto directly in front of me. The more the ship rolled, the more boisterous they were with their gorging and smacking sounds. It was too much. They showed absolutely no respect for a pregnant, seasick woman! I dove for the bunk and turned to the hull side to avoid looking at them. Their laughter drowned out the slapping waves until I mentioned that they would have to take care of little Stevie. That immediately dulled their enthusiasm for torturing a pregnant woman!

The next day brought calming weather, still cold, but not so damp. And Stevie's condition had worsened during the night. He was pale. His chest and throat were clogged with mucus, and he would flush with every cough. I placed him in a warm baby blanket and laid him on my chest to give him a mother's comfort and warmth. His head nuzzled next to mine as he wheezed constantly. Every groan drew him closer to me. I watched his face, gently stroked his cheeks, and studied his closed eyes for any indication of coming out of it, but his lung congestion was obviously getting worse and I became much more apprehensive. John came below decks to check on Stevie.

"He's not improving. We need a doctor . . . and soon." I said quietly to John.

"I'll add a twin spinnaker to port to give us more push." He gently placed his huge sailor's hand on Stevie's head to check his elevated temperature and then went above decks.

We passed many grim and anxious hours. Stevie's temperature climbed to one hundred and three and I decided to administer penicillin for the first time, by hypodermic. I agonized as I pushed the cold merciless needle into the upper, outer portion of his buttock where the muscle mass is greatest and there is less danger of damaging the nerves serving the leg. I then bundled him and cradled him, red-faced, in my arms. Neither of us slept that night. All our hopes and plans were crumbling from the unknown pathogen attacking our son.

I gave John childcare duties and went above decks to steer the last few hours before dawn. I was in a state of exhausted semi-consciousness. Then I heard a horrifying crash come up from the galley. I scrambled below and then stopped dead in my tracks halfway down the stairs. Stevie sat there, peering over the bunk boards, contemplating a pile of John's navigating books, sailing directions, and precious copies of great philosophical tomes that he had hurled off the shelf.

"He's better!" I gasped, picking up the little hellion.

"He's more than better, I'd say," said John, bending to scoop up his books. I snickered silently as John assessed the damage and rejoiced as Stevie worked hard at his old job of wrecking the contents of the boat. True, he was still wan, feverish, and shaky, but he was in his typical destructive mood and conclusive evidence that he was getting better. Our family dream was on!

The sun broke through that day, the first sun in five days. The cockpit dried out, the blankets and bedding and clothing were brought up above decks to air out. Using the sextant, John plotted our position at latitude 26 degrees and 55 minutes west and longitude 117 degrees 40 minutes west. A westerly slapped us along and our thoughts turned to the northeast trade winds. Ah, it was the perfect time to do five days of laundry! John helped me hitch a fifty-foot length of half-inch line to the rail. Near the line's end, and between its strands, John pulled a corner of a dozen diapers, a leg of Johnnie's trousers, and a sheet. Four hours of dragging these astern through a rippling wake and they were clean. I hung them to dry on a line strung in the windward rigging.

"What a washing machine! I wonder who first thought of that?" I queried.

"Yeah, it's the only way to go . . . that's how I washed all my clothes—when I had them—on PAGAN in '49."

John was claiming credit, of course, for this obvious laundry day innovation at sea! Johnnie, oblivious to it all, fed the large brown albatross that would strafe the boat as he threw bread high into the air.

"Mom, more bread!" he shouted, pointing to the circling birds.

"OK, one more piece and that's it!" I admonished, using the bargaining strategy every parent grows to know and hate. I continued folding the diapers, not looking up to avoid eye contact with the pleading monster.

"Aw jeez!" came the expected retort. Of course, one piece of bread led to another then another until an entire loaf was gone and the game really was over. But that was just fine with us. Little Johnnie, in the innocent excitement of youth, had captivated these noble soaring birds of the open seas.

4

Searching for the Trade Winds

We were nine days out and still searching for the northeastern trade winds that would carry us across much of the Pacific. The expected winds were weak to nonexistent and John was quite depressed. He and I spoke idly but with a tone of helplessness. We could only wait. Then suddenly we heard the boat's gear chatter and clank. The decks swayed and a distinct freshness came into the air. A great field of cat's-paws, riffling and graying the surface of the sea, moved over us. The wind grew from the right direction, and in a few moments John and I were both sitting up ecstatic that the trades were finally filling our sails. Our sea days would become more routine for the foreseeable future as TROPIC SEAS spread her wings.

I awoke every morning with Johnnie and Stevie crawling over me, yelling and screaming like little warriors, attacking my arms and legs. My boys were always ready for rough and tumble, but at such an early morning hour all I could do was watch the cabin sway in circles and listen to the creaking sound of the vessel as it plied through the calm waters. The routine for those weeks of pleasant sailing was always the same: once the boys were up there was no such thing as going back to sleep. I would quickly make myself ready for the day and get the breakfast going. While the oatmeal boiled John would undress Stevie and place him on the head. Above decks I would make the complaining boys fasten their lifelines, which connected to the mizzen.

"Why do we have to?" Johnnie would chronically complain before I cut him off.

"Get them on or you'll be grounded below decks all day!"

Then we would have canned orange juice, and eggs (which were soft-boiling on one burner as coffee percolated on the other) served with biscuits baked in the primus oven. Afterwards we would tend to the morning dishes. I would wash them in the bucket and lay them to drain in the small metal bathtub. Johnnie was always a particularly eager washer, washing them over and over, but the breakage was appalling and so after the third day I told him that "Mommy needed to do the dishes." The sad look on his face was enough to make me cry with guilt!

The mornings were now just incredibly beautiful. Easy-going white-crested rollers pushed the boat, and the air grew balmier with each day passing. We were all elated to the point of bursting with unsung joy. The whole family would whistle and break into song whenever the mood urged us to do so. This is not to say that things were always calm. The boys were sometimes mischievous to the point of distraction, with their constant pounding on each other. They jabbered incessantly, jumping up and down as they pulled on our clothes, questioning, demanding, and crying for favors. But we expected this. They were children full of life and despite the constant attention they required, they were the joy of our life.

We went through our ritualistic bathing every afternoon. Seawater was bucketed into the tub, and the boys were immersed, fighting and splashing each other. While they occupied themselves we lathered them up and then rinsed them down with overflowing buckets of seawater. When they had been thoroughly scrubbed we pulled them out of the tub like puppy dogs, our hands under their armpits from the back, our fingers covering their chests to prevent them from slipping out of our hands, as they struggled with their little legs kicking furiously into the air. After a brisk rubdown we would lay them in a sunny spot on deck, their naked butts pointed skyward. Then John and I would wash unabashedly naked in the same tub and afterward lay down in decadent sun worshipping (no sunscreen back then) for as long as we pleased. There could be no more blissful, back-to-nature days than the ones we experienced as a family at sea. No television. No phones. No civilization to interfere with our lives. Nature in the raw allowed us to experience and live life to the fullest.

By noon John would be in the galley boiling the night's offering of flying fish, warming soup, and heating up water for tea. I would make sandwiches from biscuits filled with meat spread or cheese. I would open a tin of pork and beans and another of fruit and pass all of this through the hatchway to the waiting hands of Johnnie, who rarely failed to dump the sandwiches or wash down the cockpit with tea. The best part of lunch was that it was leisurely—not the hasty stuffing-of-the-face during office hours. Instead, it was a time for special indulgence; we actually tasted the food, remarked on its quality and realized that it did not matter in the least if lunch took one or two hours. Who cared? There was no clock to order us back to work.

After lunch, John would bed the boys down for a two-hour nap. Suddenly a calm would spread over the boat. Some days, while the children slept, we would just sit on the deck and contemplate in disbelief that we were thousands of miles away from the nearest land, not even close enough to see sea birds. We could feel the faintest zephyr of wind, hear the slap of the waves on the hull, talk languidly about absolutely nothing, then read whatever we wished as we periodically looked up and watched the ocean in the distance. John called his delving into philosophical works his "vita contemplative," after Descartes. But I avoided the verbal morass of the philosophers and would dive into my trashy novels that I found much more stimulating and closer to the human condition than any obtuse discourse by Nietzsche. John would say:

"You're frittering away your life on cheap detective novels. You're trapped by the blood and gore of common murder and skullduggery!"

But I would respond in kind:

"And you are not in charge of my intellect!" That always

seemed to quiet him for a while, until I finished a novel and tossed it overboard.

"Now you're polluting the Pacific with your printed tripe? You'll kill the fish!"

But I would just laugh and he would grin out of the side of his mouth because he knew he would never win this battle. His lofty readings never rubbed off on me!

Below decks, John often burdened himself with the comprehension of over fifty weighty tomes of philosophical mishmash to fill the hours; but I was frequently drawn to reading my trashy novels while steering the boat. For some reason I loved being in charge of the direction the boat was taking so I frequently called down to John for the state of sea and the wind, which he dutifully delivered in a booming captain-like voice. Sometimes I could tell by the tone of his voice that I had interrupted his concentration of a particularly difficult passage and I would smile to myself. I also gave him all the responsibilities for seagoing information, galley cooking, engine maintenance, cruising hints, and precautions if shipwrecked. These were his domains. I really had no interest in being at sea and reading about it too!

Too soon the two-hour nap would be over and our bounding boys would tumble onto deck demanding cookies and other goodies. If they took a good nap and had kept property destruction in the morning to a minimum, we would plan an afternoon party. Out came the phonograph; up came the box of indestructible toys; cookies or candy or tinned fruit were brought on deck; popcorn popped in the galley; and gay cowboy music would waft across the deck to confound a shoal of flying fish or a passing seafaring bird. The rumbling of trucks, the toot of trains, and the thunder of aircraft were interspersed mysteriously with moments of silence. The food would disappear as John and I drank our afternoon tea, bringing back a little of Australia to our mid-ocean adventure.

Every other day John would slip below deck and return to perch atop the sliding hatch with his sextant in hand, an instrument

John with his sextant in hand

designed to determine our location on the planet. He would take into account distance run and direction, and with solemnity he would announced our position. We then studied our location on the charts and tried to act surprised: We were making slow time. But we did not care; we returned to our fun. This, after all, was what we had always dreamed about. Our family was at sea without a care in the world, riding a sturdy boat on the northeast trade wind across a balmy tropical ocean. We were so much closer as a family. I think we intuitively and reflexively understood each other as few families ever do. We could breathe! What was the hurry for anything? Sometimes the biggest concern on our minds was whether or not we should brush our teeth immediately after a meal or wait a while. Usually it was "Let's wait a while."

Later in the afternoon John would pull in the laundry line, yank away the sea-washed items, and string them out on the rigging to dry during the night. As the days passed I began to take more and more control of the tiller and John began to pick up the domestic housekeeping slack below decks. He would tidy the cockpit as well as any woman and begin to cook dinner. His meals were good but guided by bachelor simplicity: curry and rice, spaghetti and meatballs, macaroni and cheese, wieners and sauerkraut, stew. Because most of our food was in cans the can-opener was our most important tool aboard. Losing it always created an uproar that required immediate attention. When there were complaints from the younger crew, he would often remark, "We can always have cold salt horse and stale sea biscuits like they were forced to eat on whaling ships of old!" It was an idle threat, of course, and with dinner balancing on our knees, we would talk in soft tones that seemed to blend in with the dark as it slowly immersed us. The setting sun at open sea is always a beautiful and frightening experience. We felt so alone in the dark of night with strange sounds engulfing the boat, thousands of miles from the nearest landfall, but yet we were never lonely.

When bedtime arrived it was John who typically went below to put Stevie in his diapers and sleepers: new pajamas given by his grandmother before we sailed. He would trundle them to their forebunk, lay and adjust them carefully as if preparing them for a launch, and adjust the fish netting on the sides of their bunks to a tauntness that would prevent them from rolling onto the sole in their sleep. Then he would carefully adjust ten specially made pillows against the bulkheads to shield their little heads from bumps. He was a strong man and often bull-headed, but he was a watchful father. The children, exhausted by the day's activities and the fresh air of the open sea would fall asleep just moments after I kissed them on their foreheads. Quickly the mist of sleep would take them over and the peacefulness on their faces is something that I have never forgotten.

John and I would remain on deck for another hour or so, captivated by the cooling air of the sea night and the mystery of the stars that literally hung from the sky, radiant without interference of light pollution from the cities. The moon would always cast a shimmering roadway across our course. We would talk for a few moments and then words were out of place. We sat. We watched. And we listened. We would begin to drift off and I would leave first, giving John a goodnight kiss before turning in below. John would remain a while longer, perhaps thinking of Plato as he flashed his searchlight across the deck and through the rigging for a final check. After everything met with his satisfaction, he would then accompany me below for a few minutes before taking up his watch.

Throughout calm nights TROPIC SEAS would be by herself, unwatched and drifting silently on the rhythms of the ocean. But most nights we took turns at the watch: two hours on, two hours off. We always lashed our storm lantern to the top of the cabin as a warning to any ship that although unlikely, might pass nearby. John was always a fitful sleeper and he would awake every hour to see to the decks. Occasionally I would also look in on the boys where they lay behind the fish net, swaying gently in the ship's roll. But we returned easily to sleep until predawn when I would hear Johnnie's fingers searching across the table in the gray light, looking for cookies placed there for him and Stevie in order to hold back their hunger until daylight, which was their signal to attack us in our bunks.

A week of this idyllic pace placed us in latitude 16 degrees 20 minutes north and longitude 122 degrees 10 minutes west, roughly twelve hundred miles west of Acapulco. We had two thousand miles yet to cover until our arrival at Taiohae Bay for the birth of our third child. We had been banking on forty to eighty miles a day but had only made twenty. At five knots we would be doing about sixty miles a day; with an ideal wind TROPIC SEAS would be doing about seven knots. We talked it over and decided to raise the main and mizzen and take off the starboard twin spin to help speed our passage. I unlashed the helm and with our regular sail and the port spinnaker pulling, we made great time with a lessening of motion. That night we saw John's cherished old friend, the Southern Cross. John and I had courted beneath these stars and we selfishly thought of them as ours, especially now that we were headed back to Australia. We sat up late reminiscing over those days of the war and our first meeting, when we served together in the Royal Australian Air Force in Canberra.

"You thought I was cute back then, admit it," he said.

"Perhaps a bit," I responded with a tease.

"And to think I had to swab the floor in your office as punishment for flirting with you!"

"Well, I was watching your rear go back and forth. Quite nice, it was." I reached out for his hand and patted the back of it with my other hand.

"So I was just a cheap sex toy!"

"Absolutely . . . you still are!"

"Oh, that's *it!*" And he chased me around the boat until I allowed him to catch me.

5

The Doldrums

Our greater speed required that we take turns with periodic night watches. This altered the routine of the first pleasant days of plying the waters without a care, riding the trade winds. Because we were often tired in the morning, we were required to take both morning and afternoon naps, which meant less party time for the boys. Fortunately for the coming baby greater boat speed translated into distances of a hundred miles or more per day. But boredom and lack of adult attention brought mutiny from the boys. It started when Stevie, in an unguarded moment, threw John's navigation notebook into the toilet. The first fifteen days of our voyage were lost forever. Next, Johnnie filled the ship's clock with water. John had to rinse it clear with kerosene. On June 5 we had an additional surprise. A big black cloud bringing a massive rainsquall caught up with us from the northeast. Within a few minutes we had three inches of water in the cockpit that should have drained out immediately. John investigated and found the boys had plugged the scupper holes with toys, rope yarns, clothespins, marbles, fishhooks, and other objects. After cleaning out the scuppers, John made some wooden plugs to fit the holes and pounded them in place so prying fingers would be frustrated. Of course, during stormy weather we removed the scupper plugs.

We began to run out of things to occupy Johnnie in particular. Fishing was good for perhaps an hour; perching him on the deckhouse with an old pair of binoculars and telling him to watch for ships and land was good for a little longer; but the best task was having him pump out the bilges, which he did at least four times daily. Stevie was good for two hours with the galley pots and pans, but it took me half an hour to find where he had crammed them in lockers, the bilges, and other miscellaneous crevices. Other "jobs" he enjoyed were emptying the contents of the silverware drawer onto the floor, rolling the fire extinguisher through the main cabin, and smearing oleomargarine atop the iron ballast.

But this was just the beginning of the obvious signs of impending mutiny. We once let Johnnie wash the dishes, alone. He did a wonderful job. Not only did he wash the dishes, but also our tools, the alarm clock, and our only two flashlights. The flashlights died that night, which left us lightless on pitch night watches—not a good development when the swells picked up. Two days later, the clock died the same faltering death as the flashlights. Shortly after, Fraidy Cat turned up missing. We searched the boat thoroughly and thought he had gone overboard during the night, perhaps chasing flying fish on deck. Then, a day later, we heard a pathetic wail from deep inside TROPIC SEAS and we found Fraidy Cat where Johnnie had ensconced him—in the wood stove. Finally, Johnnie required the administration of well-meted corporal punishment after he was caught pumping our freshwater into the galley sink!

June 12 dawned as a classically tropical day: warm and breezy with blue skies. We carried on long conversations about what our friends must think of us, how carefree we were, and how we were blessed to be experiencing such a wonderful adventure. Ah! The brush of the gentle breeze, the sea spray, and the starry nights! Who could possibly ask for more? But as the day grew, long shocks of cirrus clouds began to creep up on the horizon. We called them "serious" clouds because they always warned of impending storms. By noon ugly knotted nimbus heads washed over us, bulging and darkening the sky, closing us in. The air grew more humid and soon our booms were lurching back-and-forth across the decks. John lowered the main and sent the kids down below just as a fifty-mile-per-hour wind slammed broadside into TROPIC SEAS. Our panicked cries greeted each other in mid air as we scurried to tie everything down.

"Hang onto the tiller!" John screamed.

"Watch out! The boom is flying!" I shouted back.

Then, as quickly as the storm had appeared, the sea calmed. But that was just the beginning of a string of violent storms. All night long we were beaten with a series of squalls that made us wonder where we were being carried. That night we thought many times of our fortunate friends and relatives who were undoubtedly lounging in their dry, stable living rooms!

The next day presented us with unsettled weather and a disturbed sea. Squalls marched across the horizon in regular procession. I was constantly seasick but I felt most comfortable steering the tiller, so John thoughtfully placed a heavy pot at my side for vomiting before he went to tend to the flapping sails and swinging booms. Earlier we thought perhaps we had crossed the doldrums and into the southeast trades. Now, John pointed out to me the unmistakable signs of another gathering gale.

"Look, Mary! You can see it building on the horizon. Watch those distant crests." He pointed to white caps far in the distance.

"How do you tell which ones will be the worst?" I shouted over the increasing gale winds.

"Look at the width of the wave; the bigger the width, the greater the power. The root of those waves runs deep. They can really take you for a ride."

The seas grew and finally began pouring over the port bow. John secured the children in their bunks with toys and tightened the netting that prevented them from being thrown onto the floor. I recall being not only sick to my stomach but terrified at the specter of the ocean's water shooting over the deck and piling up six inches deep in the cockpit. John lashed on the storm sail and I lashed the tiller hard alee. We then battened ourselves in, brought the boys from their bunks to the main cabin and went into the galley to fight for a steaming "homemade" meal—canned chicken this time. Something about hot chicken that soothes almost every human woe. I placed a wet towel across the table to anchor the pans of food and we all ate as though it were our last meal. Then we went for candy and the cookie jar. That's the way to get through a gale at sea—*eat!* A full stomach is protection against seasickness. The sea howled outside and we bounced around like rag dolls inside the cabin, but we were together and determined. No gale was going to put us out of business!

By morning the wind had died and now calm became our tormentor—the doldrums we thought we had already crossed earlier now wrapped their fingers around us in a tight grip. But several days later gales sprang up again, with whitecaps crashing into TROPIC SEAS from every direction. John cried out to me:

"Steer tight!"

That meant to move the tiller only if necessary. I was an expert by now and fearlessly worked the tiller, bringing us back to main course time and time again. I was secretly proud of my abilities and the admiring look in John's eyes agreed with my personal assessment.

"Not bad!" he shouted. I just grinned.

And then once again the deadly calm. It was hard to decide what we preferred: moving in a storm in the southern seas or experiencing the bobbing motion induced by the deadly calm of the doldrums. A few hours later the sea changed again, and seemed to change with each passing minute, first a south swell followed by the down-rolling of northeast surges. There was still no wind and the seas often broke ranks and charged us from left and right. We would climb great peaks and then drop sharply into a valley between the waves. To keep our seats we were forced to brace ourselves across the cockpit and hang onto the coamings.

"So these are the doldrums?" John shouted almost accusingly to me.

"I thought we'd have flat seas and a blinding sun like you told me."

"Well, I'm not in charge of the weather!" he shot back.

All around us were hillocks of pitching water running in every direction, with rain, overcast, and cold. John had had enough. He fired the engine. We ran true south to cross the punishing doldrums quicker because the constant shouldering by charging seas in every direction is harder on the hull and more damaging than a full gale's pounding. A gale hits from one direction, but these doldrums seas would one moment twist, the next buckle, then bend and lift both bow and stern at the same time, or drop from under and come back broadside. The seas were deadly but the screams of joy from the boys every time the boat lurched added a comic irony to our situation.

"More!" Johnnie would scream from the cabin below. "More!"

We waited and said virtually nothing to each other, watching the passing waves as we plowed through them. Then I noticed the wide lurching of the mizzen sail flogging in ever-increasing circles.

"John, look out!" I screamed.

John was horrified to find that a clamping U-bolt that held the shrouds around the mast on the opposite side of the cheek block had slipped. This was really bad news. The mast could go any moment, leaving us as helpless as a duck without a tail.

"I'm going to lower the sail! Steer low in the pit and watch your head!"

He lashed the shrouds together with heavy line as high as he could reach. With luck the mast would hold until morning. Without luck we would lose it and the helmsman, compass, tiller, and rudder might be seriously damaged, hopelessly stranding us in the middle of the Pacific at the whim of any weather or current that came our way.

"Honey," he screamed, "get below *now*!"

Under normal circumstances I would fight this, but this time I listened, too terrified to drum up any complaint. John raised the main for stability and then long hours of drizzling rain trickled out of the blackness. The mainsail ripped in three places at the clew so John took it in. We struggled under engine power and finally about eight hours after first turning it on John noticed a stir in the air. I went above decks for a moment to see how he was doing. The wind had shifted.

"I think the wind's from the south," I said. He nodded his agreement.

The wind, as it freshened, was actually southwest so he double-reefed the main. At two o'clock in the morning the wind was a steady thirty miles an hour and lasting. We both breathed a huge sigh of relief. We lashed the tiller and struggled below to our dry bunks. We had crossed the doldrums!

6

The Marquesas

June 16 brought us infernal drizzle, blustering squalls, and pounding cloudbursts. When the air cleared the same miserable weather surrounded us for as far as we could see. Finally, about midday, clear skies and a heady wind broke through with a vengeance. The strong winds forced us below decks, with the boys and Fraidy Cat snuggled forward in a knot, and John and I in our bunk, fortified with a store of books. We were driving hard through the rough water and meals were difficult to manage. The boys occupied themselves by opening the chain locker and climbing forward to sit on the anchor near the eyes of the boat. Here the motion was the most turbulent. To dissipate some of their boyish energy John would also stand them up in the hatchway where they would whoop and scream with every breaker that sent ocean spray down into the galley way. For three days this ferocious weather prevailed. Three days of whining rigging, draining skies, jerking decks. Our canvas was beginning to show the effects of stress.

On June 20 we broke free into a tropical blue sky with a more relaxed wind. Now we were aimed due southwest, for the Marquesas. We were near the equator, just 6 degrees 5 minutes north.

John and I took turns at the tiller, as I tired more quickly now because of the advancing pregnancy. But I never complained; that would have been beneath me. We were on deck discussing the seas when we both realized that something was wrong down below. There was silence. That is always a bad sign with small boys. We both rushed below, John first, and I heard him scream, "Oh no! Not the sextant!" I peered over his shoulder just in time to see it bounce across the cabin floor. It was completely dismantled. Parts were lying on John's bunk, others on the transom seat, and much was just scattered on the floor. John's look was of one of murder so I quickly stepped between the boys and him and started to pick up the pieces with the intention of changing his look of murder to one of salvage. But it was more serious than I imagined at that time: the sextant was our compass across the seas. John's look of murder changed to one that smacked of terror, although he never let on to it. He collected the remaining parts and screws. The sunshade for the index mirror was hopelessly smashed.

"Is that important?" I asked naively, secretly hoping all was well.

"Well, not really," he mumbled. "Hey, could you get that screwdriver away from Johnnie and that hammer away from Stevie?" I complied, huddled the boys together and watched as John fumbled with the mess.

"Daddy," Johnnie said, "Stevie and me fixed your sextant just for you, but I had some trouble." Murder returned to John's eyes.

"Oh, Johnnie," I said, "Daddy thinks you and your brother did a really good job. He's going to be busy for a while helping to adjust the pieces, OK?"

"OK! Did we do a good job, Daddy?"

"Why don't I take them on deck for a while?" I said, gathering both of them up.

There was no answer as John puzzled over the index arm that was stripped of its adjustment and sprung from the arc. The telescope, its bracket, and the horizon glass were also off their frames. Three hours later John came up with the reassembled sextant, but it did not look the same and it rattled. Not a good sign. That was an unforeseen turn. We had only one sextant and I knew from the disgusted look flowing over John's face that we were in trouble. We had no way of navigating other than dead reckoning and we were now sixteen hundred miles from California and two thousand miles from Panama, which lay virtually due east. Then I saw a smile creep over John's face.

"Well, honey, I dead reckoned my way for a thousand miles without even a compass after PAGAN and I survived the hurricane. Looks like I'll have to do it again!"

John knew I was strong and surprisingly calm in a crisis. John told me the Marquesas were a large target, offering over one hundred and eighty miles of intermittent island shoreline from north to south.

"What are our chances of finding the Marquesas?" I asked.

"About fifty-fifty," came the reply.

"And if we don't find them?"

"We'll either have to try south for the Tuamotus, or continue west and take a stab at Samoa."

"Let's find the Marquesas."

The wind shifted toward southeast and we were caught in the refreshing southeast trades.

Several days later we noticed that three dolphin fish were following close to the boat. Johnnie named them Tom, Dick, and Harry. The next day we were observing the three giant silvery fish when John disappeared down below and reappeared with a spear that he promptly and adeptly threw into Tom's side. A moment later, John lifted Tom and spilled him in the middle of the cockpit where he flipped wildly in three-foot leaps. Stevie yowled in disbelief, kicking and clawing at the flapping fish. Johnnie scrambled below decks and Fraidy Cat flew to the bow to stare at the commotion from a distance. I remember standing up in disbelief, eyes wide open. I dropped the tiller and rushed to rescue Stevie from the fish's tail, my heart exploding with a mother's adrenaline.

"Look out for Stevie!" I shouted. John stood there, paralyzed. Just at that moment, Johnnie rushed up with a pillow and using it as a shield, leapt on top of the fish. We all then joined in the melee until the fish lost its fight. We dined on poor Tom that trade-wind day. We had a huge feast with boiled potatoes, canned string beans, hot biscuits, and steaming tea. I wondered what dumb sort of luck brought that hapless fish just close enough to the only boat for hundreds of miles of empty ocean. Perhaps we were destined to have a similar, equally ridiculous fate.

John had to use certain stars for navigation: Spica in the constellation Virgo, Alphard in Hydra, and Rigel in Orion. Going toward the Marquesas I imagined how we were like the ancient Polynesians who accomplished even greater, more dramatic voyages, judging from their distribution across the Pacific, and with far less equipment than we had. During the days we busied the children with games, songs, and of course, the ever-present toy box. John dressed in one of my hats and pretended he was King Neptune. The fish spear was his trident. The boys gave him only derision, despite his commanding voice. I made some cute little certificates for shellbacks with whales, turtles, sharks, and sailboats sketched in the margin, hoping to capture the imagination of the little terrors. Stevie promptly doused his in the bath.

Other days we listened carefully for seafowl. I was the better of the two in that regard, but sometimes when you are searching for something in the wind your ears can deceive you. June 27 found us watching the stars with concern. Spica was high in the heavens and we opined that the Marquesas lay just a mite south of us. In the middle of the night Alphard marched right over the circling main. Then, in the morning Rigel shined brightly in the eastern sky. We were elated: altogether the assembled facts said we should quickly head due west, while keeping our eyes open for bird life that would signal land was near.

Four more days passed with pleasant sailing, but we began to worry when suddenly we heard a shout.

"Bird!" screamed Johnnie, pointing to the horizon. "Bird!"

We grabbed the glasses and saw a sleek gony with a dark body and white wing tips. Yes! Land was nearby, maybe only two hundred miles away. That was July 2. And then more doldrums set in with a cloudless, windless sky. Two days later we speared and ate poor Dick, who was apparently oblivious to the fact that Tom had suffered a terrible fate. Then later that day—the Fourth of July—I spotted a light bulb as it bobbed by.

"We've got to be close," I shouted.

"Yeah," John replied. "That bulb was *intact!*"

We discussed the pros and cons of that single light bulb for nearly four hours, dissecting its brass screw-on base, the clearness of the glass, the position it took while it floated by, and on-and-on, arguing over details, like fraternity boys discussing the best way to hang toilet paper.

The next morning Johnnie once again spotted birds, this time a pair of frigates holding high to the sky and soaring in a close circle.

"Less than a hundred miles to go," John said confidently. I rubbed my belly with affection as if reassuring our unborn child. That afternoon we saw many more birds: dark terns, gonies, frigates, and a solitary white tern—the harbinger of land close by.

"Land by morning," John stated flatly to me.

"You sure?" I asked.

"I'll bet my PhD," he replied.

"You don't have one yet!"

He smiled mischievously. The night came quickly, as it always does in the tropics. Then, on my watch, I saw a blur in the solitude of the reflecting ocean. It sat there, unmoving, silent and mysterious. I called John up from his sleep.

"Land!" I whispered excitedly, hoping I was right.

"Yes!" He said, rubbing the sleep from his eyes. "I guess my PhD is safe!"

It was then forty-two days since we had left Catalina. John anxiously searched for the bold bluffs of Cape Martin, the same high, jutting rock face he had sighted six years earlier from the decks of PAGAN. But we were off Hiva Oa, some ninety miles southeast of Nuku Hiva—not bad considering we had to dead reckon the last thirteen hundred miles without our sextant. Several hours later we sculled by the fantastic island of Ua Pou, which resembled a moonscape with its lofty, pointing thumbs of rock. By nightfall we were off Cape Martin. Behind it lay Comptroller Bay, the locale of Melville's thrilling *Typee*. The foreshores thundered and flashed silver in the dark to the surge that rolled around the cape. We finally entered the calm bay and looked at each other with a surge of warmth generated by the indescribable beauty and quiet of a tropical island after 42 days of heaving seas. Johnnie heard the clatter of our arrival and broke the silence:

"I don't wanna be alone," he said.

I went down below and gathered the boys.

"Come on," I said, "we want to show you something."

They stared at the island, unimpressed.

"Look, there are cliffs and valleys and palm trees!" I exclaimed.

"*So?*" Johnnie said flatly.

"And many famous people have been here too . . . like Jack London, Harry Pidgeon, Alain Gerbault, Allen Petersen, and Irving Johnson." John chimed in.

"*So?*" Johnnie said.

"So," I said, "thousands of people died here from diseases brought in by white men on whaling ships."

"Wow!" said Johnnie. Stevie clapped his hands not because he understood much but because his brother was excited. Apparently that was more exciting than the beautiful sleeping bay that surrounded us.

I was startled the next day with a rapping on our hull.

"John! Someone's here!" We quickly got dressed. Above decks we were greeted by two tall, barefoot natives, François and Joe, who represented the local French government. They were very friendly and through John's stilted French we learned that François was Tahitian and Joe was Marquesan. They welcomed us with a palm-frond basket of glistening bananas and papayas, which we gratefully accepted. In five minutes they cleared our paperwork. Then they mentioned a name that drew an excited response from John.

"Bob MacKittrick!" John exclaimed.

"Oui," came the response from François. John turned excitedly to me:

"Every sailor throughout the South Seas knows of Bob MacKittrick and his adventures. We've got to meet him!"

François and Joe nodded excitedly and moments later we piled into a sturdy outrigger—basically a hollowed log with a floating balance pole, rigged off to the side. Here we were in an authentic Polynesian canoe, the same craft ancient adventurers had used to explore the entire Pacific Ocean. I was thinking how primitive and exciting it all was. Then I heard a whir at the back.

"What's that?" I asked.

François and Joe proudly pointed to a beautiful five-horsepower outboard engine! Needless to say, it was a fast ride.

We met Bob on his veranda, lounging in a pareu, his bare feet working the sand. John introduced himself.

"John Caldwell!" he exclaimed. "The voyage of PAGAN?" he asked.

"Yes, one and the same," replied John proudly.

"Well, you must tell me everything!"

Now, that was not what John actually wanted. His desire was to hear about *Bob's* adventures, not his own. So after several hours of interrogation, John carefully shifted the conversation. Finally Bob started his life story:

"I've been in the Marquesas for over forty years. I know every island and every cove of every island!"

As he spoke the whole family sat cross-legged on the floor, Stevie snuggled in my lap, munching a breakfast of bananas and drinking from green coconuts brought to us by beautiful brown-skinned children. Johnnie made fast friends with Tiva, Bob's grandson, and the two ran off to launch the outrigger on the lagoon.

"Don't go too far!" I screamed at their disappearing bodies.

Bob laughed. He had been around the world and experienced many hard-fisted adventures but had also known years of sameness that would rot the hearts and brains of most people. Now he welcomed all people—the rich with their huge yachts and the poor with their pulpy hulks—with the same earthy smile. Every time he stopped, John would say, "then what?" and Bob would wind up again. Finally, lunch was brought in—banana poi, baked fish, avocados, baked yams, breadfruit, papayas, and coconut milk—they really outdid anything John or I have ever prepared for our family. Listening to Bob's adventures became a part of our own adventure.

Before sunset we were rowing back to TROPIC SEAS.

"That's how I want to live my life!" exclaimed John.

"But you *are*!" I protested.

"Yeah," John said, "but we're just beginning!"

"I know," I said, patting my tummy, and we both laughed.

We had landed at Nuku Hiva just a week before the Bastille Day celebration of July 14. We were urged to sail to Tahiti because its celebration was reportedly spectacular, but we chose instead to spend idyllic days in Taiohae, doing whatever we wanted. John and Johnnie would take off to climb a distant verdant crest or shoot and butcher a wild boar in a nearby valley. I urged them off the boat every day. I preferred to stay with Stevie, walking the palm-studded beaches and swimming in the crystal clear waters, admiring the multi-colored reef fishes, and reading my trashy novels on the beach with Stevie sleeping beside me. He did not seem to be developing properly and I often worried about his health. My pregnancy was progressing quickly and already I had recurring backaches and the need to urinate more often. Sometimes the baby would kick against my diaphragm and make me short of breath even after modest exertion. But I could not imagine a finer place to spend my mid-pregnancy than the tropical blue waters of Taiohae Bay. Here I was at peace with myself with my little man by my side.

John made good friends with a Marquesan named Kipiri who was an expert wood carver. Each piece of Nukuhivan rosewood was etched intricately, despite the use of crude tools. John and Kapiri would talk for hours, lazily watching little Johnnie chasing Kapiri's pigs. The days were long and easy. No appointments for John and no routine for the boys and me. Then came Bastille Day and the island celebrated by wallowing in a drunken orgy without any homage paid to the meaning of this special day of freedom and democracy. It seemed frivolous at first, but the celebration spiraled progressively downward toward public vomiting, cursing, and fighting amongst the participants. As the evening progressed it was difficult to find even a few men sober enough to engage in foot races, dinghy rowing, and horse riding. I left with Stevie to admire the dancers who could not afford to be drunk. Many of the dancers came from the outlying valleys of Nuku Hiva to compete for money prizes with their adorned, gleaming, and swiveling bodies. Among the dancers was an all-male group.

"Why are there no women in this troupe?" I asked a young woman.

"Because all the women are pregnant and unable to dance," she said, laughing as she stared at my bulging belly. I understood their predicament!

The celebrations for Bastille Day went on for another five days.

The morning after the Bastille "week" the wild celebrations ended and John and I decided to move on. We knew we had to navigate the ragged Tuamotus, a dangerous archipelago of islands, before arriving at our destination in Tahiti, so John took his broken sextant to a native Marquesan who was also an excellent navigator. "Pas bon," he said, urging John to throw it overside. In broken French John learned that it was far better to navigate by dead reckoning than set a course from a faulty sextant and risk shipwreck. The Marquesan marked our charts, correcting errors in the position of islets and reefs, and gave us good information concerning local ocean currents for the month of July.

The next day we weighed anchor. I looked around slowly, drinking in the deep-seamed, green-clad hills of this gorgeous bay. The boys were playing at my feet and I turned to John.

"It seems a shame to seek out this incredible paradise and then in just fifteen days decide to leave what we had most wanted for years."

"Yeah," he said. "I didn't want to tell you that a friend had offered us a house in the back valley. Johnnie and I went to look at it several days ago. There were plenty of food trees and it looked perfect for our family."

"Why didn't you say anything?" I asked incredulously.

"Because I knew we weren't finished," he said solemnly.

Just then Kipiri and Tiva came out in Bob's outrigger with a huge stalk of bananas. We thanked them profusely. We took a circular route in order to skirt the shore near Bob's house, to wave a last and fond farewell, and then we were on our way.

We passed through Comptroller Bay, and at its head, the wide rich valley of Taipi Vai. The greenery was lush and seemed to overpower the valley. John slid the anchor in and turned to Johnnie, playing with a truck at his feet.

"Johnnie," he announced proudly, "we are now in nearly the

same place where Jack London anchored the SNARK during his cruise of the South Pacific, and where the great writer Melville set his adventures. Are you up for a search for the village?"

"Yeah, Dad!"

John floated the dinghy and they paddled away, fully clothed.

"We're going to try that stream mouth over there," he shouted back to me, pointing to a small rivulet entering the ocean.

"OK, be careful!"

A moment later I watched in horror as a huge curling green wave came out of nowhere and struck them from behind. The foam of the breaker crashed over the dinghy and took both of them under. It seemed like an eternity before I saw them bob up in the surf, entangled with each other, the boat now heading to shore and the paddles going in different directions. All I can remember clearly is Johnnie's screams as John pulled him to shore and then a fit of laughter from the hills as the native Marquesans emptied out of their huts to come and look at the white fools, fully dressed and dripping wet, trying to claw their way out of the water. Then, through my binoculars I saw another wave come up and dump the dinghy on top of John's head. The laughter grew even louder. John and Johnnie regained their composure, gathered the oars and re-floated the dinghy, directing it toward the stream. The natives eventually disappeared, but I could still hear occasional howls from their huts for nearly an hour afterward.

John and Johnnie started their return a few hours later, but only after the dinghy was once again swamped by a wave, and once again howls of native laughter hung in the air over the lagoon. This time John was forced to dive into the water to retrieve what he had bought ashore: eggs, papaya, bananas, and a chicken. They were plagued by a swarm of vicious *nau-nau* flies and humiliated by the booming laughter of the men on the beach all the way back to TROPIC SEAS.

"Not a good day, honey?" I asked mischievously as John clambered aboard. There was no response.

Several days later John and Johnnie accompanied a young man named David up the palm-grown and jungle-clad mountain of Taipi Vai to the giant tiki gods. They could hardly contain themselves upon their return.

"Mom, you shoulda seen it," Johnnie said excitedly. "We saw six fat stony gods on the hill!" He looked to his dad for support. "Dad chased me all around the statues and said I was gonna be a sacrifice!"

"What a great dad you have," I remarked calmly. John smiled.

"Yeah, we had a grueling climb and saw these squat, bald-eyed, fat gods, just like Johnnie said."

"That's eerie," I said.

"Especially when you consider what macabre scenes those stone gods must have witnessed . . . you know, torture, human sacrifice . . . eating the vanquished."

"You mean cannibalism," I said, cocking my head to one side.

"Yeah, that too," he laughed.

John went on to describe how the modern islanders slaved as gardeners under the hot tropical sun for meager results and virtually no economic gain. Yet, this was the land of Melville's *Typee*, where centuries ago virile men locked in deadly combat and where men really did eat other men after victory. As we talked a huge biting swarm of *nau-naus* covered the boat forcing us to weigh anchor and flee for a distant green peninsula that juts out into Comptroller Bay. Here ocean winds kept the nasty flies inland. John and Johnnie climbed one more magnificent mountain that day, earning what they claimed was an unparalleled view of the Pacific. They spent hours just watching the shoreline below as it suffered from fierce crashing rollers spawned a thousand miles distant.

When John came back he was trailed by seven outriggers carrying thirty-seven people, all of whom proceeded to pour over the rails of TROPIC SEAS.

"Meet my new best friends," he said dryly.

A parade of natives crawled aboard. John went below and brought up the phonograph for them, proudly playing his cowboy music: "Tumbleweed," "Deep in the Heart of Texas," and so on. The Marquesans were impressed and told John that they were truly honored by his visit and that foreign ships were very rare in these waters. The only other ships they had seen in twenty years were the QUEEN ELIZABETH and the QUEEN MARY! John told them he was "proud to be in the same company." Then John made the mistake of asking me how I was doing with the ship's log, a tedious project. Being pregnant and having to entertain thirty-seven new friends had put me on edge:

"By the time I take care of the kids, do the housework, and scratch my *nau-nau* bites, there's no time left to do the log!"

He didn't bring up the topic again.

We decided to run for Anaho Bay, just past the sheer face of Cape Martin. A disturbing backwash rolled off the land, catching us in a cross sea. Finally the last surly headland was rounded and we entered the fairest, quietest bay of the Marquesas. We dropped anchor at the foot of a lush slope overgrown with palms, at the side of a dazzling coral-grown reef, below an overtopping sheer cliff face.

The bay was a sandy-edged bowl of tropical beauty. We smiled at each other in mutual appreciation and stayed for several weeks, happy prisoners of morning swims and afternoon spear fishing on the coral ledge with the boys. The sand of Anaho Bay was deep and golden and clean. The sea was tepid, rushing forcefully in and shoving you about gracelessly as it foamed around you. These were natural Jacuzzis long before their commercial invention. The native boys dove rhythmically and with their lightning fast spears would impale huge reef fishes. Johnnie and his native friends would often munch on cuttings of raw fish just as we would eat a cookie in the States. We spent listless days there, idling away the time. When we announced we were leaving, our native friends were deeply saddened. The weeks had flown by and we were on our way to Ua Pou.

7

Peaches and Ruita

We parted Anaho in the predawn of the second of August, heading for Haka Hetau Bay. Soon we could see Ua Pou's rocky spires breaking up the contours of low fluffy clouds. We dropped anchor just off a reddish bulb of rock and immediately felt at home with the ambiance the island exuded. It was the beginning of another unforgettable family adventure.

Johnnie and John went off daily with a huge Rapa man, a longtime seaman and father of eleven children. Each day I would watch them time the rollers so the dinghy would forge through the waters safely. We loafed quickly through five weeks of fishing, diving, horseback riding. Haka Hetau was a "children's village." I saw many families with ten or more children, all busy playing in every conceivable manner. Johnnie had free access to every home and Stevie was a human doll to all the young girls who came for him every day to bathe him, comb his hair endlessly, and wash his clothes. The island appeared to be disease-free: We never saw anyone sick and so our concerns with Stevie's health disappeared into the tropical mist. The young ladies would actually compete for babysitting, a fact that I greatly enjoyed as they were all excellent mothers.

When we left Haka Hetau the local butcher's wife gave us a devilish-looking six-week-old goat to be butchered at sea. I was horrified with our "gift," which proceeded to rip apart the boys' bunks, before jumping onto the set table, scattering food and breaking dishes.

"*Out!*" I screamed. "Get that damn goat out of here!" I took the broom after her and the goat scrambled up to the deck. John blocked any further attack by inserting his body between the goat and me.

"But honey," John lamented, "you're talking about *Peaches*, and besides every Polynesian will agree that it's bad luck to turn away a gift when you are at sea."

"I don't care a whit," I shouted, trying to clean up the mess.

"Besides, sweetie, Fraidy Cat and Peaches are becoming good friends.

"Good," I said, "then we'll eat both of them!" Johnnie was horrified and even John seemed certain that I would follow through on my threats. Johnnie grabbed Peaches and hung on to her for dear life.

"All right," I finally said, "but keep her away from me or she's stew!"

After that outburst John dutifully tied the goat up each night to prevent nocturnal misadventures below decks.

The next three days just disappeared. We found a beautiful tropical cove off Haka Maii where we dropped anchor. John loafed every day and while he busied himself writing a paragraph here and there I had Johnnie row Stevie, the pets (including Peaches), and me ashore every day to swim and play. One night thirty islanders paddled out to visit us on their outriggers. They brought steaming banana poi; a bowl of raw fish in a sauce of coconut milk; two baked breadfruit; some *fei* (cooking bananas); and two golden pineapples. I remember the items well because neither of us had to cook for days afterward. The natives stayed late strumming their guitars and filling the sweet air with songs and laughter. We played our cowboy records for them in return, but in the wee hours of the night the ocean turned sour with huge green swells and the party broke up shortly afterward. I assumed my post at the tiller while John guided us into open waters, steering straight into the hellish foam as we guided the boat through a thin passageway created by huge jutting rocks.

"Hold on!" screamed John.

"My God, we can't come much closer!" I shouted back.

"Sternway!" he screamed, kicking the throttle fully open.

TROPIC SEAS trembled and headed for the open seas, with John dead reckoning our passage in the moonlight for Takaroa atoll in the Tuamotus.

The Tuamotus are an empire of iron-bordered ringlets of land lying dreadfully low on the unknown currents that wander among them. Unseen reefs have rent the bellies and exposed the innards of many seafaring vessels, both large and small, along the hundreds of miles of their oceanic domain.

"Four hundred miles to Takaroa," said John with certainty.

"I've got some hot curried rice and biscuits down here," I responded, immersed in my own conversation.

"That shouldn't be more than four days, don't you agree?" he added.

"How about a tropical fruit salad and coconut milk?" I continued.

"Yeah," he said.

"Yeah," I said.

The next day Peaches really got to me, perhaps because John and Johnnie were pestering me with their requests for making Peaches an honorary crewmember, thereby granting her immunity.

"She bleats the entire night . . . you know I'm a light sleeper!" I charged.

"But she's just a *kid*," John lamented.

"That's not funny. She drinks my tea, raids the icebox, poops on the deck, pees in the galley way . . . and you guys take absolutely no responsibility," I said, hands on my hips.

"Well, how can you get angry at such an amusing, cute little goat?" he asked, feigning helplessness.

I thought about it for a minute and my anger subsided as I looked at the cowering boys.

"Well, for goodness' sake, at least keep her on the leeward side so we're not downwind!"

The boys agreed and we separated, each having won the battle. That night we entered a hissing sea of squall lines, thrilling us with bursts of speed that our boat had never felt before. The hourly watches took a toll on John's coral-poisoned instep, an unexpected "gift" he had received earlier in the week from Anaho Bay. He could not sleep because of the throbbing pain, and the foot was swollen and black. I knew what we had to do.

"I'll get the lamp," I said.

"OK," he whispered hoarsely.

I prepared the penicillin mixture, somehow drew it into the needle despite the throwing seas, and as John lay on his stomach straddling the cockpit coaming, holding a light over his back, I jabbed the needle deep into his gluteus medius. It was an act of pure acrobatics and to be truthful, delivered some unexpected joy (to me!). Until this day I cannot believe I threw that needle so perfectly into his sea-worn derrière. Afterward I made John stay below decks as I held us on course for the remainder of the night. The next day the festering had subsided and the pain was diminishing. Despite the vagaries of the weather, we figured we had covered nearly one hundred and fifty miles during the night of squalls. We searched anxiously for the signs of land.

"Over there!" I shouted to John, "see that line to the southwest?"

"Yeah . . . *yeah!*" he exclaimed. "Looks like a line of palmtops!"

"Is it Takaroa?"

"That's it, sweetie, that's it!"

Our approach eventually guided us along a stone jetty toward what at first glance seemed to be a ghost town. Not a cottage doorstep showed life. The narrow sandy avenues were dead. The jetty, fronting on the pass, and to which we would tie, was desolate. But the place was beautiful, picture-postcard gorgeous with its coral atoll. The wood and cement homes were surrounded by fences, flowers, hedges and lawns—very peculiar for the Marquesas. Then an old man tottered out, clad only in shorts and a hat. He grinned toothily, shook hands, and sat to study our boat. Then another old man came out. Neither spoke English or French, but they pointed to the open lagoon and spoke excitedly. Finally an old Frenchman emerged. His name was Louis Arhan, originally from Paris, and he served as the government radioman for the islanders, all of whom were presently engaged in diving for pearl shell. Nearly four hundred souls were involved in the mass collection.

As we walked down the main street we saw a tall Mormon church, which immediately explained the differences in the construction of homes there compared to those of other villages in the Marquesas. As we walked along the beautiful beach we could see a galaxy of lustrous shells and just offshore some of the most vivid reef fishes we had ever seen.

On Monday a handful of villagers returned. They came in little open boats, pushed by outboard motors. We met Ruita, a tall, friendly, narrow-waisted girl with a ready smile and sparkling eyes. Her nickname was Kete Kete (black black) because she was darker than others on the island. She introduced the entire family to the spectacular underwater shows of the surrounding reefs, pointing out octopuses, eels, fishes, shells, and corals of every conceivable structural array: castles, antlers, mushrooms, and brainlike growths. Every morning Ruita would bound through the knee-high water, running barefoot on jagged coral for a hundred yards or more (a run that would have ripped our feet to the bone), herding fish schools into the shallows. In just a few minutes she could string up twenty fish, which she dragged behind her, their blood spilling into the open waters.

One day I asked her how it was that she was never attacked by sharks, which often mauled and sometimes killed Takaroans.

"If the Takaroa shark is ignored it does not attack," she explained.

"And that is why others have been attacked, because they did not ignore the sharks?" I prompted.

"Yes," she replied. "The islanders who have been chewed had wounded a shark."

"Have you ever seen sharks approach you?" I asked curiously.

"Mais, il passe par la," she said in island French, "et il ne mange rien." (He just went on by, and he didn't eat anything!)

I was amazed at her fearlessness. A few days later, Johnnie and Peaches moved ashore to Ruita's cottage. We saw Johnnie each day, and each evening Peaches came to the jetty to bleat for a bowl of tea to which she had become addicted. Ruita and her sisters came daily to take Stevie until dusk giving freedom to John and me for the entire day. We roamed the sandy shores, strolled through the village, rowed over the shallow, almost surreally colored reefs, and fished in the teeming waters of the pass.

One day Ruita, John, and I decided to take an outrigger between two large rocks leading away from the lagoon. The water looked placid enough until we got closer. A moment later we found that we were being sucked toward the outer whorls of a great foaming whirlpool. Our boat started to rock back-and-forth and swirl around crazily, aiming for the reef that surrounded us on all sides. Ruita, who was with us, tried to guide us through *Charybdis* (as we had dubbed the whirlpool).

"Brace the tiller!" I shouted to John who had already anticipated my command.

The coral reached out for the sides of the boat and the bow faltered, then finally cleared the coral edge. A moment later we were once again in placid waters.

"What was *that*?" I shouted.

"Dangerous!" cried Ruita. "Many boats lie at the bottom, even the bones of many of my people."

"Thanks for the adventure," John said sarcastically. Ruita just nodded and smiled, assuming that we really did like the ride.

Every day we saw small outriggers from all over the Tuamotus and Tahiti sailing toward the bay for the shell diving. They sailed without compasses on ridiculously small boats, without log line, without even a bilge pump. The natives operating these outriggers were ocean hustlers, and the shoreline was beginning to bulge with shaky trading stores selling bar soap, flour, rice, kerosene, cloth, beef, butter, and cheese. We anchored because Ruita wanted to join the diving fray, but she told us she usually avoided diving in water over one hundred feet deep because she could only hold her breath for about three minutes at that depth. John and I just looked at each other in disbelief.

From a stout line Ruita lowered a rope basket into which she would place the day's shells torn from the ocean bottom. She then prepared a heavy lead sinker that would help her reach bottom quickly. She fitted her mask, slipped her right hand into a protective canvas mitten, paused, bent her head reverently and asked God to be with her in the dark shadows below. Whistling softly to clear her lungs, Ruita took a lungful of fresh air, grasped the sinker, held her nose, and slipped gracefully below the water. We watched her form shimmer until forty feet and then lost her. A half-minute elapsed, then a minute and a half; then nearly three minutes and she finally broke the water with three hand-sized shells.

"You open the shells and make them into bait!" She gargled.

John followed her instructions and baited a thick line with a sinker. Ruita turned and dove again. John threw in the baited hook and watched the marked line gurgle through the water and finally stop at the bottom.

"She's working at nearly seventy feet!" he said in amazement.

A moment later came a tug, and then another. John looked at me excitedly.

"I think it's a big shark!" he said confidently, struggling with the taut line. The fish fought like a mule and John leaned backward to pull in the monster. But it was only Ruita—laughing so hard she was choking on the salt water running down from her nose. I never let John live that one down.

We stayed at "the plunge" as we called the diving area for seven days, meeting many natives from different islands. Each night we gathered at Tommy's hut to listen to native songs describing the lonely life of the atolls. Tommy was a man of easy cheer: plump, dark, and intelligent. He made his money diving for shells three months out of the year and loafed the remaining nine months. One day in the village, after exploring a shipwreck caused by a hurricane, we came upon a small youthful procession headed by Ruita who bore, at solemn arm's length, a black furry mass dangling by the tail.

"Jawney, Jawney!" she cried, "le chat est mort!" It was Fraidy Cat for whom they marched, a victim of the fierce Takaroa dogs. Taking the limp cat we rowed to the reef edge and let him sink near the Takaroa whirlpool, where he probably was a morsel for the sharks. Later, the young islanders came penitently with replacements for Fraidy Cat: A pig, a young chick, two cats, and two dogs. John looked at me with plaintive eyes, but I was prepared.

"I've already got two boys—no, make that *three*—and a goat," I said flatly.

"Mary," John feigned. "We'll hurt their feelings for penitence if we don't take the animals."

"*NO!*" I was adamant.

"But Mary . . ."

In the end we signed on one cat, one dog, and the chick.

"And the pig?" John whined. I was unmoved and crossed my arms tightly.

"*NO!*"

"Who's captain of this boat?" he queried with care.

"Who do you think?" I responded dryly.

"Never mind," he said and turning to the islanders he graciously declined the pig. We called the dog Pedro after our homeport, the cat Fraidy II, and unfortunately there was no opportunity to name the chick because that night Fraidy II made a meal of him. Because both animals were born on the atoll they had known little else besides copra (dried coconut meat) and raw fish as food. Catching fish usually meant paddling past the jaws of *Charybdis* in outriggers that were quite unstable near the swirling waters. It required heavy stroking to get past its swirling jaws.

The fish traps on the reef were really large tidal pools enclosed by coral blocks. At high water they were immersed and as the tide ebbed they were exposed, trapping the fish within the shallow pools. Sometimes a pool would capture a school of several hundred glistening green mackerel—of which we would harvest about fifty. At other times John and his friend Vahna would take their outriggers to the edge of the reef and line cast for tuna. Pulling in a wild beauty exceeding fifty pounds was not uncommon. More than once sharks attacked the struggling tuna as the men pulled them toward the boat. John had hated sharks ever since his desperate voyage in 1946. Even now, years later, he would pull six-foot jagged-tooth monsters out of the water, dock them near the side of the outrigger, and beat them senseless with a hatchet before cutting out their entrails. Their blood would foam red in the water. He then would remove the hook from the shark's mouth and watch the dead monster slide headfirst toward the shallow bottom. In seconds a gory submarine brawl would break out as other sharks attacked their dead comrade, tearing huge chunks of flesh until moments later there was nothing left. The killers were always quick and efficient. "Another vermin of the sea gone," he would say. I understood John's hatred of sharks but yet I was always repelled by it and would sit aghast and say nothing as he butchered the creatures, without a word, before our eyes.

I watched from the shore one day while John and Vahna fished at the reef. A tremendous strike hit the line. They locked their shoulders together in an attempt to subdue the fish. "We thought it was a huge shark," he told me later. The next second I could see there was trouble: the fishing line had fouled the anchor, pulling it away and dragging it off the edge of the reef into deep water. I watched in absolute horror as the fish began towing John and Vahna seaward. I could see a number of sharks thrashing behind the boat.

"John! John! John! I shouted. I pointed in vain to the trailing sharks.

I saw the outrigger pole rise crazily and then in seconds the boat was swamped by incoming waves. I could see the fear in their faces as they fell into the water. By then they were a good one hundred feet from the safety of the shallow coral reef.

"Swim to the reef!" Vahna screamed to John. "Swim! Swim!"

I paced the shoreline, screaming at the top of my lungs, pointing to where the reef was shallow. It was all I could do and although I knew such gesturing was hopeless I did it anyway. My heart was in my throat as I watched the men thrash wildly toward the reef. Then in what seemed an eternity I watched as they pulled themselves upon shallow staghorn corals where they collapsed, finally out of the reach of the marauding sharks below.

"I could see them below us, tearing the other dead sharks apart" said John later. "I expected to feel the impact and wrench of their damn teeth at any moment, but then we saw gray, then white—and I knew we made the reef! I think the other sharks were distracted by all the dead sharks we were sending their way."

"Don't do that ever again!" I said, tears welling in my eyes. He gave me a hug and assured me that he would not. Vahna laughed, though, dismissing the whole crisis. It was just another day's adventure for him. Then John pointed to the old outrigger as it drifted out to sea.

"I was going to build a new one anyway," Vahna said, and they slapped each other on the back, laughing hysterically until the tears filled their eyes and spread over their cheeks. They had become brothers.

8

Leaving Peaches

On September 2nd we left Takaroa. It was painful leaving and we would have stayed longer but my pregnancy was progressing rapidly and nature was pushing us on to our next destination, Tahiti. Never again would our family swim on the sand patch off the reef, across the pass. Never again would we fish in the cool tropic evening on the jetty with the gay Takaroans. And never again would we visit in their friendly homes. Along with many gifts they loaded us from our ears to our shoulders with beautiful leis of frangipani and tearfully sent us on our way. Johnnie lay at my feet, sobbing and dejected, clutching Peaches, Pedro, and Fraidy II. We looked backward often until Takaroa faded from view, then I went to business, filling in the log. Barely a capful of wind was astir, but it was free, and we ran with it.

That night I thought John was waking me for my watch. I rolled over and felt a snout, then a tongue licking my face.

"*John!*" I screamed, "Get this bastard goat out of here!" The goat, terrified, scrambled clumsily up the stairs and came to rest at John's feet, trembling. Amazingly, the boys slept through the commotion. Later that same night Fraidy II and Peaches got into a wild fight. The flying fur and bleating woke up the whole crew this time and I was livid.

"I told you we didn't need a *damn goat!*" I screamed. "What the hell were you thinking?" John just stood there, statue-like, taking the volley of my verbal punches. Never wake a pregnant woman!

I was tired the next day and obviously cranky. The pets stayed away from me and the boys clung to their father. A long nap on calm waters under the beautiful tropical skies, however, refreshed me and after awaking I gave them all smiles and hugs rather than sharp remarks.

"Are you *better*?" Johnnie asked carefully.

"Yes, Mommy's better now," I said softly. They were relieved that the monster was gone.

We had an easy run down a coastline of reefs and islets—pretty little isles of swaying fronds with golden beaches and foaming, echoing surf. We rounded Pakaka pass in Apataki and as we neared the cement jetty, friendly hands crowded together to bring us in to dock. Apataki seemed to be more of a distant cousin than a brother to its fellow atoll Takaroa. Compared to others we had seen, this village seemed graceless.

Soon we learned the reason for this: its economy was based purely on copra (dried coconut meat). Times were sometimes good and sometimes not so good; they were now not so good. Copra prices were down, and little things pointed to Apataki's current poverty such as shabby streets, hungry dogs, patched clothes, shy friendships. But sincerity and honesty—rare qualities of human nature—were there. We developed many friendships but the closest was that of Teuira, who was island-borne and part French. He had sailed the world, only to return to the beautiful sameness of an atoll existence.

Teuira led us, as had Ruita at Takaroa, on field trips over the sunny reefs where we shelled and fished. He pointed out a great channel that once was an island covered with palms. The channel was a reminder of a great hurricane that had left the islanders clinging desperately to palmtops as they watched their villages disappear. Some lashed their children to the trees to weather out the storm but many Apatakians, especially children, were cruelly missing after the great storm. Teuira spoke of that meteorological terror in dread, quiet meek tones, as though any mention of the storm would bring a return of the savage winds that had destroyed their island and decimated their villages. I looked at my husband and children as he spoke and held them closer.

We often visited Teuira's palm-frond home. Our friend and his wife—the mother of twelve children (which made me feel some-what insecure because of the way she deftly handled herself and her children, seemingly without effort)—would serve us afternoon tea. It was nice to sit with these plain and simple people who displayed no airs and held no pretenses, who spoke candidly but modestly of the things they had done, and who held malice toward no one. I remember those warm, gentle visits with great fondness. They were rare, honest, good people, and they made our days complete. Here was isolation in the classical escapist setting: thousands of miles from any mainland, swaying palms, moonlit lagoons, the roar of the plaintive reefs, and friendly smiles from sun-bronzed islanders without agendas.

Teuira took us lobster fishing one evening in an old outrigger. We carried flashlights and a kerosene lantern and anchored where it was shallow, with sand and coral bottom. We hunted in the night-gray water with spent waves rolling over our legs. The surf broke in thundering rollers across the outer reef, adding to the surrealness of the scene. But there were many dangers. The eels—thick-necked, vicious things, lying and slithering like dark stubby snakes—were out attacking anything that moved from their dens. An ankle carelessly placed could be savagely bitten. A crevice in the coral could trap a leg at the moment the sea strikes and a bone could be broken. Or, an unexpected heavy wave could send you sprawling across coral spikes that could scar you deeply and forever. As I contemplated these possibilities, John shouted:

"*Eel!*"

I stopped, pitched over and frozen in an awkward position, not daring to move a muscle.

"There!" he pointed and Teuira nodded. John's spear lashed out at the ugly-headed devil and in one deft motion he speared and tossed the writhing creature into the open water for the sharks.

"Good enough for any eel," he smirked.

Then Teuira spotted a lobster, a bright blue one. He held it captive with his foot and manipulated it with his toes until he could safely lean over to pick it up with his hand. By the end of the night we had nine lobsters and two nice fish. I boiled three lobsters immediately upon our return to the boat and we sat there in the still of the tropic night smacking on the rich meat, drowsily recounting the night's adventures.

"Good thing I was there for you, huh, Mary!" John started as he began his heroic re-encounter with the eel.

"Well, perhaps it was because you realized you needed someone to cook the lobster?"

"Absolutely, good point, good point!"

"As always," I said, eating more lobster.

The evening drifted on with aimless ribald banter, everyone playing in the verbal game of sparring.

We especially looked forward to the evenings at Apataki. The villagers came to lounge on the jetty, in our cockpit, and on our decks. There were plenty of boys for Johnnie to roughhouse with, and of course, the young girls all vied with each other to take care of Stevie. Peaches and Pedro pranced on and off the boat at will. There were fishing and guitar playing and singing, and of course, inevitably, John's cowboy records. I knew every scratch. Fishermen would casually invite themselves aboard and would pull up good catches. Sometimes, however, they came up with poisonous fish that they carefully tossed in a writhing pile on the stern. Later we would shovel the poisonous catch over the side and then John would train his heavy light onto the bubbles they created, waiting for the eighteen-foot Apataki sharks to finish them off. John turned to me one evening as we watched the slaughter:

"Their arrogance is unbounded," he said.

"I hate the hissing sounds their dorsal fins make," I said observantly.

"And I hate the way they stalk like vultures."

Soon the wolfing ended and the gaunt, lean shadows swung themselves in slow death circles, thrusting themselves back into the depths to wait for more hapless prey.

The next evening John tried something different just to have fun. He unraveled the mizzensheet, and bent to it a length of cable with a nasty steel hook attached to it. To this rig he snagged a fat squirming fish. At the same moment John shoveled the catch of poisonous fish overboard he also threw in the line with the struggling bait. The terrible denizens of the deep came open-mouthed, champing and gulping at the sides of the hapless fish. Then the line went taut. The mizzen, to which the line was tied, began to rattle and TROPIC SEAS heeled as the shore lines straightened dangerously tight. Johnnie hopped up and down, shouting and clapping, but below Stevie wailed—I was trying to put him to bed. I ran up the stairs and accosted John for his silliness.

"I told you that would happen!" I shouted, hands on my hips.

"Not now, Mary! I'm busy." Actually, he was overwhelmed.

Native men rushed in to help as I watched the shark leaping clear of the water, shaking the mizzen rigging to the core of the boat. Then there was a pause in the struggle.

"He's weak, now," said Teuira, huffing.

They began to pull the shark toward the boat when suddenly it exploded again with more strength and fire than ever. The giant fish flailed against the side, stretched the mizzensheets, and nearly pulled a cleat from the mast.

"We're losing it!" I shouted, pointing upward.

John and Teuira redoubled their efforts, inching the beast to the hull side, working him astern, and then to the jetty, where he staged a final brawl with a desperate, bruising encounter on coral and cement. Finally, it was over. Four men dragged the four hundred pounds of eating machine to open ground where they clubbed him to death, turning his cartilaginous head to mush with a boat timber. After he was still, save for reflexes to his tail, they disemboweled him and pulled out huge octopuses, many fish, and the tail of a much larger fish. I sat on the boat, arms crossed, disgusted with the entire event. Then a man came up to me and spoke.

"This shark eats men," he said simply. "Last year a shark ate my wife's arm. Do not feel bad for the shark."

The men dragged the brutalized monster to the jetty and slid him back to the sea. It spiraled in a crooked plunge and as we watched by lantern light, his jackal brethren came, bolting with open maws and gleaming teeth. They tore hunks of red, raw meat, then turned and ran, making enormous swallowing movements with their necks and jaws, only to return, still choking down the previous bite, to bury themselves once again next to the eyes of their gaping victim.

The next day, seven days after our arrival, we were ready to depart. The normal good-byes were said, but there was one difficulty and I finally put my foot down in a brief "discussion" with John.

"It's Peaches or me," I said. "If Peaches stays, then I go to Tahiti on the MOANA (a commercial fishing boat moored nearby)."

It was an ultimatum. I knew John and Johnnie could never handle TROPIC SEAS by themselves, and he knew it also. He also knew I needed rest—I was tired of sleepless nights because of the capers of a pet goat in the galley way!

John turned to Johnnie and said:

"Johnnie, I think we've finally settled our long-time argument about who *really* is the captain of TROPIC SEAS . . . and it ain't me."

Of course, I agreed with him immediately and congratulated him for his insight, honesty, and candor. Soon after, Johnnie and John led Peaches away to the children of the island who had fallen in love with the goat. I took great care to explain to the islanders, in front of Johnnie, that the goat was never to be eaten. The children thundered their understanding and thanks with the song "La Marseillaise!"

9

Onward to Tahiti

$\mathcal{A}$n hour later we were in a saucy wind bearing our way past Kaukaura—the last obstacle before reaching Tahiti. Our sailing plan was simple: we would dead-reckon for Papeete. We had to pinch ourselves: Tahiti! It was true! It thrilled us with a giddy expectancy. On every island, in every anchorage, from every mouth we had heard of the ardent romance of Tahiti. This was one of the cornerstones of our dream back in California. For several days we languished on the open seas, reading books, and playing with the boys. The baby was kicking more furiously now and the children enjoyed feeling my stomach and listening to the gurgling sounds within. Suddenly an unexpectedly strong squall ripped the forestaysail full across and brought the tiller to my ribs. John fought to bring the sail down to save it from certain parceling. The next moment it was calm, and then an hour later we were just two miles off Point Venus, riding a thirty-mile-per-hour wind. In the distance the island of Moorea began to show her towering heads still lost in gleaming rain clouds.

"We're here! Tahiti!" He exclaimed with an enthusiasm I have rarely seen. I gave him a big hug, partly because I still felt guilty about abandoning Peaches. Johnnie and Stevie went crazy, chasing each other around the boat, doing summersaults, and roughhousing with the pets. John fired the engine and soon Papeete splashed into view as the weather cleared. The waterfront was tight with sea craft, and behind the marina were the verdant hills, the deep vales, and the tropic-clad ridges of paradise.

Papeete was surrounded by a ribbon of exotic reef, which we cleared quite easily. As we neared the harbor we were inundated with the rain-clean freshness that ran off Papeete's lush, silent valleys. We put down the starboard anchor and reversed to tie stern-to on the Papeete sea front. A curious crowd gathered to see what the sea had tossed on their shores. In the faceless group a head and shoulders stood out to John.

"*Well I'll be damned!*" John said, turning to me with a beaming face. "It's Johnny Litten, the man who sold me PAGAN in Panama in 1946!"

"Oh, you're kidding!" And I waved to him as hard as John. We scrambled off TROPIC SEAS and onto the boardwalk where John and Johnny hugged and slapped each other on the back. I introduced myself to his wife Jeanie and their daughter Katie. They were in Papeete, in turned out, to wait out the hurricane season, as were we.

"My sons destroyed my sextant," John told them, "and I've been dead-reckoning ever since!" He laughed.

"Well, you're in luck," Johnny said, "I have a spare sextant I'll sell you!"

"Damn, I'll take it!"

The rest of the night was filled with uncountable sea tales, many undoubtedly with more than a modicum of exaggeration, but it hardly mattered. Why let the truth get in the way of a good story! Other water-fronters came aboard—freebooter adventurers, sail men, a schooner captain, and island traders. Now so many sea stories filled the air you could cut the fantasy with a knife.

In the weeks that followed, Tahiti proved to be everything we had envisioned it to be. It was the hub island of a wide-flung sea empire of coral atolls and volcanic dots, and to this archipelago menagerie came a fascinating mix of humanity from around the world. I found out schooling was available, so Johnnie's daily shell-seeking on the beach was limited by classes with children from Tahiti, China, and France. The language of instruction was French, but the language of play was fully Tahitian. Johnnie was soon using queer, lilting words, but I feared he was largely a daydreamer, learning little from the formal instruction.

Scarcely a week later, I awoke to uterine contractions. My pelvis ached and my back was breaking.

"John!" I called with deliberation. "It's time!"

He ran and found a taxi and minutes later I was in the hospital. It was excellent timing and within an hour the baby was born, a strapping eight-pound boy with deep blue eyes and lungs like a foghorn.

"Look at his *hands!*" John said excitedly. "He's got the hands of a seaman!"

"What else would you expect coming from us?" I answered, cuddling the baby close to my breast.

"We'll need a real seaman's name, then," John added, excitedly.

The doctor and nurses laughed and they all clamored to help us. As I nursed our baby, John went for a tall, cold glass of beer, so exhausted he was from the birthing ordeal. A few hours later he came back.

"Tuborg Caldwell! How's that for a seaman's name?"

"You mean the *beer* Tuborg?" I scoffed.

"Well, yeah, but who will ever know?"

"Well," I said, "If you will remember, many years ago when we created a list for our first ten kids, the third name on the list was Roger, not Tuborg." He was obviously taken aback.

"How can anyone remember such minutia?" he complained.

"Women have strange ways unknown to men," I said, cuddling Roger Caldwell. There would be no dickering with the name; after all, John got to name the goat Peaches. So it was *Roger*, there was no sense in arguing that point. But Roger's middle name was an unconditional surrender to our wonderful Tahitian friends who insisted on Hiro, an ancient god of the islands and a famous navigator who had steered the great sea canoes to Hawaii and back in the olden days. The name was clinched: Roger Hiro Caldwell—a real seaman's name! Roger proved to be a bargain: his birth cost $29—hardly a tenth of what it would have cost back in California.

I immediately went to work rearranging the entire cabin. The older boys at first seemed miffed and they sized up Roger rather skeptically. But by the time I was finished, all was well. I found a locker for Roger's gear and I placed him happily in the little blue bunk John had made from spare wood and sailcloth. Roger was a seaman at six days.

Roger's lusty bawl attracted many curious Tahitians, among them our future friends Kauku and Roiti, husband and wife respectively. They came in the evenings, usually bringing a fish, which Roiti and I made into *poisson cru*. We would then while away the Tahitian evening, dining on the delicious raw food and listening to Kauku's guitar. Through them we found out that gossip is almost *everything* in Tahiti. It is not vicious or vindictive, just casual conversation and information about others. However, we also quickly discovered that gossip is only second in importance to Tahitian culture. The first is sex. Sex is the most discussed, practiced, and hallowed topic, and for outsiders it sometimes was the most enterprising sin of the islands.

Sex depended on the *wahine* or island girl—a slip of a thing, carefree, laughing, uninformed, going about barefoot wrapped sensually with something minimal and colorful, her hair flowing in the breeze with a flower behind her ear. She was easily approached and easily had. John would invite these irrepressible, colorful girls as guests aboard almost nightly. I found it irritating at first, but then I realized they were really just part of the social landscape and I should not be one to judge. They came with guitars to sing the lilting music of the distant atolls, of the outlying isles, and the back valleys of Tahiti.

One wahine, Tiare, came to Tahiti at the age of sixteen. Now, at twenty-three she would spend many hours in Quinn's bar until midnight, then stagger, arm in arm, into the byways with a teetering American merchantman, her new best friend. One night she might spend the night in rich splendor with a balding tourist, the next she would be found asleep on the walk in front of the Union Steamship Company wrapped in a sleeping mat. Despite her promiscuous activity, Tiare was more religious than most people I knew, at least from the waist up. She neither smoked nor drank and never drank coffee, and she treated all people fairly and with respect, even the drifters attracted to Tahiti for nefarious reasons. I came to love the wahine and care for them as I would my own children. When we stop judging others, life is sweet and easy.

The dreamy pleasantness of Papeete's weather during September, October, and November gave way to dreariness in late December. A fearful eleven days of tropical rains and brutal squalls swept the lagoon. Three to five blasts per day roared over us, drenching us in biblical deluges, ripping off rooftops and blowing down trees. Christmas for us was a day of watching our anchors, of eying the hulking schooners on either side lest they drag over us, and of sizing up the ferocity of each squall as it slanted past us. But the New Year ushered in a change of weather: the skies shone, the water grew clear and blue.

In the last part of January we were awakened at sunrise by a smile from a friend we shall never forget: it was Ruita, our island girl from Takaroa, freshly arrived aboard the WAHINE TAHITI. She gave us news about a thriving Peaches at Apataki; a schooner captain passing through gave her a playmate. Ruita proceeded directly to spoiling Johnnie and Stevie and gushing like a big sister over Hiro as she called Roger. She sang Roger a Tahitian song about their island hero, the legendary Hiro E. I remember that day well not only for Ruita's visit but because it was the day that John and Johnnie nearly drowned in a sudden squall spawned over the reef where they were shelling.

"I left Johnnie in the boat for just a few minutes," he told me later that day.

"Just a few *minutes*?" I whispered back, not wanting to alarm Ruita who was playing with Roger and Stevie.

"Well, maybe a few more, but the weather changed like that," he said, snapping his fingers loudly. "Next thing I knew the boat capsized over the reef and Johnnie was under the water."

"Oh God!" I said.

"I got over to him in a split second and he was treading water like a trooper . . . not a whine or a cry out of our boy."

"So you got to him quickly?" I needed to hear his story again. Was John telling me all?

"Yes, " he said. "The sharks in the lagoon were my biggest fear."

"*Oh God,*" was all I could say again, folding my arms across my chest.

"I swam for what seemed like eternity with Johnnie clinging to my neck. I got a finger-hold on some coral and clung to it with Johnnie until I had rested. A longboat from a copra schooner rowed over and picked us up at the channel buoy. I don't think I've ever been so scared . . . not for me, for Johnnie." He shook his head and looked out across the bay. The weather was tropical and beautiful again.

"I think we need to leave Tahiti," I said, as if it were something definitive to say after such a frightening experience.

"Yeah," he replied solemnly. "I love it here, absolutely love it, but I had a dream about Moorea and Bora Bora last night."

"Not Australia?" I added. "Don't forget Australia! I'm always dreaming about home."

"Yeah, of course," John said quietly, "Australia too!"

We looked up to see Ruita coming above decks with baby Roger and our conversation ended.

The next day we hauled TROPIC SEAS into dry dock to be scrubbed and painted with poisonous copper to destroy the larvae of teredos and other invertebrate creatures that abound in tropical waters. The cost was three times what it cost to give birth to Roger! John was furious with the French authorities, but they just shrugged their shoulders knowing that we could do nothing without them. Then even worse news came.

"Honey," John began. "I hate to break this to you, but we're broke."

"*What?*"

"We've only got seventy dollars left in the bilge cranny and my check is late from the publisher."

"*So now what!*"

"Well, we have at least three months' food in our lockers and that money should buy us enough meat and vegetables for a month, at least."

"And what about *incidentals*?" He hated it whenever I mentioned "incidentals" in a discussion.

"Well, I can't say," he said, "but there are schooners that could use a captain for a five-week run."

"Absolutely not," I said flatly.

"Well then, we'll be broke in Tahiti, just like the natives. The French are the only ones making any dough here."

"Well, John," I said plaintively, "I'm really worried!"

"We're broke all right, but we're in the most beautiful spot in the world! Broke or not, that's true."

John tended not to worry like me; he would reason his way through this mess. It would be business as usual for him, so I gave him a reassuring hug.

"OK."

We stayed a month longer, hoping for monetary relief from John's publisher, but nothing came. One day, while John was casually reading a novel, I remarked that our reserves now were less than one hundred francs. I started the battle by pointing my finger at him:

"How can you loll around contented when our funds are barely enough to buy three more good meals! We have children to feed and you are being totally irresponsible! You're not all by yourself anymore!" He put his book down slowly and his eyes narrowed to fine slits.

"I'm not lolling, I'm *thinking*, and I know we're down to nothing, but panic never got anyone anywhere!" He stood up quickly and bolted below, returning with my sewing machine.

"This will save us, are you willing to let it go?"

I hesitated.

"Yes or no?"

"OK, *Yes!*"

John jumped off TROPIC SEAS and flagged down two passing Chinese merchantmen. It turned out he had overheard them talking earlier about their need for a sewing machine. In short order he returned, the two Chinese waving happily and John with five thousand francs in his hand—enough to pay for another month in Tahiti, but not enough to pay the exorbitant port fees charged by the French.

"I'm not done," he said flatly.

John was strangely irritated to the point of boiling over. I watched him walk over to the Post Office. He opened the door and nearly ran into a patron leaving with a large package. The door slammed shut but even from a distance I could hear his booming voice and what seemed like enormous pounding. I knew John was delivering volley after volley of verbal tirades and orders to the French officials, demanding his money, demanding that they check the back room for mail. I saw several French postal workers scurrying out of the Post Office and I worried about the police. John could be very intimidating. About fifteen minutes later the pounding and shouting stopped and John emerged from the Post Office. He saw me on the boat and waved excitedly with a large envelope in his hand, and as he broke into a trot he shouted:

"The little pricks had this money six weeks ago! It was tucked away in a drawer in the backroom! They scurried like sea rats to find it!"

"*Those bastards!*" I shouted.

After that we cursed every French official in the universe, paying particular attention to their total lack of professionalism, expertise, and everything else—especially colorful aspects of their sexuality—for the next six hours. I've always believed that cussing is better than a psychiatrist, and a lot cheaper.

The next day our friend Oscar chauffeured us around the island to say our goodbyes. He drove us with beaming pride along the lush overhung roads of Tahiti's outer districts. Each curve revealed vistas of unbelievably beautiful seacoast, and when we looked past the white foam of the Pacific collapsing upon the distant reefs, we suffered heartfelt pangs knowing that soon we would leave this legendary paradise. Oscar kept us occupied for the moment, however, with a fascinating run of anecdotes and stories about his youth.

One anecdote was particularly bizarre. Oscar told us that his father owned property where at one time a crazy painter had lived. As a lad, Oscar had been sent with several laborers to tidy the ramshackle hut some years after the painter had died in the Marquesas.

The crazy painter had embellished the windows, the door panels, even the walls of the hut with wildly colorful oil paintings. There was a sea chest stuffed with canvases of tropical paintings—dozens of them. Legend said the painter—in a rage—had killed one of his babies by burying the infant alive. Local people claimed the baby still could be heard wailing each night. Oscar, being extremely superstitious, admitted hearing the infant's cry at night as well. His laborers deserted him because the eerie night cry meant taboo. In fear, Oscar set fire to the hut and then returned to his father. Years later the world would discover genius in the remaining works of this crazy painter, Paul Gauguin. I hesitated to imagine the many millions of dollars of priceless canvasses that Oscar torched that fateful day and the terrible loss to human culture.

Oscar had friends in every corner of the island and they treated us like royalty. All were greatly saddened by the news of our departure. Tahitians deal poorly with departures; in some personal way they feel that they have somehow failed their visitors. To make up for this supposed inadequacy, they party like there is no tomorrow. The guitars are brought out, singers wail out old Tahitian songs, and an overabundance of fine food is placed in front of you. I always smiled—a very meaningful gesture to the women and children.

"We love you, Mary," they said. "You keep the sea in your blue eyes."

"Thank you so much. I love you too. You are so *lovely*," I responded.

"Here, you need more food!" And they would bring me yams, bananas, taro and the inevitable poi—papaya poi, tapioca poi, breadfruit poi—every kind of poi that I absolutely abhorred, but John and Johnnie loved. I smiled through it all. The evening was topped off with a delicious serving of sea centipede, a type of shellfish.

10

Death Taints Paradise

The next day six months of blissful Tahitian living came to an emotional end with over one hundred people bidding us bon voyage. The deck was covered with gifts and food, much of which we knew would spoil, but could not be refused. We were missing two of our crew: Pedro and Fraidy II had succumbed to the lure of Tahiti and had no intentions of returning. Although I had felt anxious about feeling "trapped" earlier during our stay, that episode had been largely related to lack of money and the fear of being stranded. I honestly loved Tahiti and its people more than I could say.

"When are we coming back?" asked Johnnie, standing on a box, watching the receding saw-toothed mountains.

"Soon, Johnnie, soon," I lied, looking wistfully at the sea foaming around us.

"OK, Mom," he said and proceeded to tease Stevie into a lather.

Not long into our voyage we could hear Moorea's reefs thundering in the distance, and its mountainous spires that had always tantalized us from the mountaintops of Tahiti now came into relief. I pointed TROPIC SEAS down into the deep blue arm of Cook's Bay. As we tacked closer the vast still beauty of Moorea towered over us, dominating our view. The fingerlike peaks were spectacular in their cascading descent upon the ocean.

"Look, John!" I pointed excitedly toward the beach.

We could see laughing people outside thatch-roofed cottages that dotted the shoreline. Men and boys loaded into colorful outriggers fished with nets along the nearby reefs. Even the thunderous surf failed to muffle their communal joy. None of us had ever seen anything like this before, not even in Tahiti. It was hypnotic. I maneuvered TROPIC SEAS around in the very corner where Harry Pidgeon had anchored ISLANDER twenty years before and John secured the boat in the lee of a sandbar.

"Let's go swimming!" Johnnie screamed.

We stripped shamelessly and dove into the water, swimming and splashing with abandon. The boys bounced up and down in ecstasy while John and I lolled in the water with baby Roger. For three days we swam, bicycled, fished, and napped as a family. We danced and sang under a full moon beneath the palms. On the fourth night a high French official on his vacation joined us. He donned a grass skirt and showed us things that we thought French officialdom could never do in public. We witnessed the dazzling firelight hula of Moorea's beauties, with the Frenchman singing and dancing while abusing our guitar. We finally came aboard at a frighteningly late hour.

We had planned to stay just a week, but three weeks passed in a blur of activity. Cook's Bay had pirated our family! We lived a lazy, but beautiful and meaningful existence. Each afternoon, young girls came aboard to care for Stevie and Roger, allowing John, Johnnie and me to ride rickety decrepit bicycles to tour the bay. One exceptional tropic afternoon we stopped to watch a nearby horse rollick in belly-deep water. Dripping and sleek, he cavorted with abandon.

"He's just like us!" I remarked.

"Not a care in the world!" John said, reaching for my hand.

Just then, Johnnie screamed and pointed. The horse shook and whinnied. His eyes blazed with fear as he kicked violently and started for shore. A second later he stumbled forward and was dragged under by some unseen force.

"*Sharks!*" John shouted as he ran down the beach, pointing his shaking index finger at the sinister forms breaking the water. "*Sharks!*"

Their cruel angular fins broke the water in mob violence

around the struggling horse. Then there was silence, except for the splashes of gray fins at the kill. For moments we held our breath, drawing closer to the macabre scene. Suddenly, the horse came up, twenty yards away, the water pouring crimson from numerous gashes. He whinnied piteously, his great white eyes staring, transfixed. One leg was already gone and there was a yawning ragged hole in his flank bleeding profusely, strings of sinew and muscle hanging from his side. He thrashed, staggered, and again was dragged into the widening red pool of blood.

"My God, do something!" I pleaded to a fist-clenched John, but I knew there was nothing he could do. John just shook his head as he brought Johnnie closer, stroking his hair as we watched, petrified in horror. I leaned my head on John's shoulder. I now understood his fear: I needed only to experience the terror first hand to understand the lifelong hatred John had for these biologically programmed killers.

Then shouts erupted from cottages and men rushed for their outriggers. But it was hopeless. The horse appeared once more— only his head this time, with dulled eyes in the throes of death. It thrust up several more times from the boiling crimson sea foam surrounding him. Then he coughed a half-drowned cry, shuddered and disappeared in a boil of water, pulled by the gang of sharks below. A huge gray shark broke the surface seconds later, his teeth grasping a still-quivering chunk of blood-oozing flesh. He gulped and champed violently until the dripping lump went down his throat, his gills flaring at the sides. The water grew bloodier and more silent as the unseen slaughter below came to its grisly finish. Now there was only a fin here and there breaking the surface as the blood-crazed sharks swam in circles, fiercely crossing and crisscrossing, ready at any moment to turn even upon each other.

We looked at each other, and then hugged. We were shaking, pale and drawn by the horrific event we had witnessed. Moorea's charm had suddenly showed its fatal side. Our dream island was now an island of terror.

"Mom," Johnnie whimpered softly, his head hanging low. He was unable to finish but kept muttering "Mom" with tears in his eyes.

"I don't know why things like that happen," I said with anticipation. "They just do. That is Nature's way and it is impossible to understand why. Sometimes we must just accept things and move on."

"Damn sharks are devils," I heard John say quietly to me as we walked away. "I always told you they were and nothing is going to change that!"

"I understand," I said, "Now I understand you." He nodded, shaking his head slowly from side-to-side.

As we pedaled back to TROPIC SEAS we discussed in muted tones our need to move westward to the next island, Huahine. The following day we packed before dawn and sailed with the early sun. We landed in Papetoia and stayed for seven days, swimming in the shallow bays, dining at night with the natives. The boys lived in the water, and little Roger, who was just beginning to sit, showed his Tahitian roots. He screamed happily when we stepped onto the beach and bawled with a fury, his legs tucked up in anger, whenever we picked him up to extract his struggling little body from the water.

More Adventures

Since leaving Tahiti we covered only twenty miles in twenty-nine days. With Australia still three thousand miles away, we decided we needed to move along at something faster than a snail's pace. We weighed anchor and eased past Moorea's last coral barrier, catching a spanking breeze just off the roaring pass. We fell in with long, deep swells that whistled lightly as they hurried up behind us. Then the wind fell flat and towering ominous thunderheads erupted in the distance, marching endlessly across the horizon.

"Maybe we should motor back to Moorea," I suggested. "I can still see her lights astern."

John gauged sea and sky carefully.

"No, let's try for Huahine—I think we can beat the storm."

Two hours later we both wished we had honored my impulse to turn back. Call it woman's intuition or just a gut feeling, but shortly after our brief conversation we were surrounded by a black and threatening sky. I checked the boys below. As always, they were sound asleep, oblivious to the alarming skies above them. Little Roger, awakened by my light, yawned, listened wide-eyed to the crashing of the sea at the hull, yawned again, and settled in. He was such a little doll! Looking at him I could handle any storm, anything Nature could throw at me; nothing would prevent me from protecting my children.

The night was wild and torturous. We were flying in the mid-fury of the squall and the danger was that an unexpected reef would rent us to pieces in the darkness. These were chancy waters and our nerves were on edge. I was too much of a sailor to tell John "I told you so." After all, we were a team, and occasionally we both made serious mistakes. This one would be John's. When I came up to relieve John the wind was gusting to sixty miles per hour and steady at forty. Crested rollers piled up and I carried my bucket around, vomiting often. Even John felt queasy. We had grown soft with seven months of life on Tahiti and Moorea. Should we drive north and clear the chain of reefs, or run for it and make a safe haven at Huahine?

We decided to run for it.

John hoisted the storm sail to port and the twin spinnaker to starboard. Bursts of crackling thunder split the entire night. Fork-tongued shards of lightning revealed the fury around us. Steep black hills of ocean stood up, twisted us crazily, turning us every which way, and then finally collapsed under us. Each roller was more terrifying than any theme park ride of today. I carried my bucket from chore to chore, so sick, but thoughts of sleeping innocent children gave me a will of steel that no storm could ever break.

"I love you," screamed John at one terrifying moment. I just looked at him, smiled and nodded; I had just vomited in my bucket again and I could not talk. The worst times were the moments following lightning, when thunder and sea crashed together around us and there were minutes of waiting as unseen wild waves tumbled over our decks like boiling water, hissing and tossing us helplessly about. By dawn the storm abated and John and I were exhausted. For eight hours we had wrestled with a sea that cared not one whit whether we made it to safety or not. Mother Nature simply does not care.

The boys awoke full of their typical devilment. Johnnie emerged first from the ruckus.

"Did you sleep well?" I asked Johnnie carefully.

"Yeah, why?"

"Oh, nothing," I said, smiling at John. "Just a little storm last night and I wanted to make sure you slept well."

"*Storm?*" he asked.

John and I laughed until tears poured from our exhausted eyes.

We had to sit down on the deck to keep from falling overboard. Johnnie just stared at his bizarre parents and then without a word went below decks to tease his brothers once more. The tension of the night was gone and things were normal again. Before us, some five miles distant, lay the long, blurred line of Huahine. Directly ahead lay the spouting reefs, each wave killing itself on the shallow coral barrier.

We decided to stay on Maroe Bay, which we could reach only with a treacherous but short run through Farerea Pass. I manned the tiller and John took his station in the fore rigging to spot the pass and guide us through it. On either side of us huge arms of coralline rock groped for our hull. A side current tried to sway us, but I held fast, dominating the tiller. Then a huge swell breached and buried our bow. I lost John's voice in the sounds of the wind and sea. TROPIC SEAS lifted and twisted and sheered to port like a train. John motioned to me frantically and I heaved hard back against the tiller: No time even to vomit! We straightened for a moment until another sea ran over us, dousing us with a hissing spray over the stern. TROPIC SEAS' bowsprit went under; she rooted dangerously, deep in the water, and charged again off course with seas upending the boat all around us. John flailed his arms frantically but I could not see how we stood in the water. Another crashing wave and our stern reared up and slewed over. Fists of coral scraped our boat, but somehow we straightened once again. Just when I thought we would be fighting this passage for hours, we literally shot forward into the easier water of the inner pass. John jumped down from his perch.

"*Damn*! That was something else!" We embraced just as Johnnie stuck his head up from the hatch.

"Mom, Dad," he started, "we can't play, you're moving the boat too much. Can we anchor and swim?"

Once again we had our comic relief provided by the children. We hurried across the white blown water into Maroe's broad, deep basin. Low green hills, with a thumb of rock here and there, beckoned us. Waving shore palms never seemed so friendly. Natives paddling three outriggers came out to greet us. A gnarled old man with a leather-brown face silently took our starboard anchor and pulled us onto a shallow arm of sparkling coral, and there we lay, in a bight of coral, unbelievably snug on the flat water. Then the visitors came on deck as they always did, and as always, Johnnie, the perfect host, provided the entertainment. We were not such good hosts and while Johnnie entertained we fell dead asleep, exhausted from fighting the sea.

When we awoke we apologized to our guests who were still being entertained by Johnnie. Among those on board was the massive chief of Maroe, Hiraii a Teata, a man of rare girth and with a tall, rounded frame. Johnnie stuck his finger in the chief's huge stomach and said, "You eat too much." I was horribly embarrassed, but the roar from the natives, especially from the chief, set us at ease, and the chief promptly adopted Johnnie and asked permission to take him ashore to live for the week with him while we remained at Maroe. For the next three days we were blasted by gales with winds of sixty miles per hour and more, first from the east, then from the northwest as the huge system passed through us. We were happy we chose the pass and not the stretch to another island that was scarcely protected from the open ocean.

Johnnie came aboard each night bringing with him a group of eager singers. He would take his place on someone's lap, as would Stevie and Roger. We would place the kerosene lantern in our midst and group ourselves around the mizzen, our knees crowded together in the cockpit. For little Roger the young girls would always sing an especially romantic version of "Hiro E." We sang night after night, our favorites being "Mauweewee ma Fatu" and "Wahine Tahiti."

"Hey," John said one night, "How about some cowboy music?"

"How about giving it a rest," I said. "We're in paradise, not Texas!"

There was no battle after that.

The following morning we explained to the Chief that we would be going away soon. He was saddened and insisted that we accompany him to see his vast bay. He seated us in a huge and graceful outrigger with three of his many strong sons paddling furiously. The

John is improving his fishing skills while Mary looks on

bay was so incredibly beautiful with its rings of palm-lined shores, sandy bays, and fringing reefs beyond description. The entire day seemed to flash by and the following morning found us once again at the open sea. I had the tiller, as usual, and John called the course from aloft. We skimmed past coral knobs at Raiatea's narrow Teava-pitu Pass, and slid TROPIC SEAS down a long lagoon to the main port town of Uturoa, which had a large Chinese population (dominated of course, by the inevitable top-heavy French officialdom).

We were in a rush to sail to Tahaa, the twin of Raiatea.

"Bearings, please!" I shouted to John from the tiller.

"To Bora Bora?" shouted John with a laugh.

"Yes, to Bora Bora."

"Your wish is my command!"

John guided us across Tahaa's foaming reefs and passed several enticing bays, but we finally tied up at a nondescript pier in a non-descript village, Tiva. The following days were filled with shark fishing from the pier, eating ashore with the villagers, and of course, Johnnie entertaining the natives with his famous Tahitian hula—hips gyrating, arms spread and feet stamping.

"Damn," John said one day. "The kid's as good as they get."

"He's better than the natives!" I added proudly.

That was the day I dropped the anchor on my foot.

"Darling," John drawled, "I am officially demoting you to cook until your foot heals."

"Not a chance," I said. But hobbling was painful. "You just want to be captain, don't you?"

"Yeah, even if it's just for a few days."

"All right, then," I conceded reluctantly. He smiled and gave me a hug.

"C'mon gimp, let's get you down below. Those wonderful children of yours need you."

So a fluke of nature reduced me to pounding the breadfruit for the poi of each meal, and of course, taking care of the children. The following days were filled with typical island activities. John and Johnnie caught fish and prepared them in Tahitian ovens for baking. Other times, everyone just loafed at shelling, spearfishing, or swimming in the shallow lagoon, just inside the corals. John continued honing his fishing skills by learning from the natives how to spear a shark. He nearly lost a foot doing so, but the monster he brought back to the boat set Johnnie's eyes spinning with pride for his father.

"That's *huge!*" was all he could say.

"You should have seen the one that got away," his father said dryly.

"Right," I said, dragging my bruised foot along the deck.

"We've got to get you to Bora Bora and a dispensary," he said, the joking gone from his voice. "Your foot's getting bad."

12

On to Bora Bora

Bora Bora was really just around the corner, as landlubbers say. It is an island that awes you: her lofty greenness reaches boldly skyward with exotic romance, into a ring of clouds that never seems to leave. A native in his outrigger greeted us and then led us into Faanui Bay, a deep and broad inner lagoon where we tied to a crumbling wharf built by Americans during World War II. I received treatment from the dispensary and when I returned to the boat I discovered my crewmates had fled. John, Stevie, and Roger were out playing on the beach and Johnnie was ashore. Johnnie was gone three days, returned homesick for one day, and then was gone again for several more. He earned the name of Poi Boy because he loved the rich-tasting poi smothered in coconut milk. We enrolled him in school to prevent him from turning into a street urchin, and every day we would watch a procession of native children and Johnnie, riding with three friends on a crippled bike. (Johnnie would ride the handlebars, one would stand on the pedals, another would actually ride on the seat, and a fourth would stand with a big toe gripping the rear axle on either side. Now that took balance!)

The Americans of World War II had enlivened Bora Bora's placid life. Nowhere in the world had Americans been so loved as here. For four years the natives enjoyed Yankee luxuries: PX shopping, movies, ice cream, soft drinks, canned food, electric lights, dances, paved roads, and whizzing jeeps. During the Pacific War the Americans had armed the island as a rear base, and when the Americans left the Bora Borans wished in their simplicity for another war—to bring the Americans back! One good friend, G.I Joe, would come to visit nearly every afternoon, stroking his outrigger (laden with bananas a foot long just for us) across the lagoon.

"Let us pay you!" I would always demand.

"*No!*" he would say, shaking his head. "This is for Uncle Sam!"

One day he brought with him a beautiful pale-skinned, blue-eyed girl of nine, with a fleck of gold in her hair. She was perched with the agility of a cat on the bow of Joe's outrigger. Joe pointed to her with admiration:

"She's my granddaughter, Nina," he said proudly. "She's a Yank! They left her here. Her Pop's from New York."

When Johnnie returned aboard from his runaway life in the village he would often bring Nina with him (she was one of the children who rode the bike with him to school every morning). She could speak no English, but she told me one day in French that she wished to go with us to America to see her father. It was more of a dream than a wish, Johnnie later told me. It would remain a fantasy that would never be fulfilled.

One night we went to the Bora Bora Yacht Club with Francis Sandford, a new friend who had been the French liaison officer to the wartime Americans. We became honorary members of the Yacht Club simply because we had made it to Bora Bora. Francis was pleased to have us aboard.

"You know," he said, "there were more than six thousand Americans on the island for several years and when they left there were only one hundred 'American' babies."

"What do you mean by *only*? That sounds like quite a few." I said, thinking he was putting me on.

"Well," he said, "the Bora Borans thought that was a rather poor showing!" He laughed at his not-so-subtle put-down of American reproductive abilities.

Later that night we built a great fire whose light danced against the overarching palms at our back and upon the rigging of our yachts tied up against the mole. The high point of the night was a fiery and blood-warming rendition of the "Ori Tahiti" by Germaine (John had spiked this sultry and beautiful woman's drinks prior to her dancing exhibition). It was said that her fiery "Ori" was unmatched in all the Societies. She shimmered and swirled before us, sensuously, teasingly, and unforgettably sexy—at least according to John. There were demands from the men for many encores. She flashed every available bit of exposed flesh in provocative ways that I could only imagine. I thought to myself: "We've been in Bora Bora for twenty-seven days. Perhaps it's time to move on."

The morning dawned with TROPIC SEAS under my command headed toward Suvorov atoll—a mere hump of coral and sand midway between Bora Bora and Pago Pago in American Samoa. The sun was warm, the sky blue, and the wind gentle. Johnnie's tears from the heartfelt goodbyes to his school friends in Bora Bora were now drying up and the emotional storms were abating. John took this as an opportunity to celebrate by filling the washtub to the brim with seawater. While the boys frolicked in the tub, splashing and dunking, I guided the tiller as usual. It was then that I noticed a huge shark slipping quickly up to our stern timbers, turning half on his side, and then with mouth agape, shooting past us with a flash of curled teeth. He repeated this several times and it began to unnerve me.

"*Shark!*" I shouted to the boys.

They hurried out of the tub, grabbing their clothes to participate in the upcoming adventure. John peered overboard and watched the smirking devil. Quickly he ran below and came up with my huge butcher knife, which he lashed to the end of a boat hook. A moment later John stabbed the beast in the gut. The shark wrenched a half turn and there was a loud crack. The knife blade snapped off at the handle. The shark was instantly gone—with my knife. I was incensed.

"Hey, if you guys want to spear sharks, use your own knives!"

"Yes, captain," John retorted. "So sorry about that. It won't happen again!"

"Of course it won't," I charged, "I only had *one!*"

A few days later we were clear of a fringe of coral reeflets lying a hundred miles out from Maupiti, and ahead was the deep blue to Suvorov—nearly six hundred miles of open seas to go. To pass the time, I busied myself by designing a dream ship. I showed my plans to John:

"We could finish our voyage around the world with this 45-footer," I said dreamily. "It's got everything!"

"Damn, that's a hooker of a boat for any ocean," he responded appreciatively.

In eight days we were near Suvorov, and a storm was brewing.

"Same damn waters that nailed PAGAN in 1946," John told me flatly, scanning the ominous skies.

"Are you feeling superstitious?" I asked timidly.

"No, but this area is a well-known storm tract and I won't take it lightly." He turned to the children:

"C'mon kids, time for bed!"

I took the first watch and John had just fallen asleep when we hit something hard that jolted the boat and sent me flying backward. A fountain of water sprayed over the deck.

"John, John!" I shouted. "I think we hit the Suvorov reef!" John ran up pale and alarmed. The water once again shot up alongside the boat, drenching us. But somehow we were still under way. We both looked into the darkness but could see nothing.

"I swear," I said excitedly, "we hit something *solid!*"

"I believe you. I felt it down below."

Then I saw the huge black reef just twenty feet off to starboard. *"A reef!"*

John looked carefully. The reef moved.

"Can't be . . ." he said slowly, peering into the darkness.

"Then, what is it?"

"Damn! It's a *whale!*" he yelled with a mixture of alarm and excitement.

"Oh, no!" was all I could say.

"Yeah, and a *helluva* big one. Look at it!"

"Oh, I can't," I said pitifully. "What'll we do now?"

"Nothing. We watch," came his response.

Suddenly the monster rolled an eye toward us and disappeared with its seventy-foot hulk slipping with a hiss below the water. I sighed with relief. The whale was easily four times the mass of

TROPIC SEAS. John gave me a hug and went quickly down the galley way toward his now cold sleeping bag.

Then there was a roar, a surge of the sea and a slam to our portside; a huge hissing geyser shot up beside us. TROPIC SEAS quivered under the impact as the whale pulled up aside us. John ran up the stairs and stared, spellbound by the immensity of this creature.

"He must think we're his girlfriend!" John said quietly so as not to alarm the beast.

"I can't look," was all I could say. "I wish you hadn't broken my butcher knife!"

"No way a butcher knife would even nick the blubber of this guy."

The whale dove again. I was relieved and counted the minutes. Then, there was another eruption from the starboard, just a few feet away. The immense dorsal fin glistened and towered above us in the boat. The beast hissed and covered us with a fountain of sea spray. I could watch his nares open and close as he gulped in air. (I will never forget the fetid, God-awful breath that came from that beast. He smelled like a septic tank filled with rotting fish!)

"Maybe a couple of shots from my army rifle?" John mused out loud.

"God *NO*! You'll just make him angry." I hissed.

"Then how about shining a light in his eyes?" he pondered.

"*NO*! That'll alarm him even more!" I pleaded.

"But he could crush us with one slap of his tail!" John shouted.

"I don't care. Right now he's just spraying us."

The monster rose and fell alongside us, traveling at the same speed. He would dive periodically, his great tail rearing high above us like a demonic night shadow, until it fell with a resounding slap, sending ocean spray and a sea wave against our hull. The mounting wind of the impending storm added another dimension to the scene. So there we were: far at sea in the early night of a rising gale with an enormous whale escort enamored, apparently, with the sexy TROPIC SEAS. I held us to a firm course. I knew that even a modest collision could orphan us. For nearly an hour we put up with his antics. By midnight our brains were fried with anxiety.

Every sea that broke nearby crashed on our raw nerves. Then the lightning and thunder began. I looked tiredly at John:

"OK, here we go again!"

"I'll stay up with you, babe."

I was so appreciative! The gale was nearly upon us when we realized that our amorous friend was finally gone.

"I think the storm sent him packing," John said.

Then I let him know the truth: "Thank God! Every time he surfaced all I wanted to do was dash below to my bunk and hide under the blankets!"

He laughed long and hard. I knew what he was thinking: the captain had met her waterloo. And secretly, without saying a word, I knew inside that the storm would be nothing to me compared to the beast that had accompanied us for several hours, rubbing amorously against our hull. The wind gusted to sixty miles-per-hour and the seas howled around us as the murk closed in on TROPIC SEAS. By dawn, on every horizon, the sea was a fury of tumbling, confused foam, and the air was charged with a mist that swept off the crests. Massive wall-sided seas bore down upon us like express trains and when we mounted the height of each wave, we could look in any direction upon miles of angry white water. The din of wind and disjointed sea drowned out our attempts at conversation. The kids stayed below with their bananas, their glasses of condensed milk, their boiled eggs, and their jam sandwiches. These were "storm rations" as we called them. I was still at the tiller; I had lashed it down to be sure our course was steady. John occasionally read passages from Smollett to me. He loved his caricature, his satire, and glib humor. Finally, I asked if he could read to me from one of my detective stories. After that request he chose to slink down below to play with the hellions.

For three days the storm howled, challenging our endurance, both mental and physical, as well as the strength of our boat. The wind would gust to 70 miles-per-hour and blow steadily at nearly 50. Often TROPIC SEAS was sucked to her deck level by a raging comber, or the boomkin would actually dip into the water, but every time she rose again to meet the next sea.

13

To a Tuvuthan Reunion

The afternoon found us just sixty miles east of American Samoa. Hours later we caught a glimpse of Aunu'u Island lights on the eastern corner of Tutuila. Our eyes glazed over with pure joy: Once again we had beat the odds.

As we neared Pago Pago the winds died as an oppressive calm settled on the water and the air grew close and sticky. But not long afterward we were swishing before a forty-mile-per-hour squall. Heavy rains would be followed by tropical sun. Back and forth the weather sawed. We were exhausted and made a pot of coffee. Now, the aroma of steaming coffee is a shot in the arm for me. I love the smell and taste of coffee. I especially looked forward to this pot, but a sea wall hit us and the pot toppled to the floor.

"Damn it to hell!" I said.

"*Mary*," John said, "was that *you* I heard?"

"It'd better not happen again!" I stooped over to soak up the mess.

I made another pot and just before it was fully perked another sea hit us, spilling the hot coffee all over the primus stove. The string of foul language that burst forth from my mouth probably still hangs in the air over the wild waters around Swains Island, so devastated was I at the prospect of not having had even a cup of coffee in three storm-filled days! John just stared at me.

"Truck drivers would be proud of you," he finally said, laughing. "It's a good thing the children are still asleep!"

"I'm *not* asleep!" Johnnie said. "I've heard Mommy say things like that before!"

John snickered in silence as I refilled the pot and held it to the stove surface. Minutes later I had my coffee.

"Half-hour to go," John shouted as he climbed the stairs to the deck.

Pago Pago looked easy to bore into from the open ocean, except that there is a mountain on the northern edge of the island called the Rainmaker. As we approached we could see that every blade of grass on its green slopes lay flat from the constant force of the wind. Suddenly the harbor ahead grew whiter. The wind picked up and within minutes it exceeded fifty miles an hour. There was no time to take in the jib and reef mainsails. The boat was almost on its side. Something sounded like gunshot, then a screech of flailing canvas. It was the forestaysail, ripped along its entire length.

"*I got it,*" screamed John. He scrambled to pull it down.

Then another rending rip went off in my ear. The mainsail tore completely away. It flailed beamward, shivering and destroying itself. I opened my mouth to scream to John, but not a sound came out, so deafening was the wind. The wind then became so strong I could no longer stand and John was having a terrible time managing the torn sails. The wind speed increased to nearly 80 miles per hour, coming directly off the Rainmaker. The exposed reefs loomed closely, threatening our very existence. We were all alone; not a single other boat could be seen in the harbor. The minutes became an hour and we inched along, barely skirting the coral heads. Finally we spotted a steamer's buoy and tied up. We thought we were stuck there, but fortunately, a powerful 50-foot naval launch came out a short while later and pulled us to the safety of the inner harbor. On the ocean, even in an apparently tranquil harbor, things can be deceiving and change dramatically within minutes.

John and I were drenched, red-eyed, and exhausted. TROPIC SEAS was a disaster, with sails torn nearly completely through. The natives were awed by our appearance, John's in particular, with his tousle-hair, beard, and shirt in shreds from the wind. We must have looked a sight. Within two days we met Suzie, a dark-eyed, brown-skinned girl from an outer Samoan village who offered her services as a baby sitter. She fell in love with the boys, especially little Roger, whom she sang asleep every night with soft Samoan songs. The respite at Pago Pago gave my foot a chance to heal completely and also turned me from a boat designer to a house designer. This was a talent I had learned from my father, who was a carpenter and had sketched many house designs in front of me as a little girl. I drew floor plans by the hour, dozens of them, and was keenly devoted to furniture, color schemes, and gardens. To earn some badly needed money, John took a job taking a small copra vessel to Swains Island and I agreed to keep our crew intact at Pago Pago. The week flew by and John returned smelling of squealing pigs, smelly copra, and seasick passengers.

We stayed in Pago Pago for nearly six weeks, but because of the influence of Americans it lacked some authenticity. The average Samoan was confused and disturbed; perhaps frustrated is the best word. Americans, as colonists, are as bad as everyone else in the Pacific. One of the charms for John and me was that during our stay Johnnie and Stevie spent most of their time in jail. The Samoan police force adopted them and shanghaied them often to the jailhouse. The policemen taught Johnnie to blow bubble gum—a harmless enough diversion ashore, but a sticky business on a boat. The parties were numerous and long; in the end we grew tired of them. We, like the boys, could be shanghaied for breakfast, swims, cocktails, or full dinners, and as a result, we had no time to ourselves.

We parted in the late afternoon with the wharf filled with well-wishers, waving us good-byes. We sailed to Apia, Western Samoa but only stayed two weeks because the port was too open to the sea: the harbor was strewn with the bones of American and German seamen; six warships sank in one hurricane during World War II. The only way the British ships avoided the same fate was to steam out into the open ocean into the teeth of the storm. This way they avoided the treacherous coral reefs. Socially, Apia did not rank highly on our list of islands; at that time it was full of thieves who would filch anything unattached from our boat.

While in Apia we had just enough time to sew the rips, reinforce the patches, and strengthen the seams of our sails. I would finish up all the chores of a housewife and then dash off to my house plans. I avoided the bustling town because it reminded me of the busyness of the States and furthermore the people were not nearly as friendly. Of course, we were afraid to leave TROPIC SEAS because it would be stripped to its keels of anything removable if we did. We virtually had to stay within her sight. It was ironic because Upolu, where we were staying, had fifty-two churches in 20-odd miles. The island, though beautiful, is a patchwork of castlelike edifices that cast dark shadows over the meager earthen-floored huts beneath them.

John was at least historically interested in Apia because it is the island where Robert Louis Stevenson, the author of *Treasure Island*, lies buried.

That afternoon we left Apia, headed for Apolima and the Tongas. A wild-sea caught us near Apolima and nearly capsized us, and well into the next day we fought tongues of angry water as they lashed our decks. Johnnie would sneak up and scream with delight at each onrush of sea. He liked it most when the bow went down to sea level, the deafening thud of the waves against the hull, the explosion and boil of the water over the decks, the spray into the rigging—all the playthings of a little boy!

"I think we've lost Tonga!" John shouted over the wind. "How does a direct shot to Fiji sound instead?"

"Fiji sounds great!" I screamed back.

"At least we'll be out of this storm!" he shouted again.

"Then let's get on to Fiji!"

"Amen, Captain! I was hoping you'd say that!" he finalized. I smiled. I loved John for his humor even during the most dreadful situations.

Cooking was always a challenge in a storm-rocked galley, especially since I had to care for the children and cook at the same time. Because the boys' bunks were lying on the side facing the brunt of the open seas, I moved their mattresses into the main cabin. There was less motion low in the boat and they slept there relatively peacefully, compared to the wrestling matches John and I had with the tiller above decks. We rigged a tarpaulin to keep the deck-washing seas off of us and I kept my barf bucket close by. For three days we struggled with rough seas. We were headed toward the Nanuku passage of the Exploring Islands of eastern Fiji—a graveyard of iron-hard coral with uncharted reefs, one of which claimed John's PAGAN in 1946. Many of the reefs are not associated with any landmass and they appear suddenly, it seems, during stormy weather.

John would navigate three times a day, swearing so loudly from the shrouds above that I could often hear him below bellowing "son of a bitch" and "bastard sea" to the skies around him. Of course there were many other colorful phrases, perhaps learned during his World War II days in the Merchant Marines. We finally made it into Nanuku Pass in the pitch of night on the fourth day of high seas. While I took turns at the tiller, John chartered our course into Fiji's reef-bound Koro Sea. Because we were so exhausted we set our deck watches for an hour on and an hour off, rather than the customary two hours. We took a meandering dogleg track around Thakau Moma, a huge mile-wide circle of coral that had claimed many ships. When daylight came we spotted Ovalau, green and lush, off to starboard.

"How about a rest?" John shouted from his perch in the shrouds.

"Twist my arm!" I shouted back.

With that we pulled into the reef-enclosed port of Levuka, nestled upon a palm-grown foreshore. The overt friendliness of the villagers and their countless gifts of food cheered us immensely. A throng of sober-faced Indians and grinning bushy-haired Fijians came to visit with us. We were treated like royalty and stayed five days, but in the end John told me late one night:

"Mary, I love it here but I want to return to Tuvutha soon to give the gifts we bought to the villagers who saved me."

"Oh," I said, "we absolutely must! How much farther is it?"

"About one hundred and fifty miles from here."

"Why, that's just a few days!" I commented.

"Tomorrow, then?"

"Yes, tomorrow for sure!" I gave him a big hug.

Several days of sailing passed before we made out Tuvutha's clean silhouette in the distance. It was just a droplet of an isle. Before long we were just a thousand yards from the village across the lagoon—Loma Loma.

"It hasn't changed a bit!" John shouted, spotting the thatched huts through the binoculars.

"I can see villagers on the beach!" Three outriggers started out to greet us, but all three floundered immediately in the treacherous waters around the reef. The outriggers turned back to the village.

"*Damn it,*" John said, "We've just got to get in there!"

"We will, *damn it!*" I responded. He loved it when I mocked his cussing.

Just then I saw a head bob up from the froth at the reef edge, then another.

"*John!*" I shouted, pointing at the men, fearing they were drowning.

"Well I'll be! Hello, Joe!" John shouted with his hands cupped over his mouth. He was beyond excited.

"Hello, Johnny!" came the reply from the foaming water.

"Hello, Johnny!" shouted the other man, waving his hand wildly above him.

"Hello, Billy!" John beamed.

We pulled the men aboard; they hugged and slapped each other on the back, grunting with male appreciation for each other. And why not? These were some of the men who had saved my husband from certain death when PAGAN floundered on their reefs in 1946. I stood back and watched, not believing my eyes.

"You are fat now!" said Joe, laughing. "You were all bones last time!"

"Yes, I am strong again!"

Then John quickly introduced the boys and me. Unexpected streams of tears came down my cheeks. I remembered the terrifying nightmares I had back in Australia when I had not heard from John for several months on his voyage from Panama to Australia. Those were days and nights of constant worry I did not want to repeat. The men looked skyward and warned John about the weather. Quickly they helped us find Tuvutha's ill-defined pass, which by then was a boiling caldron of racing white water. Billy and Joe were constantly saying, "wah, wah," under their breath.

"What does "*wah wah*" mean? I asked.

John explained that "wah wah" was an expression of nervousness, peculiar to Tuvutha. With John at the bow and me at the tiller, we needed full sail and the motor to get us past. A moment later everything turned to turmoil—the crashing headers, the constant wall of wind, and Joe and Billy calling out the course of the passage to John in their undecipherable Fijian. I watched helplessly as tongues of massive coral reached out with gnarled fingers for our boat; they were always just a few feet away below us and on all sides. Then Billy came over to help me fight with the rudder. A milky foam enveloped the boat, making visibility impossible. Just then, Joe pointed ahead to pale green water—deep water—and a moment later we slipped into safe haven.

Just a hundred yards away the villagers clustered in a group on the shore. Billy and Joe quickly explained to us that John must partake in an ancient Fijian homecoming ceremony before we could all go ashore. They pointed shoreward. The village women were crisscrossing on the beach with banners streaming from poles. The banners were brightly colored *tapa* cloths, to be presented to John, but first he had to row ashore alone and collect them.

"You've got to collect the cloths from the women?" I asked, smirking.

"Yes! It's a ritual. In the olden days I would have had to chase each woman through the village and struggle with each woman for the tapa cloth. Now, it's easier—I just have to run from woman to woman."

"Well," I said. "That's encouraging. So what's the reason for the *struggle?*"

"No one knows anymore. It's just a homecoming custom."

"They should have men with *tapas* for me too!" I said.

"Maybe next time," John said, laughing at my jealousy.

John rowed ashore and ran like a wild man, laughing as he collected the cloths from the excited women. Mysteriously, he stopped short at the end of the line and took one older woman in his arms, hugging her closely, rocking her back and forth. Then he went up to an older man who stood beside her and did the same. When the ceremony was over, we anchored and the outriggers pulled us ashore. The Tuvuthan children crowded around me, amazed at my white skin and blue eyes. They wanted to touch everything on me, and did. John then grabbed me around the waist and presented the children and me to his saviors. First he pointed out the older woman and man he had hugged in the tapa line:

"This is Una, wife of Itchica, who watched over me, fed me coconut milk, nursed me and mothered me at a time when I should have died. And this is Itchica (Itchy) her husband. Without him I would have never been reunited with you!"

Tears welled quickly in my eyes again and Una clasped me closely. She wore only a skirt and her huge naked breasts pressed against my much smaller covered ones. She kept talking to John about my skin, my eyes, and my fearlessness to cross the sea. Then it was the children's turn: eager arms took Roger and Stevie. Johnnie disappeared overboard, scrambling like a monkey from outrigger to outrigger.

More friends of John stepped up: Mike and Tookai. They thumped John's chest.

"*Bula*! (strong!)" they shouted appreciatively.

"Where are Suvi and Cama, my philosopher friends?" John asked excitedly. At the mention of Suvi and Cama the villagers cast they eyes downward. John translated as they spoke softly: Suvi had died from a sudden illness and Cama had vanished on a lone fishing trip, disappearing without a trace. His empty outrigger was found at anchor in mid-lagoon—probably a shark. John shook his head at the mention of shark. Another friend, Tupa, was now a pastor dedicated to Va Kalou (God). Tupa had recently been "called" to another island.

That afternoon I made up soft drinks from a powdered mixture for all the islanders, and then brought up a sealed tin of candy for the kids. We sat about the wind-kissed decks, sipping punch, chewing gum, sucking candy, and reminiscing excitedly from all angles of history about the wreck of PAGAN and the rescue of John just six years earlier. The quiet, serene village, nestled in a glen at the base of Tuvutha's dead volcano, exuded an infectious peace. I saw John in absolute tranquility for the first time in my life, relaxing on the deck with his good friends, viewing the sleepy cluster of thatch-roof huts in the palm setting where his rescuers still lived in peace.

Whenever we went ashore the whole village seemed to follow us. John showed me where he had lived in Itchy's *koro* (house). Itchy announced to John that I was the only white woman *ever* to have landed on Tuvutha. But things were changing. Now copra vessels visited once per month instead of yearly, and there was a government-paid schoolteacher on the island with a battery-powered radio. Tuvutha had widened her horizons since John's fateful landing.

That night Itchy and Una prepared a dinner of boiled chicken for us with a side dish of *kumalas* (a kind of sweet potato). Baked breadfruit rounded out the excellent dinner.

"Look, Mary!" John said excitedly. "This table is the forehatch of PAGAN! It's still here!"

Then Una brought out knives, forks, and spoons—all from the wreck of PAGAN. We even sat in chairs made from PAGAN's beams and deck planks. It was truly a homecoming for John. Late into the evening we stayed to hear the assembled villagers sing their myste-rious, ever-varying island songs. At one point they stopped singing and called out "Talanoa, talanoa (story, story)!" John knew they wanted to hear once again of the saga of PAGAN and John was never shy about telling (and embellishing) upon a good story. When he was finished the villagers once again shouted "Talanoa, talanoa!"

"What do they want now?" I whispered to John.

"They want Yankee songs."

"*No!* Not the cowboy records!"

"No, they want *me* to sing the songs!"

"Oh, God!" was all I could muster.

A moment later he belted out such great selections as "Straw-berry Roan," "Little Joe the Wrangler," and of course, "Tumble-weed." There was an encore. He threw in "Deep in the Heart of

Texas" and "Pistol-packin' Mama" until they screamed with delight. I remembered John telling me that he was dropped from the men's glee club in college because he threw the bass section off key. It was obvious his voice had not improved but the Fijians tonight were a very charitable audience.

Before we broke up for the night, Una came to me and said something in Tahitian. I turned to John.

"She wants to know if Johnnie can spend the night ashore in her cottage. She would prepare a bunk for him as she had for me."

I turned to her and said, "Yes, yes, of course!" Her boys shouted and whooped along with Johnnie.

The next morning, John asked the chief to assemble the islanders. He had purchased a gift for everyone back in the States and had spent the night sorting things out. He explained through Samesa, his official interpreter, that he was not a rich man, that his gifts were meager, but that they came from his heart. Then he presented two tools to each man: hammers, saws, axes, hatchets, drills, pliers, crowbars, and knives. And there was tobacco, a two-foot rope of it per man. Broad, appreciative grins spread throughout the group. For each boy who looked old enough there was one tool. To the women he gave two dress lengths each of assorted bright colors, and to the girls one dress length. Each small child received a generous packet of candy, a package of gum, and a plastic toy. Then he gave each family a stack of American magazines: *Collier's*, *Life*, *Time*, *Yachting*, *Rudder*, and the *Saturday Evening Post*. To the church he gave religious pictures of biblical events, framed and done in color, as well as a framed color portrait of the Queen and Duke of Edinburgh and the royal children. Because Tuvutha was a British Commonwealth it was only appropriate, John had told me earlier, that they know who ruled over them. Finally, the gift giving ended and the talking ceased.

Billy arose. He told John he was as one with them, as were his wife and children. Then he said, "Gift" and with open palms handed John a token of the village of Loma Loma—it was a massive whale tooth, a *tambua*. It was stained and polished, a cone-shaped object, fitted with a plaited cord of coconut fiber.

"Carry always," he said in his broken English. John was visibly taken aback. Later he told me that he did not know that anyone on the island of Tuvutha even had a *tambua*, and second, he did not believe anyone would part with it even it they did have one.

"Why," I asked. "Are whale's teeth that rare?"

"They are very rare, certainly, especially around these is- lands," he began, "but the historical significance of the word *tam- bua* in ancient times was associated with the highest of traditional ceremonies. That association has been lost, but the significance is still there, and giving a whale's tooth symbolizes the deepest of sentimental value."

"It's beautiful," I said, now understanding the significance of the gift.

The rest of the morning was spent with the children, organiz- ing races for them, making sure everyone received a few shillings as "winners." As the afternoon waned and night approached, the vil- lage women daubed their faces in red, white, and black smudges, adorned themselves with garlands of flowers and strips of newspa- pers we brought ashore, and arrayed themselves in colorful group- ings on the green. It was the *meketa,* a peculiar Fijian sit-down dance, performed unaccompanied except for the lilting, high, wail- ing chanting of the women. They moved gracefully and seductively, with expansive motions of arms and hands and body, yet they sang, curiously, with faces of changeless expression.

Later that evening, John's friends took us to Tupa's cottage to partake in the traditional *kava* ceremony. The village elders were seated in a semicircle on the matted floor. John and I were given ceremonial chairs. A cloudy liquid was dipped from a deep bowl and passed around in a half coconut shell. John watched me with trepidation. I drank the mixture like a sailor then tossed the shell in the traditional manner to the ground. My eyes blinked rapidly and a weak smiled spread over my face. It was *awful!*

"Mary," John whispered out of the corner of his mouth, still smiling, "you're looking pretty bad . . . but pretend it was a chocolate shake!"

"Well . . ." I felt seasick. I needed my bucket.

"*Pretend!*" he demanded and then smiled to the entire group. I wiped my lips with the back of my hand and smiled ever so weakly. The entire group clapped loudly.

In the ensuing days Una and Itchy permitted us to make only one meal aboard PAGAN, and that was breakfast. Johnnie lived ashore, day and night, and changed families almost daily. On more than one occasion we saw him running naked through the village or swimming in the surf, surrounded by dusky bodies, or working an outrigger on the lagoon. What memories he must have stored inside his blond little head! Stevie and Roger trudged through every day with us, unless of course, they were "captured" by the native girls who constantly gushed over them.

With the approach of the hurricane season we had no more than a month before we needed to push onward to Australia. We made every day count, with numerous trips throughout the island. One day was particularly exciting. We climbed and entered Tuvutha's high crater through a northern trail.

"I wanted to do this in back in '46, but my legs were too weak!" John said, reminiscing.

Itchy led us through a tangle of bush along a well-worn foot trail that ended in a steep face of rock worn slick by centuries of hands and toes grasping for niches. We descended down the cliff face over one hundred feet and were amazed to find the volcano floor clothed in coconut palms and banana trees, like a miniature garden of Eden. There, just a hundred feet above sea level, was a copra forest surrounded by the high, rearing lava walls of the ancient volcano that had created this island. Every cranny of the volcano's sides held a bush, a creeping vine, or a tree—whatever would grow. From above, the sun's rays filtered over the crater rim through the palms, to wash the high canyon with a shadowy light that gave mystical shapes to every lump of bush or lava. Itchy explained that the valley ran nearly the length of the three-mile island, and that to the north, where a section of the crater rim had collapsed, you could walk out directly onto the beach, and this we did.

Another day we followed the south trail to the crater floor. We passed step-by-step down among the rearing castles and turrets of ash and waste. Our descent brought us to a dark, still theater deep in the bowels of the island—a round, cliff-edged bowl. Suddenly we stepped clear of lava blobs onto soft mud and found a black lifeless lake.

"This is really eerie," I said morbidly.

"Yeah," said John thoughtfully, "it's like the island died here." But Itchy had another view:

"No, this is where Tuvutha was *born!*"

On our way back we searched for the *uga vule*, the giant coconut crab of the South Seas. I spotted one of these enormous spiderlike creatures on the trunk of a coconut palm. Their powerful claws can husk and break into a mature coconut on which they dine for hours. Their pincers can also cut off a finger. Unfortunately for them, humans found them to be incredibly tasty. Una could locate them with the faintest rustle of the crab's armor in the lava clefts where the creatures choose to hide. Using pieces of copra, Una coaxed out three *uga vule*, which later were served to us for dinner. Royalty never had better food!

14

∞

Just Playing

*O*ur days in Tuvutha were blissful: we spent hours hunting for the beautiful chambered nautilus shells, fishing off the reef, or just lounging on the beaches. Each day eager arms kept Roger and Stevie occupied while John and I romanced with long walks and naked swims in the tropical water. At the end of the day Roger and Stevie would be brought back to us, freshly bathed and shiny-skinned with *wali wali*—scented coconut oil.

Often Una and Itchy would take us in a heavy ocean-going outrigger and push upcoast. Between the canoe and the outrigger pole is a boarded platform that can support a half-ton of copra. Una, the boys and I were seated on the platform while Itchy stood in the bow and John was at the stern. We poled ourselves along the shallow coral and sandy bottom of the ocean, passing palm-grown glades abutting sandy shores, with towering rims of the volcano jutting up from the island's interior. After swimming and shelling, we would camp for the night and sleep under palm frond huts on the shore. Eventually I would make the fire and Una would slip into the brush to bring back the *uga vule*. At night Una rubbed the boys down with *wali wali* and when the sun dropped like a red ball from the sky we would fall asleep to the distant muffled roar of the ocean pounding relentlessly on the reef.

On one of our camping excursions, Una and Itchy took us to the head of a palm grove. There, overlooking the beach and the sea was a tall tree. Itchy pointed to the tree and then looked at John and smiled. At first John was puzzled, then he remembered:

"Well I'll be *damned*! That's my *tree!*" he exclaimed. Una and Itchy laughed at his excitement.

"*Your tree?*" I queried.

"Yes, back in 1946 I planted a tiny shoot. Now look, it's got nuts!"

"John's tree!" Itchy nodded in agreement. Under Itchy's supervision we dug four holes to plant four ripe nuts: One for me, and one for each of the children.

"Some day," Una said, "you drink from the nuts of these trees."

"We will," I said proudly. "We certainly will! And when I do return I want to chase *men* with tapa cloths!" They all laughed.

The next day we poled the outrigger toward a lava outcrop and into a little sand bay John will never forget: he had dubbed it PAGAN's Cove.

"It's here somewhere," he said, looking intently.

"There!" Itchy shouted.

We all looked overboard. There was precious little left, but the keel was still intact. The ravages of the sea had reduced her to denuded bronze keel bolts that protruded pathetically from the keel.

"She must have been a strong ship," I said, admiring the size and length of her bolts.

"PAGAN was beautiful," John said quietly.

"Then why did you wreck her, Dad?" Johnnie said innocently.

Our laughter broke the solemnity of the occasion. That night we camped on the shore of PAGAN's *Cove* where John had dragged his nearly lifeless body six years earlier. It was really a miracle that anyone had found him, but leave it to children to explore areas that are off-limits to them! Thank God for those children!

After camp was ready we sat around an open fire.

"It's ironic, isn't it," I said to no one in particular. "Here we are where John nearly died, enjoying ourselves in exactly the same place as if nothing had ever happened!"

The flames flickered against the palm trunks.

"Life is beyond strange," John said. "It seems like it really didn't happen . . . like it was out of one of your novels!"

"Oh, come on!" I pouted. "I was being sentimental!"

"I know," he apologized, "but really, it's such a mix of emotions. I remember almost dying; I remember being rescued; and I remember knowing that I would live to see this place again. I remember the jagged volcanic rock, right over there where I pulled myself out of the water and onto the sand. I think it was sheer will power and extraordinary luck that brought me back here again. But I had no doubt that I *would* be here. No question at all."

"You are a strong man, John! *Bula!*" said Una, grasping John by the shoulder.

"Perhaps, good friend, but if I had landed 50 feet on either side of this cove where the surf crushes against the jagged lava formations below, I doubt that I would be here today." We all shook our heads in agreement and then stared off into the surf breaking over the reefs.

The next day we poled the outrigger back to Loma Loma. We met worried villagers. It was Joe's boy, Mesake—he had a deep cut on his foot and it had turned into a serious infection. His temperature was elevated and his leg painfully swollen. I gave him a penicillin injection as a temporary measure. A quick council was called in Tupa's hut. They decided that we should take Mesake the next morning to Vanua Mbalavu, 25 miles to the north; Joe and his wife Anna would come and they would stay with relatives there and return on the next copra craft. That meant our stay at Tuvutha was ending.

We had our last dinner on Tuvutha that night. Joe killed a suckling pig; Billy brought us *urau* (lobster); and Una baked an *uga vule*. Not to be outdone, Suvi's widow boiled a chicken and Tookai came with boiled bananas, *uvi* (sweet potato) and *kumalas*. We ate with half the village standing or sitting around our table. There was a sense of imminent departure in the air. Following dinner was a boisterous *meke ta* by the gaudily dressed women. The Fijians added the *tra-la-la*—a poker-faced, stiff-legged social dance to the mix. Their outside hands were entwined in front of them. John and I joined them, dancing and clapping our hands, and when Johnnie moved in with his bizarre erratic moves the entire village erupted in laughter. He looked like a crazed land crab.

It was well past midnight when we boarded TROPIC SEAS. Johnnie, as usual, chose to spend his last hours ashore sleeping uncovered on a *pandanu* mat. We weighed anchor soon after dawn. Mike, Tookai, and Samesi came to see us out of the pass, which that day was very peaceful. We said our tearful goodbyes on the open sea. Una gave us a huge bear hug, kissed our boys, and struggled over the stern to the outrigger. Words were so futile. As the wind drew us away I could see Una weeping and a moment later John and I joined her.

We pushed TROPIC SEAS northward and by early afternoon we were navigating through the labyrinth of coral formations in the Tongan Pass, near Vanua Mbalavu. It was a navigational hell of dead-end channels with barely enough room to turn around, but we finally made it to the main village where a boat came for Mesake, Joe, and Anna. A few days later, when Mesake was well enough to walk, we left September 8 with two thousand miles to go before Sydney Harbor. The trade winds caught us and we traveled hundreds of miles in just a few days. The islands slipped by: Ovalau, Moturiki, Tomberua, and many smaller isles. On occasion we stopped, but on the shores of one island we caught Johnnie swinging a deadly coral snake by the tail and a second time at another island Roger decided to walk in the ocean until the water was over his head. Each time my screams brought John to the rescue.

15

Onward to Australia

*W*e arrived at Mbau, infamous throughout the world for its bestial, bloodletting cannibalism. At Mbau, not too long ago, reigned the rapacious, frosty-bearded cannibal King Cakobau. Crusty old Cakobau thought nothing of roasting two hundred victims for a feast. The bodies were slit open, filled with hot stones (after the entrails were removed), wrapped in banana leaves, placed on hot corals, and then covered with sand to remain until well done. The tongues and hearts were the choice parts. These the chiefs ate. The hands were thrown to the dogs and children.

John decided to sail up the mud-choked Navuloa River to take a short cut through the island. We struggled at points but native children running along the banks, waving to Johnnie, often diverted our attention from the task. Later, the bedraggled, paint-hungry homes of Indian families stared at us. The little Navuloa River suddenly spilled itself into Fiji's great Rewa River. The Rewa in turn emptied itself into the crevasses and caverns of a long arm of a heavily toothed reef.

"How about anchoring for a spot of tea and lunch?" I queried.

"Sure," John replied. "I've had enough river sailing anyway."

So, on a whim, we decided to lunch at Nukulau, September 14, 1953, instead of running directly to Suva—an action that may have saved our lives.

I called the boys when lunch was ready. We had taken our first mouthfuls when suddenly the air around us seemed to quiver. A rumbling, crunching blow struck our keel and the boat trembled.

"*John!*" I screamed. He grabbed for the rail. Then the anchor gave way and a roar filled the air. Another blow struck the keel and voices screamed from the shore. John dashed below to get the kids. I watched as the little island throbbed in spasmodic jerks. One half snapped one way, the other half the other way. The palms swayed crazily. Coconuts plummeted to the ground.

"*Earthquake! Earthquake!*" John shouted from the galley way. He jumped to the deck and in a second was holding on to me. We watched as people on the shore threw themselves onto the sand. The roar of the shuddering earth grew about us, drowning out our voices. Then a moment later it was all over. A few minutes went by and we turned to each other and laughed.

"Well, let's eat lunch!" I said, brushing myself off.

"Why not? Would you like a little more earthquake for dessert?"

"No, thanks." I smiled.

"*Wait a minute!*" John said, jumping up to his feet. "I wonder . . ."

"Wonder *what*?" I asked, irritated at his secrecy.

"I wonder if the earthquake caused a *tidal wave* . . . you know, *a tsunami*?"

We both ran to the rails, and sure enough, above the reef in the distance, heading toward Suva, we saw a white halo mounting ominously. This was not the spray from sea-pounded reefs—this halo looked like it was over a hundred feet high!

"My God, look at that!" John pointed out.

Then I glanced at the reefs surrounding us.

"John, the water's dropping around us!" I shouted.

John looked and sure enough the sand was being uncovered ahead of our bow. I panicked, but John sprang into action, working with the raw strength of a Tasmanian devil over a fresh kill, and quickly drew the anchor in. The lagoon water was running out to sea like a river and the water was growing shallower by the minute—we were in danger of grounding! Reefs near us began to uncover. I jumped to start the engine to escape the shallow chasm of naked coral walls where we now stood. As we looked back we could see the great head of water in the distance, racing toward us.

"I'm putting the kids in the forecabin!" I shouted to John.

The wave continued on hissing and churning on the far reefs, well over the height of our masts. It thundered like a distant train. Everyone in view panicked. John ran around like a crazy man trying to do ten things in ten seconds. Our propeller fouled and our engine died. We were at the mercy of the ocean. As John ran to raise sail TROPIC SEAS was thrown on her beam ends and shoved toward the beach. Water flooded our decks and the rails went under. TROPIC SEAS shuddered again as she struck hard on what was the beach just a few minutes ago.

"I've still got the tiller!" I screamed to John over the roar.

In situations like that everything is in slow motion and every word is remembered for eternity. The big wave jumped inland on Mokaluva; fortunately, Nukulau lies inside the reef so that the tsunami wave split into two massive sections. Again we struck hard; our masts quaked and the swirling second wave dragged us from the beach and turned us around like a cork in a bathtub. It pulled us out toward certain doom on the coral reef but we stopped spinning just a boat length away from its jagged edges. Water poured like waterfalls off the coral banks, boiling into the lagoon and creating conflicting hillocks of water that crashed into each other. John threw both anchors over in an attempt to secure our position, but they did not hold. Another backlash pulled us closer to the coral edge. John hauled up the mizzen, and then stood on the rising stern to fend us off a knotted coral lump.

"We gotta stay clear!" screamed John.

I fell down in the commotion and grabbed onto John's leg.

Then, seemingly from nowhere, a launch appeared in the distance with a powerful motor humming. The man looked remarkably familiar, but his hat covered his eyes and we were too busy to pay much attention to his face at the time. The stranger pulled near, tied us to his stern and dragged us over the crashing mounds of water to a deeper part of the lagoon.

"*John!*" came the voice of a friend. He took his hat off.

"Alf! Dammit!" John shouted! Alf was a Fijian sailor friend we thought we had left behind a month earlier, but some act of destiny had brought us together under the most unlikely of circumstances. So there we lay, still tossing in the lagoon center, watching the wild headers as they continued their run over the reefs and the lagoon. Fifteen minutes later the sea calmed. Everywhere the lagoon was covered with dead fish and debris from wrecked ships. Thousands of stunned fish swam feebly by our boat. A shark slid by us, swimming drunkenly on his side. I actually felt sorry for him.

Several hours later we waved a goodbye thanks to Alf after he pulled us free of the roiling lagoon. We stayed close behind him until we put down anchor off the Suva Yacht Club. There we learned that widespread damage had occurred ranging from numerous landslides, earthquake rents in the near hills and valleys, to the sinking of seven sailing craft. Many other craft in the lagoon were irreparably damaged by the tidal wave. If we had not decided to take lunch just minutes before the earthquake struck, we very well could have had the same fate as numerous vessels. John and I readily agreed that night that Fiji had suddenly lost its romantic charm. We sat on the deck for a long time just staring at the tropical seas surrounding us. Everything was so calm now, who would have ever suspected that danger and death could be seconds away at any moment? Around us floated dozens of bobbing lights from boats that had scattered for deep water in their search for safety from the treacherous reefs.

"Where should we go tomorrow?" I asked quietly, as if not to disturb the peace of the ocean.

"Your pick: New Zealand or New Caledonia."

"New Caledonia . . . it's sounds closer to home!" I said thoughtfully.

"And it's got milder winds," he responded.

"Well, I'm all for milder these days!"

We both laughed and some of the day's tension was relieved, even though we continued to feel occasional heavy and unnerving thuds against the boat, created by aftershocks of the earthquake.

The next afternoon we took a last glance at the purple towers of Fiji and turned to face six hundred miles of heaving water. John and Johnnie both became nature boys, stripping down to their birthday suits. Our sea routine came back quickly: wash up the evening dishes in the bucket on deck; pin Stevie and Roger into diapers for the night and tuck all three boys in at six o'clock. Their noises of play and shouting rose above the sound of the breaking sea against our bilges and the mutterings of our gear at work. I held the first watch from six to eight; then I awoke John to a star-filled night from eight to ten, and so on. By dawn, the children were busy with their activities of dismembering everything within reach. It was always strange to hear their baby voices over the gray face of the sea at dawn. By afternoon the boys were down for a nap again, and John would read his contemplative tomes about existentialism and philosophical paradigm shifts and I would entertain myself with my wonderful "penny dreadfuls," as John affectionately called them.

On the afternoon of the fourth day away from Fiji I asked John about Aneityum, the most outlying of the New Hebrides Islands to our north.

"We're about forty miles away," he answered from his navigational perch.

"You sure?"

"Absolutely. We're on a dead course for New Caledonia. And the weather looks pretty good from up here!"

Ah, the voice of confidence. But that was all that it was. Within an hour I saw a huge hairy arm of a cloud in the distance.

"John! That looks like a mean one bearing down on us."

"Yeah . . ." he said, nonchalantly, "I suppose it is." He scrambled down from his perch and dropped the main.

"Start the engine, honey," he said. "We'll want to stay straight in this one!"

A knuckle of black sky broke loose from the rolling cloud; the sky darkened to midnight and the sea went white. Poor TROPIC SEAS shuddered with the first blast as the wind screamed through the decks. I pushed the bow up to meet it, then heard the mizzen rip and shred into pieces. The wind shrieked in my ears. The forestaysail went soon afterward and cross seas tossed us and we went broadside into a trough. Another sea behind us crashed with the first with us in between. Both massive waves hovered above us, then met and crested right over me. All I remember is being lifted high on a crest and watching the cabin go by. I saw John screaming at me as he caught the mast, except there was no sound. In a minute it was over.

"*Mary! Mary!*" was all I could hear. I heard his footsteps running to the cockpit where I should have been. I could feel his panic but I could not move.

"*Mary! Mary!*" he screamed again, running, and then he saw me, the water still pouring off me as I struggled to my knees. John grasped me and pushed the strings of wet hair away from my face. I coughed as he hugged me closely. As soon as I felt safe I let loose with a string of foul words that almost calmed the wild seas around me. I have never felt so wonderful cursing and blaspheming like a true sailor. John held me back a bit, shocked at the tirade pouring from my mouth.

"Well," he said, "you must be OK!"

I coughed again and cursed again, shaking a wet fist at the sea.

"You bastard son of a whore!" I shouted one last time. Then my anger was spent.

"Let me check you for broken bones." He found none. My body was bruised all over but I got up, brushed myself off, and walked to the tiller.

"C'mon, John," I said. "We're still in that damn gale!"

The wind howled through the masts.

"Let me check on the kids," he said.

Roger and Stevie, as always, had slept through the commotion. Johnnie, however, was resentful, complaining that he missed the wave because water poured through the main hatch, drenching him. John and Johnnie appeared on deck and John explained to him that the wave was loud but that the bulk of the noise came from his mother. I gave John a nasty look in return. We battered that storm and half a dozen of its offsprings for several days. John decided to shoot across Havannah Pass—one well known for its sea-faring dangers. It was a risk worth taking.

New Caledonia is not easily approached from any direction. Her reefs are worse that those in the South Pacific, and they are poorly charted. They lie in great circlets and crescents, often many miles from shore. Her lagoons are a gnarl of coral heads and patches and all her passes have their dangers: treacherous currents, overfalls, and scraggy, unpredictable reefs. We approached her from the south and did well, sliding past the mammoth Tiamoru reef, where we found one vessel stranded and vacated, held fast on the coral, her back broken and her stern section already eaten by the sea. It was ample warning to be wary!

Havannah Pass proved to be child's play. We ran past tall soft-domed mountains gashed red in parts by erosion, and here and there we found giant pencil pines that reared up like radio towers. After a break anchoring, we moved onward, passed Porcupine Island, Mont-Dore, then to Nouméa, where John said he had been stationed during World War II. It was a squalid, half-hearted city, sprawling unkempt on a hillside, but French officialdom added some haughty, local color to it.

New Caledonia lies on the threshold of the Tasman Sea—moody, violent, unpredictable. We stayed for a week in Nouméa, awed by the rugged beauty of New Caledonia, but soon it came time to cross the brooding Tasman to reach Brisbane. John patched and toughened our flagging sails and I filled up on stores, did a fall cleaning below decks, and kept Stevie and Roger aboard. In my spare time I sketched our dream house. When we set sail, Johnnie, once again, had a tough time breaking away from new friends, especially Sigurd, with whom he had captured or killed numerous invisible desperados. As TROPIC SEAS departed they gave each other a six-gun salute in their space helmets. Again on the open seas, we headed toward the iron-sided jaws of Dumbea Pass, where foul currents could do great harm to even the greatest vessels. John and I looked back at the last coral reef that could wreak havoc on TROPIC SEAS. It was rather exhilarating.

That night we hit a black northeaster. I called John up before my watch was up:

"I think our canvas is going to go any minute!" I shouted over the wind.

"Damn, we're not going to end this trip beaten up by another gale! This should be over by morning!"

He grappled with the main and punched it into stops, set the storm trysail and brought in the starboard twin spinnaker. The boat muddled through the next two days before calm seas started to plague us. Our wind faltered, went into torpor, and we lay on a pulsing sea with nothing to move us. We took advantage of the calm, though, reading books, playing with the boys, storing up our hours with them in preparation for the next gale when they would receive no attention at all.

Then heavy weather hit again. A year earlier such intense gales would have chilled our blood and sent us packing. Now, we simply adjusted, familiar with the routine of storms at sea.

"Nothing to this one," I heard John say.

"No, we're old salts. Nothing will get us down again!"

Days brought storms with wild winds; then nights fell with calms and dead air. One afternoon I was napping and John was on watch when Johnnie came running down the galley way.

"Dad!" he shouted. "I see land!"

"No way, son," John said, wakening. "We're too far away from Australia to see land."

"Let's go see," I said sleepily.

Far in the distance, we could see Cape Byron, one hundred miles from Brisbane.

"*Australia!*" I shouted. I grabbed Johnnie's hands and did a little jig.

"Yeah, that's it," John verified with appreciation and relief in his voice.

We stayed at sea, skirting the coast because the ports of the Australian north coast are bar harbors. The sand bars throw up thundering surf, through which runs a wending channel among the shifting banks of sand. We preferred not to take another chance so close to Australia. In particular, we were wary of the infamous Tasman Sea, a breeding ground of storms that only loses its delinquency down the full coast.

At five a.m. the next day I called to John during his sleep.

When he rose to the deck he saw me with both hands on the tiller, feet braced across the cockpit, and pulling back with all my strength to keep us straight. He blanched visibly at the high seas—like nothing he had seen before—great white-faced mountains of water, their crests leaping with froth. They picked us up in their boiling rage, ran with us shaking in their grasp, and dumped us on their backsides.

"Welcome to the Tasman!" John shouted in my ear, taking control of the tiller. Later he told me how proud he was to have me as his wife and "captain."

"We could have easily sheered off into a great wave, but you held us steady!"

"I was too afraid to look back," I responded.

"It's a good thing you didn't . . . the giant walls of water rearing up behind us would have paralyzed you in fright!"

"That's why I *never* look back!"

"*Never?*" he queried.

"No, *never*! I never look back at *anything*!"

At that moment the skies opened up and dispensed a virtual cascade of cold, oversized raindrops. The cockpit filled in minutes. Thunder filled the air and lightning crackled all around us. We were forced below to our bunks where we both lay cursing the Tasman! We figured the winds were blowing at 60 miles per hour or more and there was absolutely nothing we could do.

Two hours later we awoke. The storm had abated. The sky was clear, except for wisps and trails of cirrus clouds on the horizon. These were "serious" clouds as Johnnie called them and they meant yet another gale was coming. We counted: in ten days we had seen three gales, two calms, and two immense thunderstorms. We had sailed a thousand miles of the Tasman Sea and had seen barely eighteen hours of good sailing weather. We admitted it to each other: we were licked, bone tired.

So we gambled. Somewhere near, we knew, was Newcastle, a mining and steel town with an approachable harbor. We slanted to the southeast and at noon we saw tall smokestacks and finally Knobby's head, which lies at Newcastle's entrance. Johnnie brought up the American flag as we motored in. The quiet harbor water was such a contrast to stormy sees that it woke Roger. Johnnie ran around the deck waving the flag, shouting to Sunday fishermen that we were Americans. We cleared officialdom in an hour and looked for something to eat, but in Australia, the only forms of business allowed to stay open at that time were churches and funeral parlors. Lucky for us the wives of the customs officials brought us fresh fruits, vegetables, meat, eggs, and bread. We feasted—in Australia, my motherland. It was incredible that I was home after all these years. That night another gale hit with a fury and we smiled at each other in our wisdom.

We sailed on a fresh mid-afternoon and before long we rounded up before the sheer-faced Sydney Heads and slanted into the broad deep lake of Sydney's unusual harbor. The ferries shuttled across the harbor with their loads of morning workers. The crowds looked upon us with cold-faced curiosity. A tug hooted a welcome. Two miles down the green-walled bay, Sydney's buildings pressed to the water's edge. Then we neared the splendid steel-arched Sydney Harbor Bridge—a showpiece on the skyline. In our courting days, John and I had crossed that bridge many times, and now, nine years later, a flood of memories came back as we sailed beneath that same bridge.

We folded our tired canvas. This voyage had ended. I was home once again.

"Uma-lava pisupo (I love you)!" I said to John.

"Uma-lava pisupo!" he returned, hugging the children and me closely.

16

Tragedy Strikes

About a year after our arrival in Australia, Stevie came down with a terrible respiratory cold followed by an intractable infection and meningitis. Just a week later his little body ceased its struggle and Stevie died quietly in our arms. He was just three and a half. John and I were simply devastated. I remember the tears pouring forth so quickly they missed my cheeks and hit the floor directly. John encircled me with his arms as I slowly rocked the lifeless body of our baby. Only a mother who has lost a child can possibly understand the grief that such a loss brands on your soul for eternity. Nothing makes it go away; there is no such thing as "closure."

"Oh Mary, I'm so sorry," John sobbed over and over as he stroked Stevie's hair.

I was mute.

I remember staring in a trance at Stevie's face, not able to believe that this terrible thing had happened to our baby. And I remember vindictive thoughts flooding through my mind: A small helpless child killed by a merciful god! Ha! It changed my attitude on life and death forever. It was bad enough when adults died, but a defenseless child? And Stevie was *my* child! A huge gaping hole was torn in my heart that to this day has never quite healed.

Stevie died of a rare congenital disease, Hunter's (also called Hurler's) Syndrome, and for that reason his immune system was very weak. At birth it was hard to believe that our perfect-looking baby would be physically disfigured in just a few years by his own faulty metabolism that ultimately would lead to immune deficiency, mental retardation, and cardiac abnormalities, among other symptoms. When the doctors diagnosed him in California we were going to give up our adventure, but Sterling Hayden (the late actor and author of the powerful memoir, *Wanderer*, as well as the novel *Voyage*) directed us to a specialist who advised us that the air of the open sea was far better than the polluted air of Los Angeles and that our baby would be happiest in the open air. He said the best thing for all of us was to not give up our dream and to provide for Stevie with all our love and attention as long as he lived. And this we did. We left on our voyage when Stevie was only eight months old. He could speak, but mostly he played below with pots and pans, laughing constantly. Stevie was a happy soul and it was easier to cope as a family with his disabilities on the open sea than it was in Los Angeles with all the additional stress of civilization.

Throughout the entire trip across the South Pacific he kept his weight and his strength; however, we were very careful bringing him ashore because of his compromised immune system. We would always check out the ports first and only bring him ashore when we were sure there were no endemic illnesses going about. The truth was, though, that he was rarely sick on the voyage. Nonetheless, caring for Stevie often created a terrible psychological and physical load on our marriage. Stevie died at the Children's Hospital in Newcastle, where we had returned for his treatment after our arrival in Sydney, and we buried him at the children's cemetery next to the hospital, overlooking the sea where he first arrived in Australia. I can still hear my baby playing with pots and pans on our Pacific voyage. Stevie is still very much with me and is always much comforted in my dreams.

17

Revisiting My Youth

Stevie's death was so traumatic it nearly ended our round-the-world adventure. It took years of weeping for me just to cleanse my thoughts about life. We lived in several suburban homes for five years—plenty of time to revisit my childhood.

I was born Mary Kershaw Taylor in Wakefield, England on St. Valentine's Day, February 14, 1923. My father, John Holmes Taylor, was an officer in the Fleet Air Arm and served as a pilot during World War I. He and my mother, Laura Ida Taylor (an officer in the Land Army), along with my two sisters, Mildred and Jean, immigrated to Australia when I was four. We took the orient line ship ORAMA and arrived in Fremantle, Western Australia on August 24, 1927. I have little recollection of the six-week voyage, except for a few odd memories such as having a bad case of ringworm and my hair cut really short because of it. I was mortally embarrassed and hung my head low, avoiding eye contact with people, because they thought I was a little boy and I hated the confused looks people cast my way.

The accommodations on the boat were typical of those for immigrants. For example, when we had to wash our personal laundry we hung them from a line to dry. One day my bored sisters and I decided to take the laundry line and rig up a swing. We tied it to the ship's rail and had a great time swinging out over the open ocean until the ship's officer and some seamen came rushing up with my mother and father close behind them.

"What are you *doing*?" my appalled mother screamed.

"Swinging!" we said innocently.

"Look below!" my father said angrily, pointing at the wild waves of the ocean fifty feet below us. "We wouldn't even know you were gone!"

With that we were reprimanded severely and sent off to our cabin, bleating like terrified lambs.

After spending time in quarantine in Melbourne we were free to depart for the farm my father had bought at Katandra, near Shepparton, in Victoria. I remember being in love with the farm at first sight and for some odd reason I was particularly drawn to the cowshed and the wide-open paddocks. The farmhouse was constructed of compressed mud bricks that kept the house fairly cool in the broiling heat of summer and insulated during the cold of winter. My sisters and I played out much of our early youth on the inviting wrap-around veranda, which attached to the kitchen and bathhouse, next to the kitchen where we had a huge wood stove that provided warmth in winter.

Another fireplace provided heat to the remainder of the house. My father, who was new at farming, became adept rather quickly at stacking the bales of hay and storing fodder for the animals in winter, but it was a difficult and exhausting existence. My mother would break up the tough soils of paddock behind a plow pulled by two huge draft horses. She loved "driving" the horses and working the land. Like my father, she was also an officer, but in the Army during World War I.

Not long after we arrived in Australia our childhood freedom ended and we were required to attend the one-room schoolhouse nearly two miles from our farm. For several years we used a horse and gig for transportation because we could not afford a car. In the beginning my parents needed the horse and gig for work and that meant we children had to walk the two miles to school and back each day.

"Two miles each way!" my sister shouted to no one in particular upon hearing of what was to be our daily trek.

"It'll build your character," my dad said with finality. At first we dreaded the walk, but later we came to appreciate it and even look forward to it. Life on the farm was consistently hard but always rewarding. We never had to worry about the future or world events because our work schedule and school kept us at the grindstone and out of trouble. Even so, there was a lot of time for wholesome play, which sometimes also brought disaster.

I remember in particular one afternoon we wandered down to find mushrooms on the last paddock of the property, quite a distance from our house. My sister Jean loved horses, but this day she wandered too close to our huge draft horse. A moment later she was struck in the head by the chain on the hoof of the horse. The impact split her lip and opened a huge gash over her left eye. At first we all screamed and jumped up and down in panic as the blood spurted from her wounds, but seconds later I made Mildred stay to help Jean while I ran like a banshee to get my mom and dad. I was screaming and yelling as I approached the house and my parents instinctively got the horse and gig ready. They were familiar with the scenario. They picked up Jean and went directly to the hospital. I remember my father in the distance shouting "Gee up Colonel! Gee up boy, Gee up!" My mother wrapped up Jean's head in towels. (She recovered completely and miraculously to this day has never lost her love of horses.) After the gig left with Jean for the hospital I noticed that my feet were swollen and painful: I had run through a patch of thistles and my tough feet, normally impenetrable, looked like two porcupines. Mildred spent many hours with forceps pulling out the painful needles.

"How long do I have to do this?" she said at one point.

"Until they're all *gone!*" I replied angrily.

There were few diversions in the isolated area where we lived: dances for the adults; games and picnics for the kids. My father entertained us every Saturday with a silent movie show and my mother, a concert pianist, played along making the movie into what we erroneously called a "talkie."

The years seemed to fly by on the farm, and as they did so, my mother's health deteriorated and she needed closer medical supervision. We were not doing well financially anyway, so we sold the farm and moved to Geelong, a "big city" near Melbourne. It was harder to say goodbye to all our animal friends, especially Jean's horse, Colonel, than to our neighbors and friends. My father began working as a manager for a relative who owed a textile mill. Our house in suburbia was pleasant enough, but we preferred the open spaces of the country to the cramped style of Geelong. I am sure this is where I began to acquire my wanderlust for wide-open spaces. Shortly after my father was made manager of the mill, he designed a house and built it in Wangaratta. It was a beautiful two-story house situated on the edge of a big park with a wonderful view of a stream as it wound its way through the valley below. Soon after, my father was promoted to a managerial position of a much larger textile mill in Sydney and we once again moved to a larger, suburban house.

A few years later my sister Mildred (formerly a tomboy) and I began to compete overtly for the attention of each other's boyfriends. At eighteen I began working in an office in Sydney, where I meet my first serious boyfriend, Keith. We went on hikes together through the Blue Mountains west of Sydney, to movies, dinners, and office parties and balls. But all that came to an abrupt halt when Keith enlisted in the Air Force at the end of 1941. In April of the following year, I enlisted in the WAAAF (Women's Auxiliary Australian Air Force) and was sent to rookie training camp. I missed terribly my family and Keith (who was stationed in England) and settled down to a dreary life of discipline and khaki clothes. Even our underwear was made of khaki. But at least our pajamas were pink!

After we were sworn in we automatically earned the title of ACW (Air Craft Woman). The tennis court served as the parade ground and we marched daily along country roads singing dull and monotonously irritating WAAAF songs. It took some doing, but I finally got used to sleeping on a straw mattress (a Hessian sack filled with straw on a folding steel cot). As a concession to the women, we were given two sheets and two pillowcases along with our blankets. The men received only one of each. After completing my rookie training I was transferred to Air Force Headquarters in Melbourne as a clerk general. When I first joined the

Air Force I wanted to do something different (such as drive a truck or a staff car or fold parachutes). As soon as they discovered that I had graduated from college as a secretary, however, I was made into a stenographer because they were desperately short of clerical staff.

18

A Bit of Texas

Despite the longer hours and lower pay than those of my civilian job, I loved my time in the Air Force. During my stint I was posted to several different stations. For nearly a year I was assigned to an operational training unit for dive-bombers. I was secretary to the commanding officer and also took down evidence at court martials. Life was exciting at the station with planes taking off and landing throughout the day, creating a constant drone in the skies. WAAAFs were allowed to fly with the practicing pilots and we had a great time flying over the headlands on the coast and buzzing the beaches. This activity, intended strictly to show off, was called "wool gathering" and it was also strictly against military regulations.

I was disappointed when I was transferred to another unit on the outskirts of Canberra. This also was a technical training unit with an airfield close by with plenty of action. My disappointment vanished when I met an airman nicknamed Tex. I was on duty in the Orderly Room and had just been promoted to corporal. Every evening trainees confined to barracks reported for cleanup duty in the Orderly Room.

"We have to report to Corporal Taylor," the handsome airman said to me.

"*I'm* Corporal Taylor," I replied, noticing his strange accent.

"*Well . . .*" he said in a drawl, looking me over.

"Are you an American?" I asked coolly.

"That I am!" he responded with enthusiasm. Of course, I *knew* he was an American. Who could have missed that thick Texas accent! In fact, the whole station was already talking about this American who had joined the RAAF. I was immediately intrigued by the mysterious Tex.

"Well, my birth name is John Caldwell," he said with a cock-eyed, confident smile smudged with a touch of arrogance. "And your full name is . . ." he continued, extending his hand.

"Mary. Mary Taylor," I said shaking his hand firmly. I was thrilled with his firm handshake and the masculinity of his touch.

We spent most of the evening talking while the other trainees did most of the cleaning. We prepared a snack for everyone by upturning a radiator to toast bread and warm cups of tea. The airmen left when the cleaning was finished but not before I agreed to go on a date with John on my first night off. Unfortunately, the rules and regulations of fraternizing with the opposite sex were pretty strict at the Station. There was a high fence around the WAAAF quarters and we had to be in by 11 p.m. on our night off or suffer the repercussions. We were not allowed to come in through the guard gate and there was a sentry there at all times. In anticipation of being late, we stacked firewood on both sides so we could approach the gate and safely jump over to the other side unobserved after hours. It worked wonderfully—and many times!

John and I had an immediate and fond relationship. I pretended to like some of his books (with the exception of those on sailing such as the *Cruise of the* TEDDY by Erling Tambs, which did not interest me in the least). Little did I know at the time how seriously John took true-life sailing adventures! He had spent the majority of his life dreaming of sailing around the world; daydreams of the open sea were an escape for him.

"Why Australia?" I asked him just hours into our first date.

"Adventure," he said flatly.

"Wasn't there enough in the States?"

"Well, actually, no. In 1941 I was a student at Santa Barbara State College (now the University of California at Santa Barbara). I got my pilot's license in the college flight-training program just about the time the Japanese attacked Pearl Harbor."

"So why didn't you go to Hawaii for adventure?"

"I didn't pass the physical. I had a punctured ear drum and they wouldn't accept me. All the other armed forces turned me down for the same reason. So I joined the American Merchant Marine and spent two years as a deckhand motoring from one port to the next throughout the world."

"But how did that get you to Australia?"

"Well, that's another story," he said cagily.

"So, tell me!" I demanded.

"In early 1944 I sailed aboard the Swedish merchant ship NUOLJA from Veracruz, Mexico to Sydney. When I got here I saw a sign that read: "Join the RAAF," so I signed up."

"What about your eardrum?"

"The Aussies weren't concerned at all about my eardrum. That's how I got here. I was in the flight-training program flying Tiger Moths, training bi-planes. And the day before I met you I was grounded and confined to the drome and told to do administrative work."

"So you met me because you were *grounded*!"

"Yeah . . . I was flying upside down over the beaches and someone reported me."

"Whom should I thank?" I asked, giving him a hug.

"Your dim-witted superiors!" he said, laughing.

Our romance continued for a full nine months. But John missed the action of the open ocean; for that reason, he asked to be discharged from the RAAF and go back to the Merchant Marines and the open sea. Soon afterward, he left the station to board the MILLEN GRIFFITH, a Liberty Ship in Sydney Harbor transporting Australian troops between Brisbane and Manus Island in the Admiralty Group north of New Guinea. (It was on one of the trips to Brisbane that we were married in Sydney on May 23, 1945. We raced through a three-day honeymoon, but that was not unusual during the war.) The ship was transporting Australian troops to New Guinea when it went aground on the east coast of New Guinea, much to the amusement of the troops on board. The troops were ordered ashore to surround the stranded ship, as they were not sure if they were in Japanese-held territory. The ship was eventually towed off and limped back to Manus. Upon his arrival John signed on as crew on a tanker. At one point his ship was torpedoed and sank in the Pacific; he spent several days in a lifeboat with the other surviving crewmembers.

John remained aboard ship, crisscrossing the globe for ten months, until the war ended and he signed off in April 1946, in New York City. That's when things started to fall apart for us. John could not find passage back to Australia because there was a shortage of civilian planes and ships. Nothing had been converted back to civilian passage service and everything available was booked solid. Looking for a ship, John went down to New Orleans and then to Galveston. He got on a ship headed for Panama, thinking at least he was going in the right direction and could surely find another ship there headed toward Australia. But in Panama, he found the same problem: no ships were going to Australia. So it was then that he saw PAGAN, a 26-year-old Norwegian built sloop, on a mooring at the Balboa Yacht Club.

John decided the quickest way to be reunited with me was to buy PAGAN and sail solo over 9,000 miles back to Sydney. Of course, all hell broke loose because frankly, John was not a sailor at that time. Before he set sail he actually bought a book about sailing aptly entitled *How to Sail* and using that attempted to sail across the Pacific Ocean alone, with two cats and a stowaway rat. There were many serious mishaps and many wonderful adventures, but ultimately he ran into a hurricane that nearly wrecked PAGAN on the reefs that surrounded Tuvutha. John told me once:

"I knew I could live a long time without food, but not without water. So the food rationing didn't worry me. But I was 49 days without real food. It was horrible. I went from 165 pounds in Panama down to 80 or 90 by the time I was rescued in Tuvutha."

John ate everything in sight: shoe leather, sea birds, and fat cockroaches were a particular delicacy.

"I would have eaten anything!" he exclaimed. "Hunger is a terrible thing. Starvation is not really physically painful but it *is* emotionally painful. You have no choice but to watch your body waste away before you. It takes twenty to forty days to die a numbing death."

"Would you have eaten a human?" I once asked innocently.

"Certainly, but I would only eat a corpse. Although I used to have vivid dreams of eating children, though."

"*Oohhh* . . . that's so nice," I said.

"Even after I was rescued," he said," I kept food by my bed so there'd be no chance of waking up and not being able to get something to eat."

Dreams of starving to death plagued John for nearly twenty years. The worst part for me was that I knew virtually nothing at that point of John's desperate voyage. He wrote a letter to me before he left saying that the boat was the smallest he had ever seen with the smallest crew, but not to worry. That was all. But John gave my address to an American GI in the Perlas Islands, and *he* wrote to tell me of the details of John's voyage: that he was alone on a boat the size of a large bathtub. I even felt guilty for not being able to worry about his fate until the last several months of his voyage, after he had already been rescued!

19

Outward Bound

*P*erhaps because Stevie died, or perhaps because the sea was never far from our hearts and minds, John and I came to dislike our lives. Small complaints lead to larger dissatisfaction and ultimately we decided that we felt "cabin-bound." It was time to resume our world voyage. At that time John was a personnel officer in the Burroughs Wellcome pharmaceutical company and I was a secretary in a shipping company on the Sydney Harbor waterfront. It was great for a while, but boredom led to itchy feet and John complained constantly about being "cold." Of course, anything below 70 F was too cold for John. Even Southern California was too cold for John! He was built for the tropics. Between the two of us, John's need for warm weather, our collective need for adventure, and the desire to give to our two children a life voyage they would never forget, we decided to weigh anchor once again and continue our trip around the world.

Now, John loved Sydney Harbor. It was a sailor's fantasy come true: it stretched sixteen miles deep into the continent, was festooned with cozy coves, and traversed by the famous Sydney Bridge. Sydney was growing like a mushroom on a warm autumn day, but the upcoming opulence was lost on John's sensibilities.

"It's just a smaller version of Los Angeles and motivated by the same public disease: *greed!*" he said one night.

"I'm having a hard time too but it's *home* to me!" I countered.

"Yes, and Texas was my 'home', for what it was worth, but now it's time for us to move on and continue our voyage! Look around us. It's just a matter of years before we're just like everybody else. I just can't do that, Mary. We promised ourselves we wouldn't do that!"

John was always very convincing and frankly, although I loved Australia, John had hooked me on the adventure of the open ocean. Nothing could buy that feeling of freedom—certainly not the perfect house in suburbia.

"You're right," I finally announced in what John used to call my unflappable manner. "I'm on board."

Our plans developed slowly over the next two years. Every night John and I talked about high seas with remote islets and slumbering bays. After building a new ocean-going sailboat we would go first to the Barrier Reef, to North Australia, through the Indian Ocean to Ceylon (now Sri Lanka), and, if the political situation permitted, on to Aden and the Red Sea. We also planned to visit England, pass through the canals of France, then on to Italy, the Mediterranean, north to Scandinavia, south across the Atlantic to the West Indies, then north again to New York along the Great Lakes to the Mississippi River, through the Gulf, past Cuba on the way down to Mexico, and across the Panama Canal, then back to the Pacific, up the coast of Mexico, California, Alaska, and across the Pacific to Hawaii, Tahiti, and again to Sydney, Australia.

Whew! Needless to say, it was quite the dream! Yes, there would be disruptions in the family life: the boys were in regular school and doing well. But a formal education would pale beside what we could offer our sons by continuing our ocean voyage. We decided that a good correspondence course for the boys would suffice for an education and I was "elected" to be schoolmarm every morning, six days a week. Once the decision was announced the boys' enthusiasm boiled over.

"Let's go tomorrow!" shouted Johnnie.

"Yeah, tomorrow!" shouted Roger.

"First things first," John replied. "First we need a boat!"

We had sold TROPIC SEAS in order to buy a house in Lindfield, a nice residential suburb on the north side of Sydney Harbor. We went off nightly to Sydney's big public library to seek out plans for a boat that we would build ourselves. It needed to be bigger than TROPIC SEAS, perhaps forty feet in length (still small by today's standards). We liked the ketch rig, two masts, with a high setting yankee jib out forward. The deck would have to be flush for space and extra buoyancy.

After weeks of searching we finally found our dreamboat design in *Yachting* magazine, with lofting plans that were easy to follow. It was a jaunty Francis Herreshoff clipper-bowed ketch, Mobjack design, forty-five feet long, with a twelve-foot beam and five-foot draft. Like all ketches, she sported two raked masts, a neat taffrail around the stern, and was rigged forward with a small jib and a staysail, which meant that she could fly four small sails at once (beginning with the aft or rear: mizzen, main, staysail, and jib) rather than just two very large sails typical of sloops. There are two advantages to this: The smaller sails on a ketch are easier to handle than the large sheets of a sloop. A ketch rig also has the effect of lowering and spreading the center of thrust in the boat, which makes the vessel more balanced, although slightly lower in the water. Balance—which translates into the ability of a boat to sail itself—is very important on the open seas.

She was a sexy boat with her clipper bow, oval stern and slanted masts. John loved her because she was practical and seaworthy. In short, she was beautiful from all angles!

"What should we call her?" I asked John.

Our collective minds set to work. Within an hour we came up with and approved OUTWARD BOUND. Why? Because that was simply our goal: to be off to seaward, looking for adventure in the sun, leaving the lights of a feverish Sydney behind.

Now we had to sell our house, find a boat builder, and move into cheaper accommodations. Selling the house proved easy. The real estate agent found someone almost immediately who wanted to settle for our former version of suburbia. Next, John found a shipwright, Bob Gordon, to build our yacht. He lived with his wife on an old boat in Berry's Bay. The yacht would be built on the shore next to his boat. We settled our accommodation problem by buying an old houseboat, and moored her alongside a boiler work, on the opposite side of Berry's Bay. We used a dinghy to cross the bay so that we could work on the boat with Bob.

We found a deserted iron keel in a slough and trucked it beside the boiler works, and there in the open, just a small island's length from the imposing Sydney Bridge, we set to building our next adventure. Bob Gordon turned out to be a crotchety fellow who quibbled with John constantly. He snorted and had fits of distemper almost daily, but he did yeoman's work of boating artistry. The work was not going fast enough for John. He resigned as personnel manager for Burroughs Wellcome to help Bob as a silent (very silent) building partner. Often they worked together for days, neither speaking a syllable to each other. John had to somehow divine his every intent and hop to it or catch his Irish ire and scowls. In a swifty sixty days Bob and John put down the keel, ribs, and planks using dense Australian gumwood.

To help with the family income I secured a position as secretary at the Central Wharf Stevedoring Company. They handled the cargo from massive ocean-going ships arriving from overseas. I could look out my office window and almost touch the bow of the ships tied alongside the wharf. After my work was finished I would stop by and help clean up shavings and put the tools away as dark unfolded, while my mother watched the children. My boss was a retired sea captain who took a keen interest in my day-by-day description of the progress on OUTWARD BOUND. He would shake his head daily and mutter, "and still only forty-five feet for the whole family! Ridiculous!"

With my mother assisting with the boys in her home in the outer suburbs, we began to make great progress on the boat. John built the main mizzenmasts on shore while my father, a dilettante carpenter, made doors, drawers, and counters to be put aboard when decks were in place. On Saturday and Sunday my parents would come out for the day and work with us. Our boys played games in and out of the growing boat while our doughty shipwright hid sullenly on his boat nearby. "I hate brats," he once said to John. It was a good thing that was said to John, not me, because I would have given him more than a small piece of my mind.

The day came when OUTWARD BOUND was planked, decked, and painted. We had a huge crane lift her high in the air and settle her gently on the harbor. That was a most amazing day: nearly a year of hard labor and all of it tied up in the fortunes of a massive crane. It seemed like the lift took an eternity. But then there she was, beautiful, settling trimly and tightly into the waters of the bay. The family and a small crowd of passersby clapped and cheered. We installed a used gasoline engine, a toilet, and two bunks. A week later we moved from our houseboat to OUTWARD BOUND. It was still a little rough, but we saved money by doing so.

From then on John labored from dawn to dusk, took a short nap, had dinner, put the clock away, and worked until he felt tired. I was always amazed at how driven he was.

"Do you know how late you worked last night?" I asked him more than once.

"No, and I don't want to know!" he would reply.

While the kids played on the piles of wood and immersed themselves in sawdust and shavings, John and I worked constantly on the boat. During the evenings I sewed sails with an ancient, hand-operated Singer sewing machine. Because I designed the living space I now felt the need to finish it. The colors I selected were gay, chartreuse, blue, lilac, red and gray. The galley was compact and the sleeping quarters were well away from the main cabin. I loved every minute of the slavery—the painting, scraping, hammering, varnishing—we put ourselves through during the two years of building OUTWARD BOUND. To save money I even made all the cushions and upholstery on the boat as well as all the boys' clothes.

A year after laying the keel we were ready to go. My parents and our sailor cronies were there for the maiden voyage. I remember them fondly, cuddling their own dreams, as they waved us away to follow our rainbow.

20

A Family at Sea

Things have changed over the past fifty years, of course, but I daresay that one thing has not: Despite all the so-called sexual and gender revolutions, the average woman's work still is never done. This is just as true today despite all the progress in women's rights as it was in 1958 when our family set sail. I had many "duties" as a housewife with children and then did double duty as a sailor and first mate. Of course, the boys were a little older and perhaps a little more responsible: Johnnie was eleven and Roger was six.

We sailed from Sydney Harbor on July 27, 1958, bound for the Great Barrier Reef on the first leg of our incredible voyage.

"Mom!" Roger shouted, "Look at the Sydney Mountains!"

I laughed, but the truth was we were overwhelmed with both apprehension and joy when we passed Sydney Heads—the landmark of Australia—gradually receding in the distance as we plowed through the waves. Sydney Heads marks the entrance to Sydney Harbor—when sailors approach from the open sea it looks at first like a continuous line of cliffs but is actually a gorgeous deep harbor split in two by the middle headland. As we passed Sydney Heads I once again felt the trepidation and excitement of myself as a small girl when my family emigrated from England to Australia. And now, the sea was opening up again in front of us, the womb of the world, a female in every right. Certainly such an untamed female would be unpredictable and organization would be our key to our success. We were re-embarking on our trip around the planet where we would be at sea for weeks or months at a time without recourse to land and the safety, shelter, food, and familiarity it offered. We needed to be prepared and self-sufficient: no U.S marine would be a match for us!

About thirty miles north of Sydney Harbor lies a beautiful inlet at the mouth of the Hawksberry River. We stopped for a few days and finished the last jobs, which included a canvas dodger around the stern—this was a safety precaution that allowed the boys much more freedom in the cockpit. We anchored in a sheltered cove where for years cruising yachts had painted their names on the rocks. We selected a flat, vertical rock and painted "1958 USA Outward Bound." It is still there today. After we left our sheltered anchorage for the open sea, we drifted up the Australian coast under light westerlies and found another snug anchorage at Coff's Harbor. There we met the captain of another boat who remembered us at port in Fiji.

"So now you have a larger boat," he said appreciatively as he looked over OUTWARD BOUND with full-blown male admiration.

"Yes," I said, "all forty-five feet of it!"

OUTWARD BOUND sailed north again and the weather was kind with westerly winds blowing steadily. We were cruising by the Gold Coast when we met a pod of whales traveling south. Their heaving bodies roiled in the waves, breaching clear of the water and then meeting the ocean on their return with a horrendous splash. One of the whales rolled to one side, eyed us carefully, and then became aggressive. He started getting closer to the boat, breaching several times as he did so, raising large waves that rocked us from side to side.

"Make some noise!" John commanded. Everyone grabbed an oar and started beating the sides of the boat to scare him off.

"*Louder!*" He shouted.

We set up a furious roar.

"*Faster!*" He shouted with panic in his voice as the whale continued to breach by our boat.

The din we created sounded like a machinegun emptying itself in a bowling alley.

Nothing happened. We feared his next leap would land him

directly on our boat. About ten feet away he rolled on his side and looked right at us with a large beady eye. I can still see that unearthly stare. Then he changed direction and swam away—perhaps he was just protecting the pod.

As we sailed through the waters off New South Wales and among the beautiful islands and barrier reefs from Queensland to Townsville, my days were filled with my share of woman's work such as cooking, laundry, cleaning, and of course, taking care of the boys—all three of them. In addition, I had my share of seafaring duties such as tending to sails, standing watch, or handling the wheel. To be fair, John and the boys handled the sails most of the time, navigated, tidied and scrubbed the decks, looked after the engine, and made the constant, general repairs. But my two small boys and husband still needed the appreciation, attention, and affection of the only woman in their life. That was something biological and the circumstances of being a mate on a ship did not diminish the responsibility that I felt.

Doing laundry somehow released stress and gave me a sense of immediate accomplishment. It was something that I could finish and check off my mental list of "things to do" even when the children were impossible and the currents of the open ocean would make me physically sick. Sometimes we would pick out appealing islands or peninsulas around which to sail and explore for a week or more. After the second day at Island Head I realized I should not use any more of the 150 gallons of fresh water stored aboard for washing. When the boys discovered a spring, we rowed ashore with soap, a galvanized tub, and a scrub brush. We boiled the spring water in the tub, although looking back, that was probably not necessary considering that the spring was miles from any source of contamination. I scrubbed sheets, towels, pants and shirts on bleached bits of driftwood, the ship's hatch cover that was beachcombed from a rambling sand spit at the head of the bay.

While I laundered, my youthful shipmates made off to shimmy up nearby coconut palms and felled fat green coconuts.

"Be careful up there!" I always shouted reflexively.

"We *are!*" They chorused back in their practiced, irritated tone.

After a simian descent they would lop the tops off the nuts with the sharp blow of a knife to drink the cool sweet milk inside. Later we would break them open and eat chunks of fresh white coconut meat. John loved coconuts and many years later he would be responsible for planting thousands of them wherever he landed in the Caribbean. There were only a few other times when I had the privilege of washing clothes in the clear waters of a bubbling creek—on the beautifully wooded slope of the inland lagoon at Middle Percy Island in the Percy Group, and in the placid pool beneath the waterfall at Nara Inlet on Hook Island. Usually, though, I did the small items in the galley sink, and kept the larger items until we called in where I could find a laundry, or borrow a washing machine. By then many of the dirtier larger items could stand by themselves.

For the most part our voyage from Sydney up to Island Head was yachting right from the pages of the most glamorous spread in the finest yachting magazines. The skies were bright, blue, and pollution free. The coastline stood out sharp and defined as none other.

"It's sooo fine!" John would always announce. "Nothing can beat this!"

And we would all agree. We had delightful weather except for the first day out when we encountered a frightening 50-knot westerly that caused us deep concern. The only other time we had nasty weather was when a testy southeast gale off Gladstone Harbor drove us wallowing and spray-swept just feet away from a dangerous rocky reef and then to the sanctuary of Bustard Head Creek, where Captain Cook had once anchored for the same reason.

The gales were not so bad in themselves. We had encountered plenty of hair-raising gales capable of inducing vomiting in the most ironclad stomach during previous voyages. Vomiting aside, my main problem and concern was how to cook for the crew when I was being tossed to-and-fro without any warning of when and how I would be tossed from moment to moment! I discovered early on how to wedge myself into a corner of the galley to gain some transient stability. As my cookery heaved, rolled, and pitched, I remember wishing frantically for at least three legs and four arms.

My job was to watch a sputtering pressure cooker while opening a tinned dessert, control the door of a packed refrigerator whose contents wanted to jump out each time the door was opened, and pass food to hungry shipmates in the cockpit who had no clue as to the difficulty of the juggling act I was performing under their direct observation. Even though I was a multi-tasking contortionist, I usually enjoyed the challenge. A seawife, like a housewife, must take both fair and foul weather in stride without complaint.

Most of our weather was fair and we drifted along, pushed by a genial offshore breeze, for many languid days on end over a limpid mirror-like sea. We stopped at numerous coastal ports and anchored at many fresh-scented Barrier Reef islands—an idyllic existence beyond our wildest imagination and certainly one most people have only dreamed about. But apart from that, each port gave me the opportunity to tend to the more mundane aspects of life, such as obtaining fresh food for salads and planning a balanced diet for the crew. This was one of my greatest responsibilities and I took it very seriously. I found that the easiest way to accomplish this vital task was to work out a menu for a single week and then order thirty-five weeks of food supplies to keep us healthy on the open seas.

Managing food stores was yet another problem. We had a kerosene refrigerator but it certainly did not perform to our expectations. Often in port, we had to wait some time for just two small trays of ice. Preventing spoilage and using food before it lost its nutritional value was often difficult. I would store eggs in salt, apples and potatoes in the cooler hold, stock canned vegetables, bring on slabs of salted bacon, and in the galley store a huge stalk or two of bananas. Another major job of mine was to administer first aid to the crew (usually I administered first aid to myself as well). The boys constantly sported small cuts, bruises, banged heads, and other typical wounds of childhood that required a mother's attention, but thankfully, our health was usually excellent and only on rare occasions did we have to call upon even elementary first aid.

"You run a tight ship, honey!" John would always say.

"Someone's got to do it!" I would always retort.

"That's why we have a wheel instead of a tiller!"

John was referring to the fact that I often steered with my feet while drinking my coffee in the morning. With the tiller of TROPIC SEAS this was very difficult. The wheel of OUTWARD BOUND made steering a more enjoyable task. And I *loved* being in charge!

In our five months' voyage to Townsville, Australia, we saw many delightful places but none more heartwarming that the lovely Whitsunday Islands. There are miles of sleeping shoreline and unspoiled beaches with every view filled with picture-postcard bays and colorful straits of unbelievable warmth. These islands were truly a yachtsman's paradise, a place where one could easily live out an entire life without complaint. There was enough food, the weather was nearly always soft and sweet, and certainly there was no need for a true job or income since one could easily live off the land and sea without stress. The Whitsundays seemed like a miniature version of the Hawaiian Islands. We did many things to fill the days: Swimming, fishing, hiking into the creek beds and up green valleys to enjoy the vistas from majestic peaks, beach combing, lazing on the deck playing cards, and just dreaming our life away bathed by the drowsy sounds of the tropic calm that engulfed us. I always thought that if Heaven were anything less than what the Whitsunday Islands could offer I would not want to go! Even at the age of 82 memories of those halcyon days still make me sleep well at night.

Eventually we sailed on to Nara Inlet, on sprawling, wooded Hook Island, where complete isolation greeted us. Nowhere had we found such total silence and such unbroken solace. A sliver of the sea meanders its way a full three miles into the heart of Hook Island, and here we anchored under stately pines surrounded by towering green cliffs of plant-covered rocks, near a plunging waterfall that made its thunder just for us. The days we spent there were bright, filled with life and full of fragrance; the nights were silent, warm, and with an ethereal calm that pervaded our souls.

21

From Townsville
to Port Victoria

Even with paradise surrounding us, we faced some mundane facts of life. Wherever we came in from the rigors of the sea, I faced some of my biggest challenges—prodding the boys to complete their correspondence courses provided by the Blackfriars School in Sydney. Under my tutelage, Johnnie and Roger studied three hours a day, six days a week. But what boy would want to study when surrounded with a natural paradise brimming with wildlife? My 8:00 wake-up call for studies always shattered the tropic calm. After schooling was finished for the day, John and the boys would go fishing or hunting up the winding verdant valleys, looking for young goats. We found the meat of young goats to be similar to that of the domesticated lamb, but slightly gamier—a taste that was easily disguised by curry or garlic. However, goat stew removed all the gaminess, and the boys would inhale their dinners.

Brampton, Lindeman, Hazelwood, Dent, Hook, Long, South Molle, and Hayman Islands all provided unforgettable times when we were brought almost magically close as a family—as family life should be. Our next port of call was the town of Bowen, famous for its large delicious mangoes, called the Bowen specials. We loaded up with enough mangoes to feed the Russian army. But the cyclone season (roughly from January to April) was closing in fast and we were forced to find a snug shelter until the return of fair weather in May.

134

We sailed north to bustling, jovial Townsville, but just hours into the run an electric storm drove us all below decks. Jagged shards of lightning struck our rigging and the sea around us as we rounded Cape Bowling Green and entered Townsville Harbor. We heaved into the main harbor without incident and secured the boat in a small creek with three anchors forward and strong lines to the shore. Our plan was to spend the Christmas holidays there, securely anchored out of harm's way. But the tranquility was not to last. A short while later the wind began to howl and scream through the rigging.

"We're gonna get hit!" John yelled. "I'm taking the sails in!"

"But we're in a *bay*!" I lamented, not believing entirely what John was predicting.

"Doesn't matter!" he shouted back as he clambered up the main mast. "Look at the creek!"

I turned to see white caps building and rolling right toward OUTWARD BOUND. We had precious little time. I marshaled the boys below. Fifteen minutes later the full force of the wind hit OUTWARD BOUND on the beam and masts and she heeled over on her starboard side, throwing us like ragged dolls across the cabin.

"John!" I screamed up the still-open hatchway. "Get below!"

"I'm going ashore to ride it out!" he shouted back. "You and the kids stay on the boat! You'll be safer here . . . I'll secure the hatch!"

We stared at him with disbelieving eyes as he shut and secured the hatch from the outside with a few nails. I watched through the portal as John got into the dinghy, water rushing over the boat and wind ballooning his shirt, as he pulled himself slowly toward the shore using one of the stern lines. The wind increased in intensity and ripped his shirt to shreds. Relief ran through my veins once he was safely ashore, but then the wind intensified to strengths I could not measure. Huge waves crashed against OUTWARD BOUND. We rocked back-and-forth in our bunks and propped our feet and hands against the surrounding walls to prevent us from being thrown out. The rain came in blinding sheets, pouring under the waterproof skylight and hatches and soaking everything in the cabin. We rode out that cyclone for an entire day, sleeping little until the next morning when a brilliant sun flared through the re-treating clouds. We would have certainly been doomed on the open sea, and John's travails on PAGAN now seemed more personal.

After the cyclone, the entire town took us under its wing, lav-ishing our family with round after round of bountiful dinners, so-cial parties, and outings. There were weeks when we spent six of seven days partying "on the town." We planned to stay in Townsville for several months so John got a job at a local theater re-pairing seats. If he repaired those chairs as well as he built OUT-WARD BOUND I am sure they are still standing today. It was while we were in Townsville that we met my parents again. They had been following us north along the coastline, towing their house trailer. Whenever I would ask my father about the most recent leg of their trip he would always respond:

"Too much sugarcane . . . blocks the view of the countryside."

Life was placid in Townsville, but its balmy quiet whetted our taste for freedom. Like a bird poised in flight, OUTWARD BOUND begged for the open untamed sea with its motley crew of four. After the cyclone season passed, we headed out toward Darwin, via Cairns. Here, we would meet my parents for the last time before heading out to Hinchinbrook Island where we had the good for-tune to meet Frank Hurley, the photographer on Shackleton's ex-pedition to Antarctica. He wanted to take pictures and circumnavigate Hinchinbrook Island and so he accompanied us for two weeks, during which time he fascinated us with stories of their voyage to Antarctica and how Shackleton's ship was hope-lessly trapped in the ice. They escaped by sailing in a small boat to the Falkland Islands over a thousand miles away. John and Frank had an immediate and deep appreciation for each other because of their near-death sailing adventures.

We flew before the Southeast trade winds on our way to Cook-town, anchoring at tropical reefs and bays during the day when swimming and fishing became our main pastime. Of course, we were constantly vigilant for sharks—even while fishing they would attack our bait lines. In Cooktown we loaded up with groceries and fresh vegetables for our long ocean voyage while the boys slid down

Cooktown, Great Barrier Reef, Australia. Mary is sitting next to the cannon sent in 1803 to protect Cooktown against a Russian invasion. Cook's Monument is in the background

the huge sand dunes that ringed the harbor. Before leaving Cooktown we visited Lizard Island, where there were fascinating ruins of a shack that had once been inhabited by a sea captain and his wife and child. Also living in the shack were three Chinese who cooked the *beche-de-mer*, a sea delicacy that was then much in demand. One day while the sea captain was out on the reef, aborigines invaded the island and murdered two of the Chinese. The other Chinese and the sea captain's wife and son escaped in a huge pot, but unfortunately perished on another uninhabited island. From these lonely ruins we remarked to each other how Lizard Island would make a great resort, and indeed today it is one of the most famous holiday resorts along the Great Barrier Reef. Back then we had the entire island all to ourselves for two weeks; the boys buried a bottle with a message beneath a cairn of rocks but I doubt that it is still there today.

Two weeks is such a short time in paradise. Every activity seems to last forever but somehow the days just melt away and blend to make one ball of time. It seemed like one long day before we sailed

Great Barrier Reef. Mary, Johnnie and Roger are collecting oysters

on past Cape Flattery with Cape Melville our destination. Strong winds buffeted our boat and we decided to anchor between the un-inhabited islands in the Flinders Group. The following morning we rowed the dinghy to shore and investigated the wild island. When we returned to the beach the dinghy was high and dry and we had to drag it nearly a half-mile through the tidal mud to get it back to the boat.

"Never doing that again," John pissed and moaned.

"I'll see that you don't!" I retorted.

The boys just hung their collective heads and plodded onward toward the ocean.

Further north on the mainland, we came across a small harbor with a house perched above the beach. It was the first sign of human habitation we had seen for some time so we entered the bay and dropped the hook. The house belonged to two men who came down to the shore to meet us. They were brothers but they had not spoken to each other in ten years. Both John and I had to serve as interpreters for this strange pair.

A day later we sailed for Escape Island and then headed through the treacherous waters of Torres Strait on the way to Cape

York. The current was tremendous through the Torres Strait and whisked us toward Thursday Island where we anchored with the pearling luggers. The Great Barrier Reef was behind us and now we sailed not north but west to continue our voyage around the world. While anchored at Thursday Island we met a Torres Strait islander who showed the boys his massive scars and the deformed sags of skin around his neck.

"Sharks got me right 'ere," he said to the wide-eyed boys.

"What did you *do*?" said Roger in awe.

"I stuck me fingers in 'is eyes!" he laughed.

"*God!*" was all Johnnie could say. For days, the boys discussed what they would have done with that shark.

Shortly after leaving Thursday Island we crossed the Gulf of Carpentaria and sighted Prince of Wales Island. There was a light-house and a jetty where people stood and beckoned us to tie up and visit, but we waved them on and several days later we rounded Cape Wessel and pushed down the coast toward Elcho Island where we understood there was a missionary station. We were sailing slowly down the coast when a small boat approached and invited us to stay for the night. It was getting dark and John wanted to reach Elcho Island and a more secure anchorage. Our new friend offered to show us the way because there were many rocks and reefs in our passage, so we invited him aboard.

All went well until dark.

"Where do we go from here?" John asked worriedly as large rocks began to loom before us.

"Mine eyes are sleeping I no can see," he said and promptly rolled over and went to sleep.

John and I looked at each other, baffled at his behavior.

"I ought to throw him overboard!" John said angrily.

"It looks like I'll be steering all night," I said resignedly.

John reluctantly took his position in the mast looking for rocks and reefs, of which there were many.

Finally after a long sleepless night we arrived at the Mission Station where our friend promptly requested $50 for his pilot service.

"Mine ears are sleeping and I no can hear!" John said, laughing, as he physically escorted the man off our boat.

We met a number of wonderful Aborigines at the station, and we were especially enamored with the children who were very friendly and liked to show their enthusiasm by pinching you lightly on the arm. This irritated the boys no end because all of their pinches came from girls.

"All they do is pinch and run!" Roger complained. "They're stupid!"

"And they laugh and *smile* too!" added Johnnie.

"That's just awful!" I said. "There ought to be a *law!*"

"Mom!! We're serious!"

"So am I," I said. "Here's a broom and a mop to take your mind off your troubles."

There were no more complaints after that. After leaving Elcho Island we sailed for Darwin where we took advantage of the extreme tides to haul OUTWARD BOUND out for a bottom paint job before starting across the Indian Ocean. The retreating tides also exposed the hulls of Japanese ships that had been sunk during World War II. Gangs of filthy, knot-muscled workmen would hastily cut pieces of metal from the hulks before the sea reclaimed them with the next incoming tide. A week later we were on our way to Christmas Island, our first port in the Indian Ocean. As usual, we settled down to our life-at-sea routine with watches of two hours on and two hours off. The strong southeast trade winds pushed us along without effort and soon we reached our destination. Christmas Island proved to be too deep to anchor, so we were escorted to a heavy mooring under the control of the Australian Government. When the Australian workers discovered we were sailing to Cocos Keeling Island the next day they brought us letters and packages for their relatives, which otherwise would have cost them a small fortune to send there.

"Well, we've really got to find Cocos now," I said sarcastically to John.

"Yeah, or these guys will chase us around the globe!"

At three in the morning we entered the pass to Cocos Keeling under a beautiful moonlit sky. OUTWARD BOUND cruised through the narrow pass and we anchored on the lee side of a reef near the northwest corner of the island, manned by Cable and Wireless personnel. We delivered the mail and packages to the grateful islanders and then headed directly on to Home Island. Here the twelve lonely men inhabiting the island threw us a party. Because there was only one other woman, she and I got to dance all night. Shortly afterward we waved goodbye to our friends at the Cable and Wireless Station and headed for Diego Garcia in the Chagos Archipelago. After a long, monotonous journey we sighted the island atoll early in the morning and entered the lagoon by the northwest passageway. The beautiful atoll was so big it took us all day just to reach our intended anchorage in the southeast corner of the lagoon. We anchored close to a wrecked flying boat, a relic of World War II, and there we met the hospitable manager of the plantation and his wife, who nearly adopted Roger and Johnnie during our stay on the island.

For six weeks we languished at Diego Garcia. It was another island paradise reminiscent of those we encountered during our South Pacific voyage. Blue skies, incredible coral reefs, and endless sandy beaches were the daily norm. Bliss once again soaked into our veins, drugging us numb with the idyllic rhythm of life around us. We have many fond memories of doing absolutely *nothing* every day. Today the peacefulness is gone: there is a small atoll north of Diego Garcia that has become a favorite anchorage for modern cruising yachts equipped with everything from autopilot to satellite TV. Back then, there was virtually nothing except nature.

We reluctantly left Diego Garcia and set sail for the Seychelles Islands. I was on watch first the second night at sea. In the distance appeared what looked like a huge black island. It loomed larger and larger rather quickly and its rapid growth scared me when I realized it was a massive storm front of a hurricane.

"John!" I called. *"John!"*

He staggered up through the galley way, half asleep.

"John!" I said again, pointing straight ahead.

"*Christ!*" That was all he could mutter.

Seconds later he was dousing all the sails and tying them securely to the booms. He ran to lash down the dinghy over the skylight as the wind began to scream and howl through the masts. Minutes later angry seas washed over the boat, throwing us like rag dolls across the decks. We grabbed onto the safety lines and pulled ourselves below, securing the hatch behind us. Heavy, ominous seas, crashed from all directions over OUTWARD BOUND, sending rivers of water through our *waterproof* skylight. We huddled below, John with the fear of the past in his eyes. He looked at me with his steely blue eyes:

"I'm not going down again," he said somberly.

I was too seasick to pay much attention to anyone but my physical sickness undoubtedly assuaged the emotional turmoil of fear to which I would have otherwise succumbed. There was absolutely nothing we could do but ride out the storm: The sea ruled us. The boys huddled with their dad for hours, putting together a jigsaw puzzle on a wet blanket, helplessly watching me retch until I thought my stomach was going to evert through my mouth.

A full day later the winds abated and we dragged all the mattresses and wet clothes up on deck to dry. Our canvas dodger around the stern was torn to shreds but amazingly the sails were intact. Unfortunately, we were blown over a hundred miles off course. And now, there was scarcely a zephyr in the air. We looked at each other, dumbfounded.

"Where's the wind?" I said after a long pause.

"Wind? You want wind? Not a problem," said John, smiling like a crazed man, "I'll whistle up a wind to settle your stomach."

"Don't you even *think* about it!" I shouted, punching him in the arm.

At that point we were so tired we laughed until we were clutching at our chests for breath. The boys just stared at us in amusement.

A hurricane can do that to you.

We eventually managed to straighten out our course and sailed across a more placid Indian Ocean to Port Victoria in the

Seychelles, a group of over one hundred tropical islands. We were more than happy to spend a few quiet days ashore while all our belongings dried out in the tropical sun. But as usual, the few planned days of rest extended into weeks and we managed to explore the entire island of Mahe before leaving for gorgeous Pralin Island, also in the Seychelles, and famous worldwide for its double-barrel coconuts. The boys ate many of the delicious nuts and we packed many more away for storage. We were reluctant to leave Port Victoria, but the sailing season was aging and we needed to be on our way to Aden and the Red Sea. We first sailed past Bird Island; people waved at us from the shore, beckoning us to visit, but because we were unsure of the entrance to the lagoon and night was falling rapidly, we were forced to wave goodbye and sail on to the north. Roger and Johnnie resumed their favorite perches in the rigging, as they always did when the seas were calm.

22

Around the Horn of Africa to the Middle East

Once again we entered a lonely sea, and once again we stood two hours on and slept two hours off. John always referred to me as the automatic pilot when the seas were becalmed. The days seemed to pass more slowly now; the excitement of the earlier travel had evaporated and dreariness of the open mindless ocean settled over the crew of OUTWARD BOUND. That soon changed. Early the next morning Johnnie spotted a large ship on the distant horizon.

"Mom! That ship's really moving!"

It was a huge Russian freighter traveling toward us at alarming speed and it looked more than ominous as its hulk churned directly toward our tiny boat. Would it deliberately try to destroy a small sailboat just because it sported an American flag—after all, we were in the middle of the Cold War? We could not outmaneuver it, but in the final moments it veered and we all huddled together on deck as the captain came out on the bridge and waved his cap. We waved back, excited and relieved. Apparently, there was no cold war at sea, only friends.

A few days later we sighted the island of Suqutra (Socotra) and rounded the Horn of Africa, heading in a westerly direction for the Port of Aden, then a protectorate of the British. As we sailed into the harbor an English couple out sailing in a small boat met us. They waved to us and we followed them into the harbor and anchored to clear customs, but not before they took our laundry ashore to be washed—quite a change from washing clothes in creeks and buckets on the dock!

The RAF literally took us under their collective wings while we were there, wining and dining us, and arranging for us to move our boat so we could haul her out and coat her below the waterline with antifouling paint. This was important because a clean bottom facing the headwinds going north in the Red Sea would give us much greater speed. After departing from Aden Harbor we anchored in the little Port of Barim before tackling the Red Sea. We found the Arab people there to be extremely friendly and very helpful by bringing us many of the necessities we needed before we entered the Straits between Djibouti and Barim.

After tacking several days up the Red Sea we anchored in the lee of a small island to get a good night's sleep. Some of the lighthouse keepers hailed us from the shore shortly after we dropped the hook to secure our position.

"Dad!" Johnnie shouted. "They want to see us! Can we go?"

Of course, the boys were always anxious to go ashore for adventure. John nodded.

"Get the dinghy," he said, smiling.

"I'll stay here and blow the fog horn in case the boat drifts," I announced in a tired voice.

"Thanks, Mom!" the boys said in unison.

As John and the boys landed their dinghy the lighthouse keepers warned them to stay on a narrow rocky trail because this tiny island was volcanic and many of the areas just off to the side of the trail were soft and hot with subterranean lava flows. I could see small fumaroles wafting upwards from the heated earth.

The following day we once again tacked back-and-forth across the Red Sea, against a stiff northerly head wind. Navigating at night became difficult because huge freighters always surrounded us, so much so that we dubbed the straits "tanker alley." A tanker could hit our boat at any time and there would be nothing left of it except flotsam.

"Watch those lights," John said ominously as I took over the watch.

"What lights?" I queried. He explained his directive: "If you can see the red port light and the green starboard light at the same time plus the two white lights lined upon the mast, call me right away!"

It was an uneasy watch with many anxious calls of alarm to a husband who grew crankier with every ship that passed well ahead or astern of our small boat.

"Don't call me just because you see a ship's lights," he admonished. "Call we when they *line up!*"

"But they always seem to line up!" I shot back. "At least for me!"

John would just shrug his shoulders and head back to his bunk, muttering unintelligible phrases. Thankfully, we entered Port Sudan Harbor the next day. For the first time on any of our voyages, we were overwhelmed by hoards of people! This part of the world was nothing like what we experienced during our voyage across the Pacific where native peoples often saw no ships for years on end. Port Sudan was wall-to-wall people, with many ships in the harbor waiting to take passengers on the pilgrimage to Mecca across the Red Sea. The prospect for meaningful one-on-one relationships seemed improbable, but during a visit ashore John and Johnnie met an Arab captain who was building a dhow. The gentleman was so fascinated by John's seafaring stories that he begged them to visit the ruins of Suakin south of Port Sudan. So while John and Johnnie visited the ruins, Roger and I snorkeled over the incredible coral gardens near sunken World War II ships still loaded with deadly explosives. We stayed close to our guide because there were so many sharks.

The few Egyptians we met in Port Sudan were on vacation and after we left the port we looked forward to meeting them again in Suez. We sailed on northward with the wind astern. I was preoccupied with hanging wet clothes and sheets in the rigging when a British warship cruised by on the way south and dipped its colors for us. We sailed up the tanker-filled Gulf of Suez and into the Suez Harbor to clear customs. From there our plan was to sail to the Mediterranean Sea. By law, we had to hire a pilot to escort us through the first part of the canal, and we were to change pilots in Ismailia before sailing on to Port Said. However, John became very

First Mate Johnnie is taking a noon sight

ill with an intestinal flu and despite the valiant efforts of the boys and me we could not keep up with the speed of the motley convoy of huge ships around us. So we anchored to await the next convoy, which angered our pilot.

Shortly afterward, another pilot came aboard for the passage to Port Said. Unfortunately, the new pilot also came down with a severe case of the intestinal flu, leaving the boys and me to pilot the ship. As he lay curled up in a fetal ball on a mattress, the pilot gave us the necessary instructions. We raised sail and negotiated the canal on the outside of the dolphins (wooden posts) that marked the deeper channel for the big ships. Johnnie and Roger loved to sit on the first spreaders, so they climbed up the ratlines, one on each side of the mast, where they could get a better view of the huge ships that plowed by us. Many of the passengers and crew of these ships stopped to wave to the boys with their American flag flying, and often the Arab captains would come out as well to wave to the strange crew of OUT- WARD BOUND. That part of the world was certainly much more peaceful and friendlier to Americans than it is now.

We spent several pleasant days in Port Said, partying with our Egyptian friends from Port Sudan. We were also entertained by the

American Ambassador. All went well until one evening when we were invited to party on a French yacht. There were a number of people aboard having a great time when suddenly a soldier jumped through the hatchway with a rifle and fixed bayonet shouting "Americans go boat!" We looked around and quickly established that we were the only Americans there. The French host was furious but John quickly excused himself and we rowed furiously in the dinghy back to OUTWARD BOUND. That same evening while getting ready for bed I was startled to see a face looking through the porthole in the cabin.

"John! There's a *man!*" I screamed, pointing. John glanced up and ran to the porthole, shaking his fist.

"What is your name and number?" he screamed. "Nasser will hear of this!"

The soldier scrambled to get his oars and rowed frantically back to the shore.

"*Get him, Dad!*" Roger screamed.

"*Shoot him! Shoot him!*" Johnnie chorused.

John ran above decks but the grimacing man was well ahead of any chase we could mount.

The next day we found out that all the commotion centered on the stevedores who for some reason had refused to unload an Egyptian ship in New York. This had angered the population of Port Said. The next day many small boats circled us with signs that read: *the Arab workers are united and will strike back violently.* It seemed like the peacefulness of our 28-day Middle East voyage was about to come to an end. Frightened, John managed to get a phone call through to the American ambassador who advised us to leave Port Said immediately. He said he would send the official over to clear us so that we could leave. But when the official came aboard he said, "Welcome to Egypt!" Obviously, the intent of the message had been confused! We had had enough of the busyness of the Middle East.

And worse, there were no islands!

23

A Dash Through Europe

$\mathcal{L}$uck was on our side. As we sailed through the main harbor an American ship arrived and thankfully attracted all the attention—freeing us to sail away cheerfully on persistent, sultry, sandy northerlies to our next destination, the island of Rhodes. We sailed under pleasant breezes and gentle seas into the beautiful old harbor of Rhodes where the first large ship we spotted was VOICE OF AMERICA. At this juncture, we began hearing snippets about the charms of the blue Caribbean: remote, emerald-green isles, amiable West Indians, and startling good weather with steady trade winds—the delight of sailors worldwide, we were told.

We found a secure anchorage and tied our stern to the quay of a coffee shop. I spent hours there and in other coffee shops sampling their exquisite blends of coffee while the boys explored the other shops. We traveled on a shoestring budget throughout town, but our new best friends from VOICE OF AMERICA showed us small open-air restaurants in the old city where we could get a good dinner for a dollar—including an excellent bottle of wine, again, for a dollar.

During our stay at Rhodes the boys spent a great deal of time sailing around the harbor in their sailing dinghy. One day a large motor yacht entered the harbor and pulled up next to OUTWARD BOUND.

"Are those your two sons sailing around in the dinghy?" the captain asked somewhat accusingly. John and I looked at each other wondering what they had done now. I cleared my throat and assumed the "defensive mother" posture.

"Why, yes," I responded nervously.

"Well," he said, "I hailed them when I entered the harbor and asked them to keep out of my way."

"*And?*" John said, waiting for the worst and getting ready to publicly scold the boys.

"And . . ." the man said laughing, "your oldest boy shouted, 'Sail has right over power!' to me."

He paused for our reaction. We looked at each other, puzzled. This sounded like a compliment to our boys.

"So . . . I just wanted to invite your family over for dinner this evening!"

"*Oh!*" I said, immediately letting down my defense. "Gladly!"

We were immensely relieved and proud at the same time because typically, the boys (being boys) were frequently in some sort of trouble. Upon our arrival on his yacht he introduced his charter guests. One of these was Lady Honor Svedjar whom we referred to later as Mrs. Guinness Stout (little did we realize at the time that we would meet her again on our own island in the Caribbean). After a week of constant partying we sailed to the island of Symi, just north of Rhodes, and entered the beautiful landlocked harbor on the west side. We explored the cove and spent several tranquil nights before we sailed onward to many other islands in the Aegean Sea, including Kos, Kalimnos, and finally Patmos on the eastern side. At each port the boys attracted local children like bees drawn to sugar. And in each port Johnnie and Roger played with a different group of "Hello" boys while we sampled coffee in the local cafes.

Thereafter, each port seemed to be a repeat of the previous one: Our sons attracted gaggles of local boys, we sampled coffee and shopped the local stores, and generally relaxed as we met and discussed our adventures on the high seas with troves of new-found friends. From Patmos we sailed west to Mykonos, a thriving tourist destination with brightly colored houses, winding flowered streets, and terraced dwellings. Ultimately, our travels brought us to Passalami Harbor in Athens where we made the obligatory tourist stops. We left Athens with the idea of passing through the Corinth

OUTWARD BOUND anchored in Bastia Harbor, Corsica

canal, but the fees would have strapped our tight budget, so we decided to sail the more scenic (and long) way around Cape Matapan,
with the plan of crossing the Ionian Sea to Catania in Sicily.

On the way we stopped at the island of Hydra with its many
colorful bars and restaurants encircling the harbor; then it was on
to the island of Spezia where we left Johnnie and Roger on board
while we shopped for provisions. In our absence a large yacht
dragged its anchor, fouling our anchor and causing OUTWARD
BOUND to drift. We were shocked upon our return to find Johnnie
and Roger maneuvering the boat to safe anchorage (we had trained
them well!). During our passage we anchored at many secluded
bays and were thankful that we did not choose the high volume
Corinth canal with all its civilized busyness.

Finally we rounded Cape Matapan and set a course for Catania on the east coast of Sicily. John met some US servicemen from
a nearby Army Base and earned some badly needed cash ferrying
them daily to a group of rocky islands called Cyclops in order to
see a smoldering Mount Etna on the verge of eruption. On his last
trip the volcano exploded with a tremulous roar, spewing out lava
and hot boulders that crashed on the hillsides below. It was

OUTWARD BOUND. *Coast of Spain*

atomic in its strength and each infernal explosion both awed and frightened us.

The following day we passed through the Tyrrhenian Sea, through the busy Strait of Messina and up to our next port of call, Messina. We passed by the mysterious island of Stromboli on our way to Naples and the beautiful island of Ischia where we spent several weeks exploring old ruins in what has to be one of the world's most intriguing spots of antiquity. Our Australian and American flags always drew much attention from the local sailors and yachtsmen, especially in the Port of Anzio, the closest anchorage to Rome.

We left Anzio after a full immersion into sightseeing and entered the Strait of Bonifacio where strong head winds split the mainsail straight across the beam. For that reason we sailed in the lee of Corsica to Bastia on the northeast coast, and then to San Remo on the Italian Riviera. It was in San Remo that I first noticed what I called the "gladioli yachts"—elegant sailing yachts with a vase full of gladiolus flowers in the cockpit. We enjoyed our brief stay in San Remo immensely, but we had promised friends and owners of the yacht TAOS BRETT that we would meet them in Monaco and time was running short.

Johnnie and Roger are rigging the dinghy while Mary is catching up on the wash

Our friends had reserved a space for us alongside their boat and it was there that we were introduced to Jacques Cousteau. He invited us to visit his Sea Aquarium situated on a cliff overlooking the coast. The sheer number and variety of the sea animals transfixed the boys. When Jacques learned that Roger was born in Tahiti, he said:

"Ah, then you are 'Roger the Frog!'" His hearty laugh filled the room and Roger's face lit up with a broad smile.

"Mom!" he said. "I'm *Roger the Frog!*"

"Yes, you certainly are!" I replied.

Jacques then autographed one of Roger's book with his new nickname. It is still one of Roger's prize possessions today. Besides being a world-class marine biologist, Jacques was an excellent driver and once took us around the winding drive along the coastline to Antibes at ninety miles per hour.

From St. Tropez we sailed along the coastline, passing many yachts and powerboats and admiring the many famous and historical towns and cities we sailed by, until we reached the harbor of Marseille, where we were reunited with many friends and met new friends from around the world. Such is the world of sailing.

At Marseille, we decided to skip sailing through the frigid canals of France. Instead, we cut our original plans short because we wanted to sail across the Atlantic while the trade winds were still blowing consistently. We left our last French port, Sète, and cruised along the Costa Brava until we anchored in the charming harbor of Sant Feliu de Guixols for one night before moving on to Barcelona. Although Barcelona was beautiful and fascinating we stayed only a few days because we were anxious to sail on to the Balearics.

We made landfall at the island of Mallorca and entered Palma de Mallorca Harbor where we heard many more fascinating tales about the Caribbean islands—some sailors claimed they were the most beautiful in the world. We stayed longer than expected, as usual, and then decided to sail straight to Gibraltar, first passing the city lights of Cartagena, and headed to the small port of Adra to wait out an impending storm. We were welcomed at the yacht club and heard the news that John F. Kennedy had been elected President of the United States, which met with high approval from our Spanish friends. Despite the celebrations we were anxious to sail on to Gibraltar, the gateway to the Atlantic. There we went ashore to buy Christmas gifts and provisions for our voyage across the Atlantic. After a few days the RAF reported that the weather had cleared and we departed immediately for Tarifa, where unbelievably, we *did* encounter nasty storms that forced us into the harbor.

24

Searching for a
Caribbean Paradise

*W*hen we finally arrived at Las Palmas on Gran Canaria (Canary Islands) we were shocked by the smelly ocean, overrun with oil tankers, and its overdeveloped shoreline encrusted with tourist high-rises. We were also shocked by the number of yachts waiting to cross the Atlantic. There were cruising yachts and charter yachts, both sail and power, all waiting for good weather. By comparison, we looked pretty ordinary.

Days of doldrums weather went by but eventually a steady breeze arose and we were on our way to the West Indies—a yachtsman's paradise, we were promised by everyone. After having sailed across the Pacific and Indian Oceans we expected some rough weather on the Atlantic, but it was almost boring by comparison. The trade winds blew steadily, there were no storms, and we crossed the 3,000-mile-wide Atlantic in just nineteen days and eighteen hours, entering Carlisle Bay and mooring at the Barbados Yacht Club of the beautiful western Antilles in June of 1960. Somehow Columbus's feat seemed less spectacular.

At this point we had crossed the Pacific, Indian, and Atlantic Oceans. Our original goal was to be the first family (pregnant and with children!) to sail completely around the world using only a sextant for guidance. We only had to sail to Panama to complete our circumnavigation.

We never made it.

Johnnie and Roger, the Atlantic Ocean

We were running short of funds and needed to replenish the kitty, but we could readily see that the island of Barbados was headed for overdevelopment and we decided not to linger. So we hoisted sail for Castries harbor, St. Lucia, in the Windward Islands of the eastern Caribbean Sea. John took work as skipper on the 120-foot charter schooner, WANDERER, owned by Walter Boudreau, a pioneer in these heavenly waters. We plied the seaways, St. Lucia south to Tobago and back north, hopping through the windward and leeward chains of the British and American Virgin Islands. It was a rewarding experience, pushing this elegant yacht around, and it showed John the possibilities for chartering our own OUTWARD BOUND.

That bit of serendipity led us into the charter trade with the venerable old commander, Vernon Nicholson, the dean of Caribbean charter skippers, out of Nelson's Dockyard, Antigua. This happenstance was a proverbial plum from the sky. We loved the work and spent the next six years of the 1960s sailing on trade winds up and down like a boomerang along a chain of unspoiled islands, from Antigua to Grenada. We took paying guests, usually a couple and sometimes three or four, careening before balmy white-capped seas. Every sailing day was a feast of voyaging, snorkeling, beachcombing, quiet lagoons, dining out, and fraternizing with newfound sailing guests/friends aboard—and being paid handsomely for what we loved to do best—*sail!* The kids stayed in an apartment in the old officer's quarters at Nelson's Dockyard, Antigua, caressed and spoiled by a local nanny. We saw them every few weeks at the end of charters and had a fantastic reunion every time we got back together.

"This has got to be heaven," John said dreamily one day.

"It's better than that," I countered, "but I still think we have a star to follow somewhere out here."

"Yeah, I've got that gut feeling too. Fate's been relatively good to us these past few years."

"And the children are growing so *fast!*"

"That's exactly my point . . . we need an anchor . . . here, in the Grenadines."

"You sure about that?"

"Yes, dead sure," came his response.

In reality, we had no clue that this idyllic lifestyle would one day phase out. We really were in heaven without a worry in the world. But we still had that distant, unresolved dream longing to reach fruition. Maybe we were too fussy and were seeking too high a goal, something that did not exist or that we could not afford. In truth, our major restraint was finances. We had managed to save only $10,000 US in five years of chartering, not much to fund an island operation, no matter how small. What we earned was sparse, but the joy of living was always there and we were frightened at the thought of giving up chartering and the freedom it allowed.

This is when John made a bizarre observation:

"Did you ever notice how few palm trees there are in the Grenadines?" he asked one day over a cup of Jamaican coffee.

"Not really."

"Well," he said, "I'm going to do something about it. You can't have the tropics without its ultimate symbol . . . waving coconut palms!"

John and Mary are transporting coconut trees on OUTWARD BOUND

"Of course not. Whatever you think, dear," I patronized, not knowing what he was really thinking.

From that day on, John carried a dozen or more small palm plants on the stern of OUTWARD BOUND, and at every opportunity, on any deserted, palm-less beach he would plant his seedlings. He meticulously followed planting instructions given to him by a local islander: dig a hole both twenty inches wide and deep. Fill it half-full with rotten leaves or soil mixed with cattle or sheep dung, and then lay the nut in, flat side down. Cover it with a thin layer of soil, water it well and place grass around it as a mulch to hold in the moisture. Finally, add small cut sections of palm frond to hold down the grass. It was as simple as that. Suddenly, John was an expert palm-planter, and from that day on OUTWARD BOUND always looked like it had a rooster tail with its bunches of palm seedlings hanging off her stern.

Inevitably, John was dubbed "Johnny Coconut" by the locals. He enjoyed his new hobby like a drug addict.

"They're an esthetic attraction," he would always say to friends who doubted his unsailor-like preoccupation.

"They're making fun of my tools," he said one day, enjoying his self-deprecation.

"Who wouldn't?" I retorted. "Most sailors don't ply the reefs with coconut seedlings, a spade, mattock, rake, cutlass, and containers of fresh water!"

"True, but they all add another dimension to my persona."

"That they do," I admitted.

25

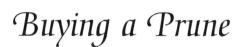

Buying a Prune

Six expansive years of blue sea chartering in paradise never damp-
ened our ardor for a slice of terra firma to seal our plans of finally settling down. And one ordinary beautiful day, it just happened. We were
sailing from Grenada to St. Vincent to meet a charter party of three
and pressing through a miniature Hawaiian chain of thirty seductive
islets and outcroppings over forty miles long in the Grenadines. Silver
beaches and snug anchorages were everywhere. On our approach to
St. Vincent we were sliding between Union Island to the west and tiny
Prune Island to the east when the latter caught John's eye.

"Look at that," he pointed, bemused.

"*What?*" I snapped.

"Prune Island. I've planted a hundred palm trees on its beaches.
It's beautiful."

"It's beautiful all right," I said disinterestedly, "but it's got at
least a dozen mosquito-ridden swamps and hundreds of thousands
of crab holes, and tangled thorny brush dating back to the time
of Christ!"

"So what do you think of that island?" he asked, ruminating.

He was ignoring me. That translated into nothing but trouble.

"Too many mosquitoes, gnats, and sand flies!" I charged.

"The Grenadine government owns it," he said, throwing a
tangent to my concerns.

"Good!"

"When we get to St. Vincent I'm going to ask them why it's just
sitting there with nothing going on . . ."

"*What?* It's a mess! Bugs and stinky goats foul it from one end to the other. It would take a fortune just to clean up the underbrush. And what about all those swamps? There must be a dozen of them."

"Eighteen," he said flatly. "I counted them."

I eyed him like a dogcatcher trailing a feral mutt.

"Who in their right mind would want that? You don't *really* want it, do you?"

"No," he said, finally recognizing my antagonistic mood. "Just curious."

But I knew he was lying. His body literally quivered with anticipation. I knew he was thinking this would be our "dream island." His eyes shifted back-and-forth and I could literally see his head fill with frantic, delicious thoughts of ownership. He was stripping that island of its jumbled undergrowth in the same manner that men eye-strip attractive women of their clothes.

"Yes, that's it," he finally said mysteriously, leaving me to fill in the blanks. "I want to be in Kingstown before noon."

I felt an instant depression come over me. I wanted to shop in Kingstown, not visit the minister's office to waste time inquiring about the status of Prune Island—aptly named, I was now sure. But John was too excited to eat, even after rowing ashore to Kingstown, the capital of St. Vincent.

We eased our sweaty bodies along a sterile corridor with dingy offices and clacking typewriters. John approached someone poring over stacks of manila files.

"My name is John Caldwell. Is it true that the government owns little Prune Island?" John was always very direct and to the point. The man looked up slowly and a flash of recognition spread over his face.

"John Caldwell? I've heard so much about you. Allow me to introduce myself. My name is Johnny Alves, the Chief Minister's Senior Permanent Secretary. So, why do you ask about the island?"

I stood there behind John, mute.

"Well," John continued, "it seems only reasonable that the government set up some kind of tourist activities there and hire some of the unemployed people on Union Island." Mr. Alves quickly rose.

"Come with me," the tall handsome Secretary said and turned down the hallway. In just a few minutes we entered another office.

"Meet the Honorable E. T. Joshua," he said. John looked into the Minister's eyes and said, "What's happenin', mon?"

"Tell Mr. Joshua what you told me," the Permanent Secretary said to John.

As I stood beside him like a dead coral, John explained how *we* planned to construct a tourist facility on Prune Island and create jobs for unemployed locals on Union Island.

"*Stop!*" shouted the honorable Mr. Joshua. He reached for his phone, made several calls, and minutes later (unusual in the Grenadines) there were five suited men, his government ministers, filing deftly passed us.

"Tell these gentlemen what you just said," Mr. Joshua boomed. John carefully repeated his comments and suddenly Mr. Joshua stabbed a finger at John's chest.

"The government has no money!" He shouted. "But . . . I like your idea. Prune Island is sitting there, dead. You should have the island. How much money will you spend?" he asked.

"One hundred and fifty thousand dollars," John replied. I looked at him aghast. We scarcely had $10,000 in the bank. My jaw hit the ground. John ignored me.

"How many workers will you hire?" Joshua shouted again.

"Fifteen," John answered after a moment of thought. Joshua slammed his open palm on the table.

"Wonderful! When will you start?" He boomed again.

"Tomorrow morning!" John shouted back.

By then I was smiling at the ridiculousness of the entire scene. But it got worse.

"You get the island!" Joshua exclaimed like a game show host.

They shook hands and we left. I immediately accosted John in the hallway.

"What *are* you thinking?" I demanded.

"Our *dream!*" He announced, smiling.

"*Our* dream?" I replied caustically, "You mean *your* dream!" Outside he turned and looked at me with those intensely blue foreman's eyes.

"Imagine a hotel on that island. Imagine our island paradise come true! We can do this!"

"What about money?"

"First you need a dream. A goal! You can always get the money once you've defined the dream. We can leverage what we already have, you'll see."

But I was still in my stubborn pragmatic streak.

"How will you get the rest of the money?" I asked with hands on my hip and head cocked to one side in my ultimate feminine display of absolute disproval.

"Banks!" he announced. "Borrow it like everybody else!"

"But bank managers are tough. They want collateral, plans, and they want to know if you've had any experience. What do you know about building a hotel? You're too cheap to even eat out in one!" I hit a nerve.

He touched my shoulders.

"Give me a couple of days," he said quietly. "I'll figure it out."

"I hope so," I responded, still in my defensive female posture.

"Hey, I've got an idea! Let's go look at the island again!"

That was classic John—the ultimate salesman, never giving up, returning when rejected, always optimistic. He could seduce the bark off a tree. That was the John I fell in love with twenty-five years ago.

John got up early and made a hasty lunch so we could sail at first light. We rowed ashore and climbed the southwest hillock, a full 150 feet above sea level (security in a hurricane!). All the way up John kept up an incessant chatter about fate, striking while the iron was hot, going with your dreams, and working hard for your goals. We reached the top and gazed with mixed feelings at the jungle and swamps below. A long pause followed.

"It's big," I finally said, trying to be vaguely positive.

"Maybe it's *too* big." he said reflectively.

He watched me in silence as I counted the five beautiful tropical beaches.

"We could build a house there." I pointed to an exceptionally lovely spot with a spectacular ocean view.

"You think?" he countered. "I'd be willing to build us a dream house there."

"It's beautiful, isn't it," I said finally.

And it was beautiful. Prune Island was a diamond in the rough. It was the island everyone dreams of possessing. John hesitated, and then struck for the gold:

"No, it's gorgeous! We just need the guts to work our tails off for a few years and go for broke!"

"We could put a bar down there, and over there the guest house and dining room . . ." I added thoughtfully.

"And a jetty there and a cistern over there . . ." he pointed out.

A few moments later we were talking like an architectural team and within the hour the island was completely developed with hotel and facilities, landing strip, jetty, cistern, and boat launches.

Our excitement grew as we descended the hill and sailed back to St. Vincent to meet with Attorney General Snagg, a comfortable, quiet, and friendly bureaucrat in his mid-sixties. His walls were lined with heavy legal tomes; his desk piled with thick manila folders. He gave us a fatherly look with dark eyes over horn-rimmed glasses. Test cricket was playing on the radio and we had to halt our discussion as his hand went up periodically to hear how each ball was played. We explored each clause of a 99-year lease with an option to renew for another 99 years. As John showed more interest in the cricket match (John hated cricket), Mr. Snagg showed more interest in John's ideas.

John agreed with Mr. Snagg's wisdom over each clause, knowing that a cricket match can go on for four days! It was time to sign the deed.

"Everything looks in perfect order," I heard John say, feigning knowledge of British law.

Mr. Snagg suddenly became solemn.

"To make this legal under British law," he said, "it is necessary for you to pay a peppercorn rent."

"What's *that*?" I blurted out.

"That, my young lady, is normal British practice," he responded.

"How much?" John asked politely.

"Well, now, it could be as much as $20,000 US a year to make it lawful."

I quivered as John looked at me. Was this the awakening that would fade the dream?

"Could it be less?" John ventured cautiously.

"Well, yes," he said, "it could."

"How much?"

"That's up to you as lessor in the transaction." His attention was once more drawn to the cricket match. Someone hit a four, meaning, four runs! He was ecstatic. The advantage was to John.

"How about $10,000?"

"Yes, yes certainly. It could be that." John was emboldened.

"How about $5,000?" Mr. Snagg now has his ear physically pressed to the radio.

"Great play!" He shouts, "Another four! And yes, $5,000 is acceptable."

"Well," John dragged on his Texas drawl, "Could it be even lower?"

"Two runs! That's incredible!" Mr. Snagg pounded the table with excitement.

"How about $1,000?" The game is boiling over now and I am smiling from ear-to-ear as I watch my husband take advantage of the situation. I stood back and let them continue.

"How much?" Mr. Snagg said, "I'm sorry, I didn't hear your offer."

"I was saying perhaps $100? Would that be too little?"

"Oh no, mon. That would be fine!"

Mr. Snagg turned his ear to the radio again. "Damn! This is a rout!" he shouted.

John went for the kill.

"Would I be thrown out of your office if I offered just a paltry

$1.00 per year for the 99-year lease of Prune Island?" I heard John spell it out and I knew that he had set the hook.

"Excuse me a moment, Mr. Caldwell." He held up an open hand, turned to hear the latest play, and quickly stood up halfway out of his chair, shouting excitedly, "Oh, yes, yes, that's not a problem! One American dollar will do!"

"Okay," John said, smiling at me. "So we have Prune Island, right?"

"Yes, it is yours! Mr. Caldwell. Sign here, please!" He pushed the paper toward John and went back to the game.

I was brimming over with inner joy. For one American dollar John has purchased our dream island for 99 years and kept $9,999 in the bank!

"They just hit another six," Mr. Snagg shouted, rising from his seat with his fist clenched.

I turned to John and lowered my voice.

"There will be something special for *you* tonight. Husband's choice!"

"My God," he laughed, "can a day get any better?" We laughed and hugged. John used his free hand to shake the free hand of Mr. Snagg who continued to listen to the game.

26

Developing the Prune

Prune Island was ours! John quickly petitioned the government to change the name from Prune Island to Palm Island, which had a more romantic ring than an island named after a dried plum used for the relief of constipation. Our first workday dawned with John in the Caldwell work mode. He donned his high rubber boots and rowed ashore. I called out to him from OUTWARD BOUND.

"Hey, you forgot fifty percent of the crew!"

It was 1966 and there were eighteen shallow swamps that needed draining. That May was one of the rainier ones on record with daily showers that brought out hoards of biting mosquitoes and sand flies. Along with them came balls of fruit flies that invaded every facial orifice (but thankfully did not bite). Together John and I walked around the 120-acre island of mostly level terrain, sizing up what needed attention first. Our conclusion was that *all* of it needed attention immediately. John kept his promise to the Honorable Mr. Joshua and his determined and socially sensitive wife, Ivy. Exactly fifteen men sailed over on an eighteen-foot fisherman, open hulled, much overloaded, and steered by a primitive tiller. Vince Brown of Union Island was the skipper and James Cudjoe, a slick talker but experienced builder, was our foreman. James and John huddled together, looking down the dowdy site on our west beach, where our Palm Island Beach Club resort would be built.

After consulting with me, they decided first to dispose of the piles and windrows of leaves and then hammer together a structure

Johnny Coconut (as John was known) is planting a palm tree with local help on Palm Island

so we could live ashore. James' brother, Prince, joined us the next day as a much-needed stout set of arms reaching outward from a peaceable, hard-working frame. He was a stalwart of dedication to the taming of Palm Island. Agatha Roberts also joined us as a general helper. She was a skinny, quiet, and dedicated young woman and a pillar of strength set in an old-fashion woman's ways.

We joined our new workers, raking the leaves into long piles and placing them in trenches we had dug nearby for burning. Afterward, we covered the carbon residue with sand. The shack took longer. I designed it on a piece of old cardboard: a two-part structure with a pitch pine framework and galvanized iron sheets nailed together to serve as walls and roof. Our room was open in the front and the west side, with a window fronting to the east. In one corner was our bed and in another corner was the boys' beds, smothered by mosquito netting, used only when they came home from boarding school in Barbados. The cabin was rustic and purely pragmatic, but had a romantic feel to it. John called it "Wolf House" in honor of Jack London.

On the other side of the house wall was the workshop with tools, workbench, and enough space to park a truck—if and when we could afford one. Each night, while building, we would row to OUTWARD BOUND, trailed by a singing, biting undulating formation of hungry female mosquitoes. As soon as we were aboard, we lit mosquito coils that drove the nastiest ones out, but when the smoke faltered they returned with a vengeance. We moved ashore after the Wolf House was built and during the day we were safe from the troops of mosquitoes. But at night it was a different story. Our humble domicile was literally flooded with mosquitoes venturing out from their swampy birthplaces, pouring in like the Richthoffen Flying Circus. They dove and tormented us from all directions. We ate dinner in bed, covered by mosquito netting. John worked at night at his desk under a sputtering Coleman lantern that seemed to melt the top of his head as he wrote "investment" letters to friends, former charter guests, and celebrities. Virtually no one responded. The truth? No one but the Caldwells was interested in our dream scheme.

One night John was particularly discouraged.

"We are like flotsam on an airless sea," he said, scratching his mosquito bites under the hot lantern.

"What do you mean by that?" I asked, looking up from my book.

"I mean that no one in their right mind could possibly care about Palm Island but *us!*"

"Well, that's to be expected, isn't it?"

"True, but our $10,000 are melting away, even when we pay the laborers just three dollars a day! I've decided to sail to St. Vincent tomorrow with Totobell to get a bank loan."

"That's fine, honey, I'll keep the mosquitoes occupied."

I was glad he was waking up to reality, and taking Totobell (James Clouden was his real name) was a safety net for him because Toto was a big-footed, raw-boned man with two hands like baseball mitts, an expansive smile and the loyalty of the family dog.

He could be *very* intimidating.

John and Toto returned completely discouraged with their quest for money.

"I gave them my best paradise scenario. And do you know what they asked?" John asked angrily.

"No."

"They asked if I was a builder or if I had any experience in hotel management. Then they threw in the clincher: 'How much financial reserve do you have?' The hell with the financial reserve crap! Why would I be begging for money if I had financial reserve? I've got sweat equity. That's all. But they're all hairsplitters and bean counters. They want you to build your hotel first and then come see them when you don't need their money."

"They're such small people," I comforted.

"Yeah, and to make matters even worse, I ran into Fred Hazell. He grabbed me by the arm and said, 'Prune Island is a mosquito factory—get out now or you'll lose your shirt!'"

"Fred Hazell the merchandiser?"

"Yeah, dead Fred! I wanted to punch his lights out!"

"I'm glad you didn't," I said, concerned.

"Anyway, I grabbed Toto and left. But I had an idea. I sailed over to see Dr. Rico on Canouan Island. Remember his 100-foot yacht?"

"Who could forget that gorgeous boat?"

"Yeah, well, you would think a man of his means would be more than ready to make a sound money-making investment, right?"

"You'd think so . . ."

"Think again! He said, 'Johnny, you're a nice guy; I don't want to see you get burnt. So many people come out here to the islands under-funded and then go bust! Down the tubes! Even good ideas need sufficient capital. My advice to you is sell out while you still have a shirt on your back!' "

"He mentioned your shirt *too?*"

"Worse! That arrogant son-of-a-bitch! Everything was handed to him. Another lard-ass born with a gilded spoon in his lily-white mouth! No pride there. I decided right then and there I'd show that decadent rich smart-ass some day, if it's the last thing I do!"

"Oh honey, you're really upset! But look, why don't you try the banks again tomorrow? Maybe get rid of the shorts and T-shirt and try a business suit? That'll impress them more!"

"Hell no! I'm not going to kiss any fathead's ass! I'll do it *myself*!"

That was John, pure and simple, a team of one, fighting the world of injustice and hard knocks. If you crossed him he just did it himself and never spoke to you again. The same moxie got him through the University of California at Santa Barbara without even a high school education. He was honest, hardworking, and independent. I stopped making suggestions. I knew when to quit.

Later that evening we bounced ideas off each other: John chartering with Toto and I running the island, but that could not bring enough capital. Hours later we decided on a list of our assets: five beautiful beaches, great coral reefs, gorgeous potential home sites that we could sell based on our 99-year lease.

"That's it!" John shouted. *"Home sites!"*

"But John, we have no money to meet Friday's payroll. The bank's a better bet!"

"Nope, this is it." That conviction again!

The next day dawned with Toto, Prince, and John making wooden stakes. I watched as he laid out 27 home sites on our flashy north end called Tamarind Beach. The lots were one-quarter acre with 80-foot ocean frontage. Then I laughed out loud as he placed bold "SOLD" signs on ten of the lots. From the window of Wolf House I could see two yachts lying contentedly off of Tamarind Beach. John approached several passengers who were ashore. It was a calm day and I could easily hear John's sale's pitch:

"Hi," John said to a tall well-dressed man beach-combing with his wife "Say, I have a lighter just like that!"

"Really?" He smiled. "Perhaps you would like a cigarette?" He offered John a Marlboro. John was trapped. He had never smoked in his life!

"Oh, my favorite brand," he gushed. He puffed away without inhaling.

"I hear you're building a hotel," said the man nonchalantly.

"Yes, should be open Christmas of '67."

"My wife's not so keen on the sailing; we might come stay with you someday."

"Great!"

"Do you own the whole island?"

"Yes. Yes, it's all mine. Would you like to see it? I'll show you around. We have a number of lots for sale. Sold quite a few in the past week, as you can see."

"Well, yes you *have!*" His wife got closer.

"Honey," she urged her husband, "Are these lots for sale?"

A few minutes passed as the wind picked up and I lost parts of the conversation but the next thing I witnessed was a check passing from the tall man to John who gave the man a vigorous handshake. Then they parted. John literally floated back to the Wolf House.

"Mary! Mary! Guess what? I just sold our first lot! Four thousand dollars! We're in the black again!"

"You're such a wheeler-dealer!" I said, hugging him as he spun me around. As always, this spinning was a prelude to making love, which took up most of the remainder of the morning.

John deposited the check with Mr. Trimmingham, the manager at Barclays Bank, who was kind enough and trusted John enough to clear the check the same day. An ecstatic John returned to Palm with a bag full of Biwis, paying off the workers as he met them. From time to time in the ensuing years we would encountered other financial difficulties, but the wonderful Mr. Trimmingham always came to our rescue, creating a strong financial and personal friendship.

Each lot sale honed John's beachside manner and in a few

months he was selling oceanside views for $20,000 per lot. Suddenly we had fifty workers on the island, and whenever funds were low it was off to the beach for John who regaled potential buyers with tales of the trade wind islands, lounging under the golden sun, while surrounded by crystal waters stalled in an endless summer.

They loved it.

27

Palm Island Stories

In May of 1966 Jonathan Roach came to John looking for a job. Jonathan was a quiet man with an explosive laugh. We immediately gave him "Roachie" as his knickname. He became our general factotum and could handle virtually any job with a warm manner and sure hands. One day a visitor from Grenada came to Roachie with great news: he was "giving" us a generator.

"It's yours, mon, for nuttin' mon," he said in his thick patois.

John and Roachie looked at each other.

"Yeah, mon. I sellin' it so cheap, mon, it is a *giff*, mon."

"This contraption is out of the Ark!" John said, laughing.

"No, mon!"

"Look at that rust! And the oil dripping out of the crankcase!" John bent over. "And smell that diesel! It's a mess!"

The negotiations were on.

As I watched, John and Roachie whittled the price tag for the "gift" down from a "tousen dollar" to just $100 Biwi. The money changed hands and John said, "OK, start it." The boys and I looked on, skeptical as usual. The visitor leaned over, making adjustments here and there, first wiping up oil leaks, and then starting the generator. It broke into life, smoking and shaking from side-to-side, giving off the strangest assortment of grunts and groans I have ever heard come from an engine. We all looked at each other and laughed as "Huffy Puffy" shook its body in the water-filled bilge of the visitor's boat.

That night we had the luxury of lights with background music

provided by the clanging Huffy Puffy. Sometimes the engine sputtered and the light bulbs dimmed to near darkness; other times the
engine roared into hyperactivity and the light intensity grew until
the bulbs exploded. A tough life in paradise, but at least it kept the
squadrons of mosquitoes at bay. John took notice of the absence of
these flying needles around the lights.

"Tomorrow we'll tackle these bastards . . . again!" His eyes
narrowed to warlike slits.

The boys hated the mosquito control work. When people asked
why we were building an airstrip Johnnie would say, "the mosquitoes need a landing strip!" Every day the workers who toiled in the
interior of Palm would rub diesel oil on their legs and arms and on
their ears and chin, a ritual that offered only imperfect protection.
In addition to diesel oil, John and the boys wore a khaki suit: long
pants and long sleeves. Knee boots, a hat that covered their ears,
gloves, and a rag around their necks completed the space suit. Still
the mosquitoes bit: right through the khaki cloth, especially when
the workers bent over. While the boys worked I tended to architectural plans, bookkeeping, and numerous other tasks. Each night at
dusk, John would stroll through the tangled scrub and bushes,
hacking his way with a 24-inch cutlass blade. Every moment I could
see him assessing and re-assessing what must be done to make our
sow's ear into a first-class tourist facility. The enormity of the task
frequently overwhelmed him.

John researched the life cycles of all the various mosquito gen-
era on the island. Several species laid their eggs in the mud and
when the rains came and covered the mud sufficiently, their wig-
gling larvae would hatch out in days and fill the open water.
Scarcely a week later they made their way straight for Wolf House
to give us weeks of misery before they died off. Another species laid
its eggs in any stagnant cool water, especially the low swampy areas.
We soon learned that a thin film of diesel oil sprayed on the water
prevented the larvae from breathing through their anal siphons,
hence suffocating them.

The remaining species laid their eggs in the mud of thousands
of holes—occupied by enormous land crabs—and when rain

raised the water level, sure as taxes, the mosquitoes would erupt from Hades. John and the workers dipped bits of bread in Dieldrin, an agricultural pesticide solution, and shoved the dripping pieces down the holes. Then Prince and John would go out daily in their khaki fatigues and shove the dead crabs back into the holes before filling them with dirt, packing them down with a blunt stick. If they ran out of pesticide, they would ram stones and small bits of co-conut shells into the holes, and the crabs, unable to dig their way out through the surrounding roots, would perish. We killed thousands of crabs on the island, which would be ecologically unthinkable today, but back then, it was a matter of survival.

Another major problem on Palm was the need for the daily availability of fresh water. Actually this was true everywhere in the Grenadines. Rain was (and continues to be) the only source of fresh water, and one of the first tasks was to build a cemented con-crete slab on the backside of a large hill on the east slope of the is-land overlooking Mayreau and the Tobago Cays to the north. This large water catchment would feed two cisterns, one up on the hill and the other at the base. With the expertise of foreman James Cudjoe we shaved off an area 90 feet wide and 130 feet deep. Dozens of men and women cast a sturdy concrete foundation, hand-pounded by three solid ladies. Other women toted buckets of sand patiently up the hill to the mixing board. One of these intense in-dustrious ladies was Loretta Mills, later to be the second cook for years in the kitchen of our resort. There was always much gusto, chatter, and joviality in this hard-working group.

We now had 100 workers, requiring two boat trips every morn-ing and two back in the afternoon, manned by Roger and Johnnie. A cement mixer and the help of an itinerant Swede, Arne Hazelquist, our long-time friend, greatly simplified this task. Even Barclays Bank facilitated our adventure, giving us overdraft ad-vances and allowing us to pay back at whatever rate possible. Once, when showing the bankers our progress on Palm Island, the bank manager sank knee-deep in a swamp, and we were sure our over-draft days were over, but he laughed until he cried, even losing his shoe in the process. Another time when a banker was visiting to check on their investment we heard a huge boom and a loud uproar of voices from the cistern area. We ran over to see flames engulfing some unknown object.

"Dey is fire at de cement ting!" shouted a trusted worker.

John ran over.

"What happened?"

"Dem workers and' dem do dat," the worker explained, "De ting stop and dem take out de plug an' pour in petrol an' strike a match to see if it need more, den up go de whole ting with fire!"

By now the cement mixer was a ball of flames shooting ten feet into the air, melting the gasoline container and anything else nearby.

John was ready for murder. In the past he would often fly into a rage when things went dramatically wrong or when he thought anyone, even his sons, were slacking at the job. Our foreman, James, and Roachie were standing beside him, subdued, looking seasick. Henry Brown, the mason, broke the deathly silence:

"It ain't no good, John. Can't mix nuttin', not even a drink at de bar!"

There were roars of laughter and a smile creased John's stern face as he realized the futility of blowing himself up along with the cement mixer. The mixer made a final popping noise following by a death rattle: more gales of laughter erupted from the workers. John's shook his head from side-to-side:

"OK, men, let's use the shovels!"

John was sure he had lost the banker's support, but the banker turned to him with a serious face and said:

"Frankly, I think you'll save some more money using shovels."

Saved again!

We finally finished the cistern by hand and turned to another vital job: the jetty. James and Willie designed it and Totobell served as foreman. We started with a big Trinidad cargo schooner tacking into our harbor and discharging 20,000 board feet of Guyana timber (known as greenheart) over the side in twenty feet of water. This Guyana hardwood is so dense and hard it will not float. There were eight-by-eights for the jetting pilings and assorted lengths of pitch pine that did float. John and the workers donned masks and snorkels and fins, and swam out and towed the hundreds of boards to the beach where the workers arranged them. They finally dragged the last timber from the sea at two o'clock in the morning.

Toto took charge of the jetty project with a team of seven workers. With cutlasses they sharpened one end of each fifteen-foot long 8 x 8 hardwood timber, and with a framework to guide the timbers, they stood on a scaffolding and pounded the pylons into the sand, using a 12 x 12 timber of five-foot length, with two pipes through crossed holes to form four handles. I can still hear them shouting "heavy, heavy!" in unison as four men drove each pylon down scarcely an inch at a time. Hour after hour they persevered bearing the heat of day until each pylon was driven a full ten feet into the sand, or until it struck hidden coral and was stopped.

Forty years later it still stands, a tribute to their exhausting work.

Our workers came to Palm Island via our CARIBBEAN BELLE, as we pompously called her, operated by Johnnie or Roger, with arrival at 7:30 a.m. and departure at 4:00 p.m. The workers came tight-packed and jovial. Despite their joviality, arrival was about as much fun as going to their mother's funeral, and departure was like loping off to a cricket match. CARIBBEAN BELLE had once had a nefarious past when she was known by her first name, JESSIE GIRL. She had been employed as a rum smuggler in Antigua, slinking in by stealth of night to sleeping bays, from St. Barts in the French islands, with cargoes of illicit rum and liquors. Customs duty was high on these popular beverages and rum running flourished profitably on Antigua's many shores.

We had once saved the former JESSIE GIRL from a fiery death when "business competitors" in the rum smuggling business tried to torch her near Palm Island. We saw the fire and called the owner who thanked us with several bottles of fine rum. Later, the boat was put up for sale in Antigua when the tariffs on rum were dropped and the cost of doing illegal business became too high. Her rigging was in tatters, ropes and lines were shredded, and she had no lights, no stove, no dinghy, no radio, no life jackets, no engine controls, no distress signals, no bilge pump, and a main sail that was about fifty percent sail and fifty percent patches.

She was a fair amount of floating dry rot with broken engine hold bolts.

The boys thought she was a great buy.

I stayed alone on OUTWARD BOUND for a week while John and Johnnie sailed the floating wreck carefully back to Palm. (Roger was back in Barbados attending boarding school and missed the circus.) I watched with fear and amusement as the decrepit boat crawled into the Young Island anchorage on St. Vincent's south shore. John and Johnnie quickly shut off the clanking, overheated motor. It had been a sixty-hour straight run and this prompted John to do something very unusual for him: he took us out for dinner—fish and chips, and a bottle of beer for the two of us. We considered JESSIE GIRL's unladylike properties and named her CARIBBEAN BELLE in jest. Little did we know how badly we would need CARIBBEAN BELLE.

28

More Palm Stories

*A*cross from Palm Island, barely a mile to the west lies Union Island and the two competing villages of Clifton and Ashton. Union
Island is a dozen times the size of Palm's 120 acres, and it served as
our support community with a population of about one thousand
sturdy inhabitants. Virtually all are Caribbean blacks, the descen-
dants of slaves. They are quiet wonderful people who had been isolated for generations and only recently touched by incoming
charters, beginning in the 1950s. Clifton, on the east side, is the main
village, blessed with a coral-framed harbor, and a mile westward of
it, over a rise and around an ambling curve and a downward slope,
is Ashton, in a peaceful valley with an avenue of rundown abodes
and paint-hungry shops, attended by the constant assembly of in-
different loiterers, sitting or standing languidly, with searching
eyes—alert and very congenial.

When we chartered, wending our way down the archipelago
bound for Grenada, we slipped behind the bulky, curving barrier
reef, called Howlands Reef, confronting and protecting Clifton,
and put down the hook in placid, azure water for a stable night.
John would row ashore with our charterers while I—the peren-
nial cleaner and tidier—tended the ship. John would bring our
guests to the Clifton Hotel to visit with Conrad Adams, a suave,
quiet man with a broad smile and low-key manner, amiable and
willing, quietly ethical. We would make arrangements for an
evening's entertainment—a "jump up" as the West Indians called
it—held in the back room, which served as a dance hall. Conrad

Palm Island charter yachts ILLUSION *and* AFOXE

would set up his hi-fi set of thunderous proportions and mock up a bar in the corner with a table covered by a bed sheet and an open cardboard box for the drink money. Behind the table was a huge tub of iced-down beer.

Word of Caldwell-sponsored jump-ups spread quickly among the islanders. "Dancin' by Adams tonight, mon," or "Mr. John goin' buy we a beer, mon." And true to almost any Afro-West Indian soiree, when ripping Calypso music blasted the walls, and dancers were packed in like sardines on an overheated floor, pure joy ensued from about 9 p.m. to the wee hours of the morning. However, the *Outward Bounders* usually folded around midnight, and departed the boisterous frolickers to enjoy a rock-like sleep on the smooth sheet of Clifton's placid water, with the gentle roar of Howlands Reef in our ears.

The next evening, we would sail around and put in behind Frigate Island, a three-acre bit of high rock with scalloped, sandy edges, 300 yards off Ashton. We rowed ashore to hobnob the night away with King Mitch (aka Augustus Mitchell) sipping beer while an impromptu dinner of young goat and local vegetables was stewed in the kitchen by curious, attentive local belles, who peeped at us intermittently throughout the evening, always smiling and giggling. King Mitch was a Grenadines stalwart, a legend of a man with quick, alert eyes and a stentorian voice, whose visage was brightened by a broad, white-toothed smile. He was affable and loquacious, the West Indian Dale Carnegie of our time; a man with a winning disposition who was a major influence in our tiny part of the globe. King Mitch could spin endless yarns borne of years of intimacy with these isles, back to when his father and grandfather served as captains of trading schooners in a day when they had no engines at all. Above all, he was the epitome of the small island businessman—nothing to him was impossible and everything was based on profit. He was the African-American forerunner of Reagan-Thatcher economics, far before their time.

King Mitch would always enthrall our guests—they had never seen a personality like his! The nights were always filled with hyperbolic stories of sea adventures as well as repetitive explorations of the world's growing problems. Even in the early balmy days of the 1960s—the lasts days of nirvana on the islands—it was painfully apparent that the social problems of the world were metastasizing and seeping into the peaceful fabric of our tropical paradise. What could we do to help? We concluded many times that there was little if anything we could do except to be honest and hard-working, give a helping hand when needed, spread joy whenever possible, and always be fair, decent, and tolerant. John and I would always stand firm on those attributes.

We knew even then that one day we would look back nostalgically on these convivial sojourns as the "good old days." We savored every minute knowing that this eternal bliss must eventually end. And end it did, when we really started developing Palm Island in earnest. The manual labor involved was horrendous, and between that and the considerable planning that was needed, our idyllic idle time was taken. Of course, Palm was not the only small island under development at that time. Yachtsman Hazen Richardson, a New England Yankee and a fellow yachtsman, Doug Therman, writer of mystery tales, were undertaking a development in the Grenadines similar to our own. Their developments, however, had the significant financial backing of corporations. Our budget operated on a shoestring and serendipity.

Let me pause here to say that there are really two Grenadine groups: the St. Vincent Grenadines, from Bequia, quiet and quaint, to Petit St. Vincent (P.S.V.). This group includes the bustling island of Mustique. Then there are the Grenada grenadines: Petit Martinique, Carriacou, Ronde Island, rocky Isle de Caille, and a smattering of islet outcroppings. In our St. Vincent solar system, Mustique shines above all. English socialite, Colin Tennant, later to be Lord Tennant, lifted it out of failed agricultural experiment and planted it in the world headlines by enticing Britain's Princess Margaret to take a hideaway home there and give the island the luster of the British Royal Family. The elegant princess made her all-night parties showpieces that attracted the moneyed set, which built lavish, escapist homes, and fueled the island into new heights of conspicuous consumption by jet setting night-lifers.

We had the pleasure of her Royal Highness visiting our modest spread, sans the snobocracy, and she pleased us with appealing smiles and nods right down the line of our staff from the family to the lowliest kitchen maid. She may have been smiling because Palm Island is surrounded by miles of colorful coral reefs, with snug coves and exceptional weather throughout the year. We have mild tides with weak currents, lustrous trade winds, and blazing white beaches. It was and is still a yachtsman's paradise throughout the St. Vincent Grenadines.

In those days the islands were serviced by mail boats, a collection of floating tubs, contracted by the government to bring the mail out twice weekly from Union Island to Kingstown. These weary old vessels were a scrubby lot—because mail payments were low—and the skippers had to rely on cargo and passengers to eke out a living in the trade. This accounted for a fascinating assortment of mixed general cargo, jammed in with assorted island life paraphernalia, including food, tools, household necessities, bags of cement, furniture, engines and spare parts, timber, and assorted bags and boxes.

At each island stop, beginning with Bequia, there would be an exodus over the rail—a river of people with packages and assorted containers—accompanied by a backdrop of loud, eager voices. At Canouan, where there was no wharf (in those early times), a flotilla of small boats (colorful but of questionable construction) would row and dock together to exchange goods as the lusty trade winds jostled them back-and-forth. Next would be Mayreau and then Union Island with its ancient and weary wharf, where a boisterous crowd would flood aboard even before the warps were made fast. Locals would swarm into the hold and toss anything aside in order to locate their items. Ashore, their colorful contents were thrown into rusting vehicles that transported drivers and their motley cargo inland.

Not everything went smoothly, of course. There were times when these hulks broke down. Radio calls would bring Toto, John, and sometimes the boys to the rescue. Many times they made night runs to a flagging ship to rescue the fresh and frozen resort provisions before they thawed. And there were breakdowns at sea—engine problems, dirt in the fuel, or lack of fuel. John and some of the workers would then sail out in search of the crippled vessel along with Mac and assorted tools, and a drum of diesel oil precariously lashed on the deck. Then there were the passengers and crews of these stranded boats singing calypsos and shouting "On to Panama!" Sometimes mailboats would crash into the cays; other times they would mysteriously burn, although no one ever lost his life.

One memorable time, John and I went up on SOLENT SWAN, better known to us as DIRTY DUCK. It was jackfish season, when local net fishermen made runs on shoals of the silvery, seven-inch creatures with piercing eyes and constantly flapping tails. We took a boatload at Palm and poured them aboard the deck of SOLENT SWAN for shipment to St. Vincent. At Mayreau more boxes of jacks were dumped atop Palm's catch. And at Canouan a record catch was shoveled on board, forming a two-foot deep mass of writhing silvery bodies that needed to reach market as soon as possible. Smelly fish, a blazing sun, and a windless sea all combined to make the perfect storm for my giddy head.

Then the coup de grâce: The engine began to cough and sputter.

"It's going to *stop!*" I said rather fearfully, thinking of the nightmare of being stranded with a boatful of ripening fish.

"No," John said.

But it did. An hour slogged by with the clinking of tools from below and finally the mechanic stuck his head up, face pale, and crawled across the slippery fish to divest himself of breakfast over the side of the boat. Afterward he curled up in the fetal position to "cool out." Now things were getting serious. The annoying roll of the ship, its oily cargo, and a dead engine all served to intensify the reeking aroma beyond human tolerance. Soon, others, including myself, were vomiting like geysers over the side of the boat.

"Fix de ting, mon, go start she up. I weary dem fish," bellowed the captain, hat pulled down low over his eyes.

"Just now, just now, mon. Don't rush me. I will fix she, mon," the mechanic said waving a flailing arm over the dying fish.

The mechanic, realizing that conditions were better below than above with the rotting fish, sighed and stepped down into the galley. Another hour went by before pouts and idle threats from the engine finally broke into a steady roar, providing limited power and movement. Meanwhile, the fish got hotter and smellier. Then it began to rain steadily and the fish became a mass of dead eyes and scales. I huddled close by the wheel to avoid the sloshing fish, and sat there, patiently, watching the land slowly get closer when suddenly two huge waves reared up unexpectedly and bashed against the hull, soaking me from head to foot. At this point I was resigned to any humiliation. I looked at John with forlorn eyes tinged with a bit of disdain.

"Sorry," was all he could mumble.

"*Jesus!*" was all I could muster.

We landed shortly afterward and with my hair in oily strings I plodded uncaringly to the homely New Haven Hotel to take a shower. Every few seconds I turned my head to watch with scowling curiosity the growing train of cats that followed me.

Back on Palm we surveyed our newly acquired Wreck of the Hesperus: CARIBBEAN BELLE (aka AFRICAN QUEEN). Our dilapidated purchase lay forlornly at anchor, unable to provide safe sea service for our employees, some of whom could not swim. She was to re-place the small sailing smacks, which were not reliable for trans-portation between Union and Palm. Nonetheless, we were desperate to get workers to Palm every day at a reasonable time. So Toto the handyman, Tyrone the carpenter, and John and the boys all pitched in to repair CARIBBEAN BELLE in a mere two weeks. This is how the entire development of Palm Island would proceed; everything was always at risk: our money, our lives, our futures. We bet it all on our-selves and our collective abilities. In the meantime, we had an over-grown island, a dilapidated boat, and a Wolf House that barely kept us dry. But our dream of making Palm Island into a tourist resort gem kept us going.

We had made progress with mosquito control, but still out in the middle of the island was a daunting patch, about an acre, of spi-dery mangrove thicket with their many-legged tripod-like growths anchoring ten-foot high bushy heads of impenetrable green. Below the root system was a perpetual muddy swamp that bred mosqui-toes by the millions. We had to destroy this subterranean mosquito condominium before Palm could be habitable.

John set out to tackle the beasts with diesel oil. Armed for bat-tle with long-sleeve khaki shirt, long pants, boots, hat over his ears, rag around his neck, gloves, and plastic eye guard, he loaded the bulky spray can loaded with five gallons of diesel. I watched from afar as John entered the swamp. Immediately, a ball of angry mos-quitoes blackened the air above his head as John sprayed the holes below with diesel. He swung like a madman at the little vipers but they found easy passage into his nose and ears. He slapped furi-ously, hard enough to dislodge a glove and his hat, both of which went sailing into the ooze below. Now the real feast began. John staggered forward in an attempt to gain his balance, but instead he fell into the ooze and lost his other glove and the plastic face visor. I edged closer.

"John, are you OK?" I shouted.

"Yes, I'm *OK!*" came the angry response. Clearly, he was not OK.

I walked down to the edge of the swamp, just beyond the reach of most of the mosquitoes. John's face was thick with the flying vipers and they were biting through his clothes. Then he had another bad slip and tumbled backward, sinking through the spidery legs of the mangroves. The tank jammed under him and his shoulders were immersed in mud.

"*John!*" I screamed.

"I'm *OK!*" he yelled. I learned never to interfere with John's macho even under the most hilarious of circumstances. He frantically rolled back-and-forth to extract himself. A boot ripped off and he sputtered as water entered his mouth, getting angrier by the second. I watched helplessly, biting my lower lip.

"God damn mud!" he screamed. Then with the blur of angry motions that followed, John literally rose from the muck with legs and arms flailing, running through the air toward the edge of the swamp, and finally collapsed at my feet in a mass of mud and dead mosquitoes.

"Honey?" I queried carefully.

"Dammit, I said I'm *OK!* Do you understand? *OK!*" he said in a thoroughly disgusted tone.

"OK," I said and watched helplessly as he struggled with his deflated ego.

He was bloodied and beaten, but not defeated. Like MacArthur, he would return to the swamp, sometimes alone, sometimes with unwilling helpers, and eventually his sheer willpower won the battle. That was John: focus and conquer; everything in life was a war. His ego was big enough to fill a room.

We developed Palm with the socially idealistic concerns of John in mind. He was tempted by many friends to make an escape for the *Rich and Famous*, but he chose to create a laid-back resort for middle-income professionals and entrepreneurs like himself. He would have nose-to-nose yelling contests with some of the *nouveau riches*, such as our Swedish friend, Arne Hazelquist, an architect. Arne was a graduate engineer with an ambition and ego that matched John's. They frequently fought over just about anything. But there was one complication that prevented all out war: Anita,

Arne's wife, was pregnant ("making baby" as the locals describe it). From my own experience, I could see that Anita would be delivering soon. Arne had pre-arranged delivery for the baby in the Kingstown Hospital when the blessed event arrived.

One day, Arne, assuming it was safe to leave his wife, went to St. Vincent with a fishing boat on a shopping run for items required by the house he was building on Palm. That same day, John and I were invited aboard the English yacht BLUE MOON at Union Island for wine and dinner. I was showering in the outback enclosure of galvanized sheeting, dipping into a bucket of fresh water and pouring it over my head when I heard Arne's manager, Ambrose, screaming at the top of his lungs:

"Anita having belly pain, de baby comin', she need your help!"

"I'll be comin'" I shouted back.

I threw on my clothes—no time for underwear or shoes—and raced up 180 steps to Anita's house, two steps at a time.

"I can deliver here!" she said excitedly.

"*No!*" I countered firmly, "not on the island!"

We walked carefully down the steps, she breathing heavily and emitting audible gasps of discomfort. John and I packed her into the sole of the boat and leaned her against a thwart with a pillow. In a rush we headed to Union, the full moon low in the west with a pale dusk closing in around us. It created a shining silvery path that guided us toward the docks.

"It's so beautiful," Anita said simply as she clutched at her belly.

On the harbor shore we took Anita into the Adams family's small hotel, fitted out like a frontier inn with just the basics in those rustic days. Nurse Clouden, general health handywoman and island midwife, was there in minutes. I stayed with Mrs. Adams while John went to BLUE MOON (docked about fifty feet away) for dinner. Periodically I would announce the birthing progress to John and his English hosts, Nigel and Pauline. While John ate a stunning dinner of steak, homemade bread, gravy and potatoes, I worked with the midwife.

"Anita is in labor, having a hard time, more later!" I shouted to them from the hotel patio to the deck of the ship.

An hour passed.

"Anita still in labor; the baby won't move!" I announced dramatically at ice cream.

Several more hours passed.

"Now the baby is moving, but progress is slow; Anita is having a rough time!" I screeched at them during their liqueur.

A long lapse of verbal bulletins made John and his hosts edgy so they broke open a bottle of wine and had the leftovers. They sat on deck, apprehensively watching the hotel deck, waiting for more announcements from me.

Bulletins four and five were rather discouraging, but near midnight I announced, "The baby has moved again!" Finally, at four in the morning I shouted, "The baby has arrived and she is beautiful!"

Shouts and cheers arose from the boat. Glasses were raised and spontaneous dancing erupted. But it was nearing 6:00 a.m., working time on Palm, and John and I were ready to go. Arne was finally reached by the "island coconut radio system" from the transceiver on the host boat and he joined us, his wife, and new baby shortly afterward. A month later, Arne came to the conclusion that Palm Island was too small for John and him to live peacefully together and he migrated over to Petit St. Vincent and then finally to Mustique Island, bonding with Lord Colin Tennant of the British aristocracy. There he went on to have a brilliant and lucrative career as guide and builder of that famous chunk of rolling tropical greenery, making a world-renowned resort island. It was his talent that helped draw in Her Majesty Princess Margaret, and a host of other *Who's Who* personalities from around the world who in turn erected magnificent villas and established that enclave of conspicuous consumption. This, of course, ran contrary to John's socialist views.

29

Preparing for Opening Day

$\mathcal{A}$t this point in time, late 1966, the foundations were dug and cast in concrete for the first ten rooms of our emerging resort. I had designed duplex cabanas, two rooms to each cottage, divided by a plastered wall for privacy. Each of the guest rooms had space for two twin beds, which when pushed together and fitted with special sheets would become a king-size bed. I designed side tables at the head of each twin bed, with reading lamp, ashtrays, flower vase, and magazines, with a drawer and shelf for small things. In my sketches I placed a clothes locker, a small refrigerator, and in the corner a writing desk with more drawers. At the foot of the beds would be a rattan divan and two chairs, with a central low table. Through an adjoining door would be the bathroom—shower, sink and counter, toilet, and locker with shelves. Out on the front patio would be a palm-frond gazebo, table and chairs, with two portable lounge divans of light aluminum.

My plan was obviously not one of super luxury, but one of sensible and adequate comfort with the convenience of our future guests in mind. It was a purely pragmatic design: no costly trifles to elevate our rates. Needless to say, John greatly appreciated my pragmatism. I did not stop there. I also added my designer's eye to the layout and position of the beach bar, dining room, kitchen, storeroom, and small office with a reception counter. Attached would be John's office with two divan beds, one for him and one for me, which would make us two of the world's shortest work commuters. In the morning we simply had to sit up, slip on our clothes, take a

The Beach Bar at Palm Island resort

few steps and we would be at our desks! While John enjoyed the temporary living quarters, I made it known early on that this was *strictly* temporary. I also made it very clear that I would not serve as the hotel chef! John was upset with my decision but he knew I was a good planner and administrator and not one to pick a fight or continue a fight. I simply stepped back when I thought John was out-of-line (until he felt guilty enough to apologize!).

Lot sales were dragging at this time, so the cheapest way to continue the development of the resort was to order what we could afford and carry on with bits and pieces of work that were the least costly, leaving the big ticket items until later. We lined out and cast all the floors for every building, even the laundry room back near what would become the staff quarters. Then we started cautiously with walls, creating gaunt, unpainted structures with square and rectangular gaps for future windows and doors when we could afford them. When sales of beach plots perked, we brought in lumber by the thousand board feet and started roofing the structures by placing boards over rafters of 2 x 4 pitch pine and then covered the boards with rolls of green-tarred felting. This was the beginning of our Palm Island Beach Club, whose name was modeled after the Galley Bay Beach Club on Antigua, where we dined often in the early years with our charter guests.

By 1967 construction was increasing at an exponential rate, with an additional six private houses for lot owners. We now had 200 workers on the payroll, not all of whom worked. But John, being a "socialist" kept them all on and even hired their families! He practiced what he preached. Union Island, with its economy boosted by another hundred employees at Petit St. Vincent, had the air of a gold rush outpost on the Alaskan Klondike. Roustabouts poured down from St. Vincent and swelled a raucous throng of beer boys, rum and cokers, gamblers, and scufflers. This resulted in a flurry of shack builders on Union Island. Anything with walls and roof on Union was used to house the multitude and the population sprouted from 900 to 1500. The economy was booming. Shops (mainly rum shops) sprang up, just as verbal brawls and fisticuffs did. Friday and Saturday night dances flourished. It was all very colorful and exciting—a hash of intrigued humanity chasing rainbows.

As our "resort" (as we pompously called it) took shape with rooms 1 and 2 and rooms 5 and 6 emerging from their construction cocoons, our galvanized-sheeted Wolf House looked much out-of-place. We loved its simplicity and coziness, and our workers related to us through our modest choice of abode. But it had to go. We dismembered it to make space for rooms 3 and 4. That humble abode was the epitome of the good old days—even though the nights were sticky and buggy and the silence of the tropical wilderness was drowned by the noise of Huffy Puffy, our generator.

At this point, we turned our thoughts to an airfield as a

means to get our future guests to the island. Way back, when we sailed up the Great Barrier Reef along the Australian coast, we landed on Dunk Island, in Queensland waters, and observed a young family hacking a hole in dense bushland for a makeshift hotel. Their development included a hand-hewn airstrip, created with cane knives, mattocks, shovels, and barrows. They hacked out the tangled growth, leveled the terrain by toting away a half-acre of coarse coral chunks in wheelbarrows, and then filled holes with rubbish and hillside loam. That memory gave John the idea.

"Forget the shovels and wheelbarrows," I said, "rent a bulldozer!"

"No money for that," John said, "and besides the closest one is in Trinidad, it might as well be in Timbuktu!"

We were in luck because Palm lay east to west but this was not readily apparent as the wall of wild growth across the interior made it impossible to see our four low hills on the south shore from the northeast point. The varied bush made it difficult to establish a line running east to west. John solved the problem by bringing in OUTWARD BOUND's steering compass. Sailing the course prescribed by the compass and some mathematics involving variation and deviation, John and the boys, along with Prince Cudjoe (James's brother) plotted an east-west pathway. The next week involved a vigorous battle with the foliage, hacking away at the evergreen growth with cutlasses to create a ten-foot path that to our glee was right on the money. The next step of airport construction was easy. With help from our employees, we created an 80-foot-wide swath from the original path, with most of the downed small trees and branches serving as excellent firewood for home cooking. Other workers followed us, setting the remaining debris ablaze until Palm Island looked as though it were being burned. Even the St. Vincent newspaper would write articles with headlines like "Palm Burns Again!"

We still needed to smooth our "airfield" however, which was a rat's nest of holes and stumps. We were saved by "Ratman" (Ralph Alves), a Trinidad-born entrepreneur who often descended upon us aboard the weekly mail boat with all sorts of equipment, machinery, and gear he had ferreted out of agriculture estates and auctions in St. Vincent. So here was a smiling and laughing Ralph, appearing on our jetty, with a brand new tractor.

"What's *this*?" a tired John asked casually.

"It's *yours!*" Ralph stated, beaming.

"What do you mean by that?" John stood back, calculating.

"I bought it for you, mon," he said.

"Look, Ratman, we don't need this, we don't want it, and we can't afford it even if we did want it!" John said angrily.

"It's *yours*, mon. You don't have to pay notin'!"

"Does the owner know about this?"

"I bought it, mon, I'm givin' it to you!"

"Listen, Ratman. You've never given me anything! Put it back on the schooner and cut the bullshit."

Ratman feigned emotional hurt and continued his love-dance with the tractor, extolling its many virtues.

"De tractor can build Palm Island!"

He shouted, "It's better than de truck; you can pull a trailer behind it!"

I started to laugh as John turned with those jaded blue eyes to take in a trailer by the jetty. It too was a "gift."

"Cheap, mon. Only $13,000 US for the tractor. The trailer's free, mon! Another gift for you! This is your best day!"

I could see the fight was out of John.

"Looks like we sell another home site, honey," he said to me.

"I'll go make the sign," I said, laughing all the way back to the workshop.

That is how we got the tractor, which really did make the job of extracting tenacious stumps easy. We also used it to fill holes in the runway with piles of conch shells. Later, Ratman also "gave" us a rusty dump truck and Chevrolet pickup, both for "free." Ratman was as patient and as persistent as a lover at full moon. His closing argument on the Chevy was this:

"Listen to dis engine, mon . . . it will last you for fifteen years!"

Indeed, it did purr like a kitten, so Ralph drove it to the generator room to park it for the evening. The next morning Mac came to see John with a long face.

"De Chevro needin' parts, mon, won't start."

And with that simple comment began three years of fruitless search by ourselves, well-meaning guests, friends who claimed they were mechanics, and anyone we could buttonhole to discover the make of its engine (it was decidedly not a Chevrolet engine but a freak monstrosity that defied description and for which no one had made parts in the past twenty-five years). So there it sat, in retirement before it even began work, slowly manufacturing rust and gaining in paralysis, with tires flattening, windshield and windows dusted over and the back used for a rubbish bin. After that "gift" Ratman was given specific orders never to bring any unauthorized vehicles or vehicle-like facsimiles onto our jetty again. He complied.

About this time, the spring of 1967, nearly ten months after our start of Palm Island, we had finished three rooms, one of which housed John and me. Seven others were in various stages of readiness. The kitchen block was roofed and we had three fine cabinet makers putting counters and lockers together: Tyrone, as handsome as a movie star, tall, quiet, and diffident; Ambrose, a staunch pillar of equanimity; and Otis, known as "Big Foot" and always barefoot, highly serious and a no-nonsense tradesman who got things done. Our tenacious Johnny Allen, one of the original fifteen laborers, was learning masonry work and to show his eagerness for work, turned up with his own trowel and float board. With his toothy smile, he applied himself to setting blocks and plastering walls, assisted by the loquacious Breadfruit, a stocky soothsayer and proponent of the mysteries of Obeah, our Grenadine version of Haitian voodoo that was followed by many.

Breadfruit claimed special powers with Obeah. He had attended sessions in Trinidad and learned esoteric practices from a bearded and turbaned East Indian. He personally had observed victims being "blown away" into thin air. He also learned the art of "bone pointing," a voodoo practice in which a cooked chicken bone is blessed and anointed with secret formulae; then its soft end

bitten off and the jagged remainder pointed at who is to be humbugged. In twenty-four hours the humbug would start its stealthy
work—the victim could suffer rotten bones or a pox on his skin, or
a dripping of blood from his heart to poison his insides. All of this
errant power was explained by a solemn Breadfruit with a cold and
knowing stare that bespoke of intimate knowledge of the world of
the unknown.

If you gave him money he would try to lure you alone to his
ramshackle abode in a plot of unkempt yards on Union Island,
where he would go into his weird and eerie act to bring down the
sinister forces from above. Johnny Allen had witnessed this firsthand. He had wanted one of his errant "wives" to be punished for
running off to Venezuela with another man. He would huddle in a
ball in a corner and whine a long discourse to strange forces that
resulted in a staring trance. He would tiptoe around, lighting some
twenty candles, and, sticking them about the floor, would walk
eyes-closed among them, face upward to outer powers, never
touching a candle. Humming loudly, he would put his hand on his
client's head with his other hand raised above to catch the outer vi-
brations and call the evil spirits down to harass the fleeing woman
and the wicked wife stealer.

Johnnie was quite influenced by this hocus-pocus and once
asked John's opinion of Breadfruit's prowess in occult matters.

"It's all baloney," he answered flatly to a dejected Johnnie. "Save
your money."

Breadfruit as obeahman also had the power to thwart the evil
intents of one's antagonists. This required, of course, more money,
the amount of which determined the extent of harm that could be
visited upon one's enemy. Breadfruit could make people sick, and
by special incantation (accompanied by another increase in fee) he
could incapacitate even the biggest, most fit man. In fact, for the
sum of $3,000 Biwi, he could explode someone into a million
pieces, causing them to disappear without a trace. He also claimed
association with jumbies—ghost-like denizens of the dark hours
who filtered invisibly through walls and closed doors to do harm-
ful acts to humbugged people. For a modest fee, Breadfruit could

assign jumbies to perform wanton acts of nighttime sabotage, but he claimed he also could enlist jumbies to perform benevolent deeds of aid and comfort to his clients. Again, the success was in proportion to the bribe.

Such was the spiritual life of the locals who participated in the building of Palm Island.

After eleven months of diligent effort we could see the bones of a resort forming and feel the heat of the impending opening date: Christmas 1967. The encroaching wall of knotted jungle growth was beaten back by chain saws and cutlasses, but it always threatened to return. The chief offender was a noxious weed that grew incessantly known by the locals as *cashee*. These plants were covered with small spikes and stickers. There was also cattle tamarind, a pleasant-looking growth of feathery green that grew rampant across the island to the height of a tall man, and which had to be dug out by its deep roots—or it sprang back again. The locals said cattle tamarind provided good protein for their cows, and the thick, stout stalks were ideal framing for the fishermen's fish pots, covered with chicken wire to form a shaped hole where unwary fish would enter but could not leave. Other offenders from the plant kingdom included maiyan, a plant that would send out numerous roots like snakes sixty feet in all directions. We had to ferret out each root with mattock and spade or they re-sprouted. The burn bush was probably the most bothersome plant: to merely touch it meant a burning misery of extreme agony.

We finally beat back the noxious weeds and filled most of the eighteen swamps by manual labor. Hefty guys like Johnny Allen, Breadfruit, Benson, and Happy Man spread sand from the beaches and dumped it where John indicated with his shovel. Then we both would spread it to three inches above high water mark in order to kill the subterranean den of mosquitoes. Our tractor, Jezebel, zeroed in on the larger swamps while the men tackled the smaller swamps.

Once the mosquitoes and noxious plants were at bay we planned a catchment for a safe supply of drinking water. In the Grenadines, water is as costly as rum. Weather conditions are divided into a wet season (summer, beginning in July) and a dry season (winter, beginning in December). Summer was the time to catch rain on our hill catchment area and store it in the two big cisterns there. With most of our roofs fitted with an efficient gutters and down spouts, rain was channeled to a number of cisterns around the hotel grounds. We designed our cistern after one we had seen at Gibraltar, just before sailing across the Atlantic.

30

A Troubled Youth

*I*t seemed quite natural for John that the first completed building would be our beach bar. Although he was a teetotaler most of his life, he saw no harm in bending the elbow for special occasions, especially if it were connected to business transactions such as lot sales. However, during the course of its construction, John began to recall his childhood and his father's alcoholism, which disturbed him a great deal.

"Sometimes I wish we could dispense with the bar," he said one day.

"Because of your dad?" I questioned. I had previously heard only bits and pieces about his father's alcoholism.

"I think so. You know, there was always booze in our house and Dad was a consummate drunk. His choice was corn liquor, which he downed neat with a twist of his face, pursing his lips with his chin bent onto his chest."

"Did you ever want to try it when you were a boy because you saw your dad drinking so heavily?" I queried.

"Yeah, many times. At least the beer. My dad liked home-brewed beer. And because it was Prohibition he was rarely hired—they could always smell booze on his breath. He was a debt collector and a weekend poker and whisky devotee. But he also brewed beer in a bathtub in our garage."

"*Bathtub!*" I laughed.

"Well, if the police came to raid us one of us kids could run to the garage from our school across the street and pull the bath plug and drain the beer into the hole below. More than once, looking out from my upstairs classroom across the street from our garage I spotted a police car pulling up near our house, the coppers getting ready to bust in. I would raise two fingers to the teacher to indicate the need for bowel relief. Then I would run lickety-split for home, enter the garage from the rear door and pull the bathtub plug. That was my job."

"So you saved the day for your dad?"

"Yup. No booze. No case. No charge."

"That's perfectly awful, a brewery in your garage, and you had to cover for your parent! That would be child abuse today!"

"Yes, it was awful, although it was a way of life and I didn't know any better. Dad would get the malt and hops in the garage and mix it in the night hours with doors and windows closed. Each week we capped the beer in unmarked bottles and boxed them for Dad to deliver. First, Mom poured the bottles. Then I popped on the caps and brothers Jack and Tom packed them in wooden fruit boxes. Dad would drink about six every evening; he stored them under a tarpaulin in the corner of the garage. The next day we would use our old topless Dodge to deliver the 'Caldwell Stuff.'" A disdainful look spread across his face.

"I'm surprised that with your family environment you aren't an alcoholic too. When did you first try a drink?"

"One day after school—109th Street Grammar School in South Los Angeles—I slipped out behind the garage and sat on the dog house. No one was around and I quaffed a mouthful, thinking it must be sweet tasting because Dad liked it so much. Instead, it tasted like dishwater. But I thought it *must* be good so I struggled and got the whole bottle down."

"*Oh my!*"

"And I said what my dad always said when he'd take a big swig of beer: 'good stuff!' Shortly afterward my head started spinning. Just then, my mom called: 'Johnny, it's your turn to wash the dishes!' I ran to the house and walked as steadily as I could to the sink. But the soapy water made me queasy and immediately after I finished the job I wobbled into the backyard and lost everything since breakfast, including the lining of my stomach!"

"You poor *boy!*" I gave him a hug.

"I felt better by dark, when Dad returned. He had a rule that we had to be in the house before dark or all hell broke loose. Of course, he was a bullshitter supreme and never minded his own rules. Sometimes he'd be back on Monday wall-eyed and empty-handed, or wall-eyed and plush with enough cash to choke a mule."

"How sad! You've had such a crazy life compared to my tame childhood." I said, putting my arm gently around his shoulder.

"The next time I drank a full bottle of beer was when I married you!" he laughed.

"Should I take that as a compliment?"

"Well, I guess," he said, collecting his thoughts. After a long pause he added: "You know, you're right: my childhood wasn't exactly idyllic."

"So *tell me*—you've never really told me much about your early years."

I settled in for a long Caldwell story, embellished, I assumed wherever necessary, but his childhood stories had a ring of truth to them and, more important, they explained a great deal of his adult character.

"A few nights after I got sick I heard someone on the back porch pounding on the door with his fists and shouting sternly for my dad. Out came Pop, groggy and half-drunk. As he pulled the door open I saw a huge pistol emerge from the coat pocket of the man outside. He quickly stuck it against Dad's belly and shouted, 'You want a lead slug in your guts?' I remember that clearly even today."

"*No!*"

"Well, Dad was mumbling something about his innocence when out came a second gun held by another man's hand in the shadows. 'I want my whisky back!' the man hissed at my dad, 'or I'll fire this gun right out of your backend!' 'Johnny,' my dad said, 'get the whisky in the gunnysack we found yesterday.' Well, we hadn't really found it; we *stole* it from a neighbor down the street and apparently someone snitched on us. Anyway, I uncovered the gunnysack from the back yard and ran it back to the men who grabbed the sack and waved their weapons one more time in front of my dad's face. One guy said, 'you son-of-a-bitch, you come snooping around my place again and you'll get some lead up your ass!' "

"That's *terrible!* And he made you an unwilling accomplice!" I said, honestly appalled.

"The worst part was my mom woke up and came into the kitchen and asked us what was happening. My dad said, 'I don't know what's going on. Johnny, where did you get that gunnysack?' But my mom knew my dad was bullshitting. I could see another family blow up coming, so I jumped up and ran into the garage and hid for the night."

"Why didn't you tell me any of this before?"

"Well, there's lots of nastiness in my life I haven't told you."

"*Tell me!*" I demanded.

Long into the night John told me of his teenage gang activities on 105th Street and Central Avenue, a suburbs of Watts. He rose up the ranks to become the leader of Dudley's Gang (named after Dudley its organizer and leader, until John punched him in the face and forced him out of office). His gang was a mix of Mex's (Mexicans) and white bitches (as John told it). They would meet the Tijuana Bastards and a black group called the Black Devils and go at it on an open lot, fighting in two opposing lines with clumps of grass, pounding each other into submission with the dirt-filled roots. This usually went on for about an hour with a respite or two during which time the boys would size each other up and re-plan their attack. This would go on until one of opposing guys or one of their own dropped his root ball and started a personal fistfight with someone from the other side. At that point they would crowd around in a ring and cheer their man on. When there was a winner the boy won for his entire gang. Then they would go into each other's territory and look for more trouble. But there were rules back then: no sticks, rocks, or kicking. When they tired, they fired insults at each other and flicked each other off, and went home to recover. It seems relatively tame by today's standards of drive-by murder.

Those were the lasts days of 1931, in an economy-crippled South Los Angeles. President Roosevelt then broke the bleak cycle. County aid was keeping most families going, including John's. It was the height of the Great Depression. America responded to Roosevelt's risk-taking ideas and began to progress toward recovery. John went on with more stories of his early family life:

"It was readily apparent to us kids that our parents were not making it as husband and wife. The stress of poverty and Dad's boozing was just too much for any kind of meaningful partnership. Dad frequently boasted that he had drunk enough corn liquor to float the battleship USS TEXAS. And it was this frequent drunkenness, with Dad locked out, staggering around in the yard into the late night hours, shouting and mumbling to himself, and later involving Mom in an insult contest, that frayed the family fabric beyond repair. Dad would slap her around in the wee hours and the neighbors would peer out their windows and we kids would peek through the doors, scared to death."

"I never knew any of this," I said quietly.

"Most people don't know me well," he said. "One night I got bold and gave Dad one beaut of a haymaker halfway between his nose and bottom lip. He had blood all over his shirt, which sobered him up somewhat, and after that he went quietly to bed. The next morning he packed his suitcase and left without saying a word to anyone. We didn't see him for four years, and when we did, I told him to 'haul ass' out of there!"

"You said that to your own *father*?" I was shocked by the degree of his family dysfunction.

"I never really had a father," he replied, lips pursed tightly. "It was all just too much for Dad—and he was dangerous around us six kids. As time passed, there were fewer customers for the 'Caldwell Stuff' so the family business went bust. His debt collecting business was also a failure. No one had any money. Gambling had lower and lower stakes. Dad was reduced from his original occupation as a lawyer to fixing flat tires at two gas stations. And worse, we were recipients of public assistance, with its meager income. Our household was hungry and there were no jobs. Brother Jack and I had to go out at night and steal vegetables in the Japanese gardens ten blocks down the road. We learned to run really *fast!*"

"But you were just children! You could have gone to *jail!*" I gasped.

He laughed.

"Jail would have been a blessing. At least we would have been fed!"

"You were that hungry?"

"Yeah. We even raided hen houses late at night for food. We got really good at lifting the hens off their roosts, stuffing them into a gunnysack, and then slinking away without making a noise. At one time we had eleven live chickens in the garage for future meals! We brought in the food by stealing it. We were really desperate! One night during a raid a rooster flew off the roost and made an ungodly scene, working up the hens into a raucous lather. The lights went on in the house and Jack and I collided running out the door, which got the hens going even louder. We ran and hid in the bottom of a weed-filled ditch that in the winter led the rainwater from Los Angeles to the sea. As we covered ourselves in the thick grass I saw the house owner coming out with a shotgun. We lay down on the hens to smother them. Just above us the owner stopped to light a cigarette. I peed in my pants out of fright but I didn't ease up off the chickens just in case they were still alive. Besides, no matter what happened, there was no way I was going to lose the family food! When the owner moved about a hundred yards away from us I whispered 'go!' to my brother and we took off like coyotes after a kill."

"John, that's just crazy!"

"Well, things changed. I had just turned fifteen when I realized that I *could* support the family. My first job was as a ditch digger with the Works Progress Administration at Avalon and 112th Street, in full view of my friends going to school. That shamed me, so I asked for a transfer and was sent to the Civilian Conservation Corps near Yuma, Arizona, repairing roads in the blazing desert heat. The CCC guys with me were hopeless: they drank, smoked, cussed, and played poker. I decided that was definitely not going to be my style. My uncle Roy saved me from a tragic life. He got a job for me where he worked at the West Coast Bake Enamel Corporation up in Los Angeles where I was employed as a hand sander for cars and sheet boards. I smoothed, painted, and baked those sheet boards sixty hours a week."

"Did you drop out of your gang then?"

"Hell, I was too old for any more gang stuff! I was the breadwinner! But my boss would've made Scrooge look like a Sunday-school teacher. I guess that's what turned me into a socialist. I never had a paid vacation, I came to work in my clothes and left in the same and was paid fifteen and three-quarter cents per hour. Not sixteen cents, *fifteen and three-quarter cents*! The depression was breaking working people. I was an extra on the job. I came to work and sat on a table by Scrooge's office door. If he walked out and snapped his finger, I got up and went to work. If by 11 a.m. no finger had snapped, I walked home, penniless. The irony was that while my family lived in poverty those 4 x 8 foot masonite sheets we laboriously hand-sanded with special wet sandpaper to a meticulous gloss finish and baked to lustrous hardness, were trucked out to Hollywood where movie stars like Fred Astaire and Ginger Rogers flitted over them in audacious twirls and pirouettes! We were so close to glamour and famous people but miles away at the same time."

"How ironic . . . and *demoralizing*!" Angry, I crossed my arms over my chest.

"Yes, true, but my experiences served me well. I never expected anything from anyone. I was self-sufficient. And, as you know, I developed a chip on my shoulder . . ."

"That's for sure . . . but that chip has not always served you well," I commented.

"Maybe, but that chip got me through some pretty hard times. My experiences endeared me all the more to Norman Thomas and his socialist leanings. I don't know how Mom managed on such a pittance. I never asked because I was afraid of her answer. She had to work 16-hour days . . ." His voice trailed off as he looked at the stars.

"Your *poor* mother! That's dreadful!" was all I could offer, shaking my head.

"All I could see then was an endless tunnel and no light. I intuitively knew that the only way I could survive was to get an education. That's when I became a Jack London aficionado. I literally saved pennies out of my allowance given to me by Mom each weekend, after the bills were paid, of course. When there was enough money I bought a dictionary from the lady next door for thirty-five cents. I read it cover to cover . . . *every* word! That dictionary opened a new world of experience for me—*words*! I loved it. With words I could speak and think in new directions. I could escape poverty! I went to the library religiously and read every book I could, but especially sea stories, adventure yarns, and Jack London's tales of far horizons and his thrilling *Cruise of the Snark*. That's why I always yearned for faraway places in the tropics and that's why I wasn't afraid to sail alone from Panama to Australia to be reunited with you. Wanting to go to sea was my salvation!"

"But it nearly killed you, John! Weren't you ever afraid of dying? Why didn't you ever talk about this before?"

"I don't know. I've never wanted to look back. I just remember a series of events that changed my voyage into a desperate one. I ran out of money and couldn't pay the port fees in the Marquesas, and I couldn't see myself sweltering away a fine in a French Bastille, so I turned around and proceeded westward to get back to you. It was only 4,000 miles away!"

"But you were alone, John, *alone!*"

"No, remember, I had my two cats Jetsam and Flotsam and my rat Stowaway."

"That's hardly company!"

"I didn't feel alone though. I had the kittens and I had a dream of being reunited with you as soon as possible, so I was really *driven.* My travails began when my watch stopped and the old sextant died. That left me with dead reckoning on the open seas . . . not a good situation. I remember running into Caroline Island by accident and being given food by the wonderful native people there. I left with their provisions and a thousand miles later real disaster loomed: squalls and heavy rains with seas that grew from threatening to mountainous, pushed by hurricane-force winds. I was petrified and fearful for perhaps the first time in my life."

John sighed and was going to stop, I could feel it.

"Don't stop *now*! I want to know *everything*! Please!"

He sat up and looked into the distance at the sea and stars around us.

31

Secrets of
Desperate Voyage Revealed

"*W*ell, I remember tigers roaring over the deck and PAGAN getting bashed from every direction. The cockpit was filling with water and at some point I realized I was in the middle of a cyclone with winds steady at nearly a hundred knots with much higher gusts. I baled out the boat for hours but white water rapids kept flowing in. It seemed hopeless. Thunder was like shellfire all around me and the lightning was terrifying. Next thing I knew I was knee-deep in water. Things were floating all around me so I threw everything overboard: mattresses, pillows, foodstuffs, water containers . . . anything to lighten the boat. Then the mast careened wildly and snapped off a foot above decks, so I had to chop at the shrouds with my hatchet to let the mast go before it damaged the deck. For two days I went through that hell, and when the weather finally cleared I was totally exhausted and my boat PAGAN was in ruins."

"I can't imagine how you went on after that! How did you feel?"

"*Numb*. That's how you feel. Everything was gone. I hauled the trailing mast on board, fashioned a jury rig with the boom and top part from the mainsail. I was hoping to run into Samoa before my rusting cans of remaining food ran out. I allowed myself just two cans a day. I only sipped water because I had so little left. When the food ran out I ate the face cream and lipstick I bought for you. I even ate fish eggs I used for bait, hair oil, sun cream and the chamois cloth I used to strain gasoline. Hell, I ate the seaweed growing on the hull, cockroaches—the only big fat fellows on the boat!"

"Oh, *John!*" was all I could mutter. I held his hand, squeezing it gently.

"When it rained I spread my blanket on the deck, then squeezed the water into a bucket. But I only rationed myself one cup a day. Days and then weeks slid by. No Samoa despite sighting many birds that I knew had to go back to land every night. PAGAN and I were crippled. We were at the mercy of the weather and sea. All I could think of was lying in your arms and eating cheeseburgers!"

I laughed and cried at the same time.

"By then I was starving. I had lost over thirty pounds and was considerably weaker. One day a flying fish landed on deck. I couldn't believe my good fortune! I scrambled over on all fours and devoured the thing whole, guts and all. Nothing went to waste. It was a gourmet breakfast! The next day I nailed a seabird flying overhead with a silver dollar I had saved as a gift for you. The bird fell into the ocean and I strapped a line on my scrawny waist, jumped overboard and ate the bird whole, feathers and all, right there in the water. I cooked the feet and beak later for a stew. At that point I ate everything raw—sea turtles, fish, entrails, everything except the cats, which were skinny but obviously surviving by finding cockroaches I could not get to."

"How did you ever sleep with all your misery?"

"I always felt drugged. Starving is actually painless. Things just shut down. I dozed constantly and fitfully with recurring dreams of food, like Mom's cornbread and buttermilk and pumpkin pie. I had other dreams too: people chasing me with knives . . . I couldn't outrun them. I tried to climb a hill with a glittering food store on top, but I couldn't make it. Mom was always scolding me: 'You shouldn't have bought PAGAN!' But dreaming of Mom like that was really OK with me. Her familiar scolding was strangely comforting, even though she was angry. She once told me she nursed me until I was eighteen months old. When I was older my dad told me that I used to chase my mom around the house saying, 'Mommy, mommy, tity, tity!'"

"So *that's* why you're a breast man!" We both laughed.

"I suppose! My hopes were fading though. I was getting so skinny and my teeth were loose—I couldn't chew the dried turtle meat anymore and the cockroaches were getting scarce. The cats looked delicious—I don't know what prevented me from eating them. After seven weeks of drifting I was eating anything organic. Life was grim. One day, I downed a cup of engine oil and petroleum and got violently sick. I must have fallen asleep because I woke up with demons talking to me and vomit at my feet. By then I was too weak to pump out the bilge water. I was a zombie, yelling at myself, 'Go pump the bilges, stupid, we're sinking.' But nothing would happen. My body just lay there. A few hours later, I saw what I thought was a mirage: a seabird preening its feathers in the hatchway. Then I realized it *wasn't* a hallucination! In a second I transformed into a violent predator. I lunged and snared the creature with my bony hands. Then I clawed the creature to my chest, holding his head in my mouth and biting hard until he was dead. I had new hope!"

John looked at me for a reaction.

"I would have *died*," I said. I was now so physically and emotionally depressed by John's story that I hoped he would finish quickly, although I felt guilty knowing he had been through so much and had never completely confided in me. Perhaps he recognized a reticence in me; perhaps I never wanted to really know what happened to him. He continued, slowly and deliberately:

"I counted the days. Day forty-nine dawned without birds, fish, or algae from the side of the boat. I chewed the bones of the bird from the day before. Never mind that they were disgusting and rank by then. I sucked on those bones for three days! But when darkness came I always talked to you, 'Goodnight, honey, I love you and I will see land tomorrow.'"

I cried so hard at this point in his story I had difficulty breathing. I was consumed with such terrible guilt for not being there to help my husband, to hold and caress his face, to do *anything* to ease his pain. Our marriage had certainly had its high and low points, mostly low for the past fifteen years, but these moments of revelation now brought me much closer to John than I had ever felt before.

"There, there," he said calming *me*!

"I'm sorry . . . go on. I'm listening."

"But I was a hypocrite too," he admitted. "In my darkest hours I was praying to the good Captain for sight of land. I quoted the damn Bible and reached out for the warmth of Jesus. But whenever the immediate crisis passed I lapsed into a deeper analysis of what life really is all about. I dissected this phony world with its billions of phony souls—the whole phony world order and I asked the inevitable questions about life and death. And there were *no* answers, just conjectures. But you know, Mary, really, it's all bullshit—baloney, pure and simple. No God with any sense or sanity would create the image of humanity and then condone its craziness! Just wayward events and things, all lost like me and PAGAN on the open ocean of the universe: We live on a disjointed, irrational sphere spinning off in space, just as it has been for the last four billion years."

"So you didn't believe in God *at all*?" I knew John was now an agnostic on his best days and an atheist on his worst.

"No, not at all. We've talked about this. You know, Mary, we are just accidents of rawest nature and history drifting along with the ebb and flow of tides, at the wind's will so-to-speak, grabbing greedily at whatever we can get. And that's the big problem— human *greed*! I don't see any cure for that human malaise. No light at the end of that tunnel! *None!*"

"How hopeless you sound, John! I would hate the feeling of a meaningless life!"

"But Mary, it's all very *freeing*! Don't you *see*? After I analyzed life for what I thought was the last time I saw something right in front of the bow—a beautiful, lush green island with a ribbon of pounding reef fringing it. I got enough energy up to do something crazy: I washed my face, combed my hair and beard, and put on my pants and shirt, or what was left of them. They hung on me like the ragged clothes on the Jews who survived Auschwitz."

"But they were human *skeletons*! Were you *that* emaciated?

How much do you think you really weighed . . . you never told me exactly?" I was searching for a tangent and an end to the horror of his conversation. It was too much to bear.

"Not much," he replied calmly.

"*How* much?" I demanded.

"I'm sure it was less than ninety pounds!"

"Oh Christ!" was all I could manage.

John continued:

"Then PAGAN encountered giant swells. I staggered back up from the galley. I felt a huge thud as PAGAN struck the reef. I instantly knew the reef would tear me apart, so I cut the mast lashing, shoved it free, and jumped on it, belly flat, clutching hard, legs and arms hanging over the sides of the mast. But I was exhausted with all the extra effort I had put into cleaning myself up—for whom I didn't know. I guess I felt that if I died and someone found me they would at least see a dressed man with combed hair and beard!"

I laughed and cried, grasping both his knees.

"I hung on and fell asleep in my exhaustion, wrapped around the mast. By some miracle I washed up on the beach, on a small sandy beach lying between two volcanic spits . . . landing on these rocks would have been instantly fatal. I remember opening my eyes, ever so slowly. *Saved* I thought! I couldn't believe it. But then a darkness came over me like a veil and I fell into a death-like sleep. I could actually feel death coming on and I didn't care any more about anything. It actually felt *good*! Hours later my stomach woke me up and beside me was a small snake. I slowly grabbed a stick and tried to pin it down but it wriggled free. Now I really felt doomed. That would've been my last meal on earth. I fell asleep again and miraculously was awakened by heavenly children's voices. I opened my eyes and knew I was hallucinating. The voices came from dark-skinned angels looking over me with heads of wooly hair. They had fear in their eyes. Then the angels screamed and ran away. A short time later I heard more voices—this time older ones. But night was falling and I thought I was dreaming again. I could not move. How ironic, Mary! I was saved only to die on the beach! That was the lowest point in my life."

"I wish I could have been there for you!"

"You *were*, honey. You didn't have to be there physically to be *there*! You were *always* in my dreams. And that night, I was saved by Unarice and Itchika and placed in their bure with the thatched roof and plaited pandanus walls. I remember raising myself up on one elbow and asking, 'Where am I?' They all shouted with glee. They knew I would live. That's why I like simple people. People who live day to day, struggling. They have no *pretenses*. They live life like it should be lived, with adventure and intent and purpose. That's why I hire all these island people even though I cannot pay them a great deal. I owe a great debt to all the people of the developing cultures of the world and it is my personal duty to offer a helping hand whenever and wherever I can."

"And you certainly have *done* that!" I said, patting his knees.

"The Fijians were a revelation to me. They saved my life and assisted me selflessly. You see, Mary, even without God we are all brothers and sisters to each other in the most real sense. Just think, I learned this vital humanitarian truth in the South Seas on my way to be reunited with you! That's why I *dream*, Mary, not for money or prestige, although being human there's got to be some of that, but because I want to be free to help others even though they may disappoint me."

"I think you've more than repaid your debt to humanity," I said sincerely.

"Not yet," he responded. "Not yet. We have an opening date to look forward to and I intend to keep it."

32

Business Begins!

*W*e were now in the middle of summer and Christmas was less than six months away. Day laborers crawled over the island every day except Sunday. Later that summer we cut back on Saturday work as well, but paid them the same rate. One afternoon during quitting time a small plane circled the island and bounced along on our new runway. The pilot's name was Frank Delisle, manager-owner of the Windward Islands airline LIAT, which island-hopped from Antigua to Trinidad in those days. Frank was easy going and explained he had heard of our operation on the "coconut radio."

"Here I am," he said amused by his own audacity.

He recounted the trials and tribulations he had encountered building his small fleet of twin-engine Britten-Norman aircraft. The next day another plane landed with Otto Gerlach and his ever-smiling wife, Biggy, expatriate Germans then living in Venezuela. We knew that we were no longer isolated from the rest of the world. People felt comfortable just flying in for a visit! After that we no longer referred to our airstrip as one for the mosquitoes to land on!

Now that we were officially "discovered" we worried about people coming by boat or plane who were not familiar with various dangerous aspects of island life in the tropics, such as the machineel tree. Its white sap bears a strong acid. Bend a twig or crush a leaf and you have an open door to serious skin burns—and eye pain, with eyes clamped shut from swelling. The best and only remedy is a thorough saltwater bath at the closest beach. These worrisome trees produce a small, apple-like fruit that tourists often

The Beach Bar. A glorious sunset

picked and tasted. The result was skin lesions and gastrointestinal burns that could remove the cutaneous lining of the stomach. So it was a constant source of instruction to remind new visitors, if we saw them first, to avoid the deadly machineel tree.

To announce our "grand" resort opening, John penned several dozen letters to a list of travel agents that I had tallied over a period of months. Ten rustically furnished rooms now awaited our first guests, and John and I moved out of the office into one of them. We had wisely listened to Otto Gerlach's advice and bought the best quality mattresses money could buy: "If your guests can sleep in full comfort, everything else will be wunderbar, OK?"

Christmas Eve 1967 dawned and opening night was imminent. The Caldwell family assembled with three guests, two from New York, lured by an overly lavish letter from John listing the tropical delights of sea and sun and our perfect Grenadines weather. Naturally, after that introduction, it thundered and rained all day and all night with windy squalls and slanting showers that found every unfilled opening and drenching everything. A morass of wetness and stickiness surrounded us. John sat at a table, head in hand, looking at our wet barroom floor as the rest of us celebrated with drinks before dinner. A number of leaks dripped in time with the Reggae music. The waitresses moved forlornly through the dining room with towels over their heads and around their shoulders. Quiet, peaceful Prince was bartender. We had rescued him from fieldwork and given him a couple dozen of drink recipes from *Playboy* magazine. He anxiously awaited his first real order. Tiny Agatha was the cook and Mary was her mentor, but Virginia Buell showed her how to cook turkey—West Indies style, of course.

Ben, our first guest, broke the morbid silence.

"Hey Caldwell! C'mon," he said. "This is just one night! You've built your resort, you're open, what more d'ya want? You'll be in business the next 40 years. C'mon, cheer up!"

"Sure," John said quietly.

"Hell," said Ben, "let Prince make you a drink. You need an official drink anyway—a *Palm Rum Punch!*"

"Yeah!" everyone shouted. Sons Roger and Johnnie were particularly enthusiastic.

So Prince experimented and we drank all night. Finally John said: "Prince, what was in that last batch?"

"Brown sugar, water, lime juice, and rum, with de Angostura bitters and de grated nutmeg."

"That's damn tangy," said John. "That'll do for our Palm Rum Punch."

So despite the leaking room, a half-inch of water on the dining room floor, and mosquitoes diving in like spitfires, Ben Quinn and Prince led us through a great opening night. Then the portable generator ran out of fuel.

"How romantic!" I gushed. I ran and got the candles.

"Bartender," yelled Ben, "Bring us your finest champagne!" Prince laughed and popped several bottles. After that, things picked up. We devised a way for Totobell and John to transfer the guests from St. Vincent to Palm Island on OUTWARD BOUND. I would always offer a warm Palm welcome when they arrived several hours later. The boys sang loud seafaring songs to keep the guests occupied both coming to and going from Palm Island. Sometimes the trade winds would send all but Toto sprawling into the cockpit. They did the trips so often I figured that OUTWARD BOUND knew the route and John and Toto were just tagalongs. A few months after our grand opening we figured that son Johnnie could relieve father John and allow him to target the endless jobs that cried out to be finished on the island. Johnnie, aged 20, was entrusted with the lives of our guests on the high seas and reef-surrounded shores, and he performed his job with great distinction.

The second Christmas was quite different from the first. We had all twelve rooms (two of them new) occupied. But just when we were about to celebrate, tragedy struck.

"Did you hear the news?" said a worker early one morning upon her arrival on Palm.

"No," I said. "What is it?"

"The FEDERAL QUEEN sank and seventy-five people drowned."

"*No!*" I shouted, hands over my mouth in disbelief.

"It is true," she replied dejectedly.

We knew the derelict FEDERAL QUEEN well. It was a thirty-four-foot local sloop that plied the Grenadines water with cargo and passengers. A few days before Christmas, she left Clifton at dusk, grossly overloaded with nearly a hundred people on deck (many still drunk or passed out) with their boxes of Christmas drinks stored below. When the FEDERAL QUEEN (loaded below her water-marks) passed Canouan, a light breeze apparently lifted her slightly and blew ocean spray over the starboard rail. A number of passengers, feeling the shock of cold water, jumped to the port side, and the boat slithered over enough for the sea to pour aboard.

The FEDERAL QUEEN turned on its side, and sank rapidly. Those below were trapped and some on deck got caught under the sail as the ship went down. Passengers spilled into the ocean and those who could not swim drowned quickly, while many of the good swimmers could not manage the two-mile pull to Canouan's northwest point. Some slipped under, only yards from safety. One girl from the sea girt shores of Sandy Bay on St. Vincent's north-east, windward shoreline, swam all night so that two men, exhausted, could hold onto a plank that could not support all three. We found out that our effervescent Ratman saved a mother and son by clinging to a spray tank he was taking to St. Vincent for repairs. Most sadly for us, twenty-seven of our workers drowned with the FEDERAL QUEEN, among these, three of our carpenters, including our handsome, and ever so polite, Tyrone. We deeply missed them all.

With our airstrip officially in operation, there was no more need for the long and tedious midnight voyages with OUTWARD BOUND to bring in our guests from St. Vincent to Palm Island. We put our trusty old girl out to pasture, snuggled in her familiar mooring out in front of the office. Roger and Johnnie proved very helpful as adjutants, taking many jobs off their parents' backs. Johnnie initiated our scuba diving operation, trained himself as a dive master and set up a scuba shack with all the required paraphernalia. Roger tucked our two generators under his wing and was El Capitan of CARIBBEAN BELLE on her morning and afternoon workboat runs. John and Johnnie took turns at running the scuba operation on Gran de Coi Reef, Horseshoe Reef, Frigate Island, Mopion Sandbar, Punese Sandbar, Chatham Bay, Mayreau, and Whale Rock. Scuba and snorkeling excursions filled fast and our bookings increased dramatically once we offered these activities to our guests.

Word got around. We really *were* open. We even had a phone! A few months after opening we discovered what we called the "Palm Island Rule." If the generator goes out for one night, guests think it is romantic. They have an exotic story of dinner by candlelight and bedtime by flashlight to bring back to civilization. Two nights and it still seems a little romantic, although the romance is quickly wearing off. Three nights without a generator and tempers shorten considerably, grumbles pervade, and some suitcases get packed. Thankfully, we were rarely out of a generator for more than two nights. But adversity often leads to progress. Our decrepit generator was replaced by a new forty-five kilowatt model, which once installed, purred for many years.

People think we lived on a perfect little island, sitting around twiddling our thumbs, hoping something would happen to brighten the day. Not so! Our island was like a farm with seemingly never-ending work and always with many adventures daily and at least one major crisis a week; such as when our jeep, *Hot Rod*, went off the end of the jetty. *Hot Rod* came to us through our old friend Ratman (who got much of his extermination business by smuggling in rats and cockroaches in jars and then announcing major infestations to the owners). After he arrived off the trading schooner with *Hot Rod*, he packed John, Johnnie and Roger on board and drove them around our tiny island at hair-raising speed, whizzing inches past me, narrowly missing coconut palms, and roaring through many muddy swamps. It was a mid-1942 vintage, without a muffler, and all four fenders nearly fully eaten by rust. As with everything we bought from Ratman, this was a "giff." Workman Mac and Mars repaired *Hot Rod* almost daily. The boys often rode *Hot Rod* as though it were a racecar.

One day a party of overweight jetsetters stepped ashore Palm from their luxurious 160-foot yacht. While the tipsy passengers refreshed themselves at our bar, their meager forty-foot "escort" began pulling away from the jetty when Bigsey, standing upright on a careening *Hot Rod*, came roaring toward the jetty, a death-grip with one hand on the wheel while he waved wildly with the other screaming, "No brakes, mon, no brakes!" A moment later he flew onto the wharf and, seeing the dramatic end to his "trip," made an Olympic dive into the ocean to avoid being taken down with the hapless *Hot Rod*. We shuddered to think what would have happened if the opulent forty-foot transport would have still been tied at the dock! Another time, a young man left in John's charge with his father's instructions to "turn him into a man" sank our small launch WOBIN on the reef. At that time, Johnnie managed the Beach Club and Roger the Yacht Club. Our boys and their sons helped manage many of the aspects of Palm Island as they got older, but helping them mature was sometimes a chore! They also learned how quickly things could go wrong.

33

Squelching a
Caribbean Rebellion

$\mathcal{A}$s 1979 eased along, a young man from Union Island named Boomba, with a huge ego and irrational goals, began stirring political foment. It was also an election year and Milton Cato and his St. Vincent Labor Party won handily. Boomba aimed his natural charisma at the disillusioned and unemployed youth of Union, and he began amateurish military exercises that no one took seriously at the time. But Boomba had confided in a worker that he had set 5 a.m. as the time one day to take control of the island (now known as the Union Island Rebellion).

The night before this "rebellion" Boomba and a few others sailed to Carriacou where they had a source of World War I Enfield rifles. Grenada and Carriacou were under the communist rule of the New Jewel Movement, and it was believed that Boomba got these archaic arms from the Maurice Bishop-led People's Revolutionary Army, a well-armed bunch, put together by Russian advisers. On the way back from Carriacou, and close to Union, the small sailing smack tipped and foundered from either too many guys on board or too many guns. Sadly, a young boy drowned, and the sinking delayed the attempt at takeover from 5 a.m. until 7 a.m., which obviously took away the element of surprise since everyone on the island was awake at that time of the morning.

Boomba, irrational but focused, set off a small charge of dynamite at the back of the Ashton Police Station, sending all the policemen scurrying into the bush. Then Boomba and his troops marched into Clifton, firing the twenty or so weapons they had, using up scarce ammunition. They proclaimed in the town center that Union Island was theirs, took over the Customs Building, cut all incoming phone lines and put oil drums on Andre Beaufrond's homemade airfield at the Anchorage Yacht Club. The inhabitants of Union Island were terrified by these miscreants. Next, Boomba with four others, wearing police shirts, commandeered Andre's Boston Whaler, and with their Enfield rifles, came to capture Palm Island, asserting to the townspeople of Union Island that his aim was to capture all the islands of the Southern Grenadines and set up his own separate state. (The truth was that he just wanted money.)

Our workers came over as usual that morning and gave a garbled account of what was going on at Union. John knew that Boomba had a love/hate relationship with him, so he ran to find our only firearm. John found his .22 rifle in Johnnie's house and the shells in Roger's house. John and I went down to the beach and spotted the archaic Boston Whaler approaching.

"It's the *police*," one of our workers shouted, seeing the police shirts of the crew.

"Why would they be coming *here*?" I asked, looking intently at John.

"No one's landing here unless they call first and identify themselves," John shouted.

John waved the workers back with his hand and then hid with his rifle behind a coconut palm. As the boat neared he fired a round at the whaler, kicking up a splash just in front of the bow. They returned one shot from an Enfield, which was very loud and frightened our workers into a panic. A moment later the Boston whaler turned around and ran toward Carriacou. We scrambled for more accurate information and were told by the coconut radio that the government PBX telephone exchange had been damaged overnight and that a general statewide uprising was indeed possible. For that reason, every policeman was needed there, but military assistance had been requested from Barbados and could be expected by midday. A yachtsman anchored at Clifton was watching matters at anchorage through a porthole and radioed messages to us. There were nineteen rebels armed with Enfields and pistols. At times, they played cards and quarreled loudly about what action to take next. Apparently, they never expected to be fired upon as they approached our resort at Palm Island!

At noon a plane with eight policemen landed at Palm. We greeted them happily! At 2 p.m. another ten policemen landed. We felt our island was now secure. At 3 p.m. John and the boys contacted the Prime Minister by radio and suggested that they go over to Union and capture the rebels. The Prime Minister demurred at first, fearing bloodshed. We argued that if we delayed and night fell, they could get reinforcements, making their capture very difficult. At 4 p.m., John and I got a radio message from Milton Cato:

"Okay, go ahead. Good luck and God bless you."

I was terrified that my boys were going to challenge some common thugs on Union Island but they assured me that everything would be all right. Who can deter young men with adrenaline running high in their veins? We only had two boats: John put Johnnie in charge of IN-THE-RED and Roger in charge of RUM-N-COKE. I saw Johnnie off in his boat with eight policemen, all bearing rifles. Roger had eight in his boat and a hotel guest. Two policemen stayed with us. Off they went to do battle, all feeling very nervous. The strategy was that Johnnie would land in a cove at the back of the hospital, and then the boys would disembark, mount the hill, and come into Clifton from the south. Roger would go straight into Anchorage. Later, John told me what really happened.

"When the rebels saw us coming they scattered and ran like a bunch of chickens into the hills, with us popping up dust around their heels. I reached the airstrip and started rolling an oil drum off the runway to clear it for landing, when one of the locals, Bibby, drunk, came up and playfully grabbed for my rifle, wanting to fire after the fleeing rebels. But a nearby policeman—thinking I was being attacked—fired a round from his automatic rifle; five or six bullets whizzed between us. I could feel them zip past."

"*God save us!*" was all I could muster.

"That wasn't the worst: One thudded into Bibby's chest, dropping him and covering my left leg, belt to shoe, with blood. He didn't have a chance!"

"You mean he *died*?"

"Yes, he died in my arms," John said, choking back his tears and looking at the ground. "He said, 'I dead, mon.'"

"Oh, God, that is so *awful*!"

"I told Bibby I was so sorry for the mistake, but he just went on: 'John, tell me girl fren' to sell de boat and keep de money. Tell me boss I sorry to drunk. And tell my muddah . . .' and then he died. I helped carry his body to a waiting plane, so warm and supple, but so lifeless."

"And all because of a couple of dozen thugs! I hope they all get prison time!"

That would not be the last serious political incident we had on Palm. But in the meantime, things returned to normal on our idyllic island. The weather was always balmy and the sun drenched us more than three hundred days a year, and our constant and steady easterly trade wind kept us relatively cool and dry most of the time. We truly had developed a yachtsman's happy hunting ground, and each season saw an increase in business as word spread about our crystal clear waters and gorgeous weather.

34

Duties, Obligations, and Principles

The increase in tourism also brought its problems. Early on John and I became accustomed to distress calls and flares from hapless boaters pinioned on the heartless coral ledges. In those days, all we had was an eighteen-foot runabout with a thirty horsepower Johnson outboard engine. Towing a twenty- to thirty-ton yacht off a ledge of coral with our inadequate pull demanded more art than technique. John and the boys learned to outwit the vagaries of the wind and sea hammering a yacht's bottom against a windward reef. First they would size up the situation as they neared the grounded vessel. Then John would enter the water with snorkel, mask, and flippers to inspect the position of the yacht in the coral and plot the closest route to deep water. The boys would then hitch up a towline and instruct the yachtsmen to adjust their sails to meet the boys' needs (most yachtsmen thought they could just "sail over" the reefs but this misconception just brought them into shallower water).

Before the actual tow was started, anchors were laid out to prevent the grounded craft from being pushed by waves and wind into shallower waters. The anchor lines led aft to the jib sheet winches and by applying a constant pressure the boat could be slowly pulled off and away from the reef. While this was going on, the boys would dive down to pull aside any lumps of coral lying directly in the path of the boat. Sometimes they would use a four-pound hammer to crack large lumps and move them aside, or use a crowbar to pry the bigger lumps away from their pathway to deeper water.

My boys virtually never failed, even when a boat was in danger of sinking. To be caught in a falling tide was the worst problem because then you had to wait twelve hours for the return of high water, and here in the Grenadines, with a tidal difference of only about twenty-four inches, every inch counted! An advancing tide always brought higher water, but also a force pushing the boat toward the beach and even shallower water. Unfortunately, yachtsmen did not always ground themselves in the middle of the day when visibility was good. Many times the boys had to rescue stranded yachtsmen at night, and sometimes they would work into the wee hours of the morning to free a boat from further disaster.

"Why free them at *night* . . . why not wait until day? Especially if they're such poor sailors!" I complained one night, unable to sleep and fearful for their lives.

"I hate to see a boat stuck high on a reef, pounding her guts out! I was there once, you know," John said reflectively.

"Yes, I know, but you do it for *free*! All these guys have the money to pay you!" My hands were now on my hips.

"True, but the islanders who rescued me and PAGAN weren't doing it for gain either! They did it out of duty, obligation . . . and *principle*!"

That ended the conversation because I realized he was right. A stranded boat needs help, not a bill in advance. Of course, this was in the "good old days" when maritime chivalry could still be found. Nowadays, backs are turned when distress is seen and the brotherhood of the sea is largely dead, killed by greed. But not John. He might acknowledge a fair tip for a full night of rescue effort, but he would never actually bill anyone for his service. During our time on Palm Island John and the boys saved over one hundred boats with only three lost to the reefs. Not a bad record.

The yachts they saved were of various sizes, designs, rigs, and nationalities. The main cause of getting lost in coral heads was just plain careless navigation; the skipper not paying attention near obstructions; cutting too close to rocky outcrops; not keeping an eye on the seas ahead; sailing into a blinding sun; or moving in overcast conditions when waters are leaden in color (in this case distinguishing the leaden sky from leaden waters is nearly impossible). As John always said, "KISS is the key—Keep It Simple Stupid!" The concept of KISS dominated his entire life. He thought of himself as rather ordinary, uncomplicated, naïve, edging toward stupidity, overly generous, and always ready and willing to help anyone in need. At the same time, however, he was seen as a bit of a demanding curmudgeon to his workers and family and certainly an eccentric by all who met him! And he was certainly a loner as a poem he wrote about himself amply suggests:

> All alone with John C . . .
> What I rank best is privacy
> Alone with books, no radio or TV
> All alone with my buddy, John C.
>
> Give me my boat and an open sea
> Let me wander in ecstasy
> Just leave me alone and let me be
> All alone with John C.
>
> I want only to be happy and free
> And let others be the same as me
> Yes, all in the world I want to be
> Is all alone with John C.

The poem speaks volumes about his true internal feelings about life and his often-strained relationships with the boys and me.

At 6 a.m. every morning John would awake, do fifteen minutes of light calisthenics, and then stride around the 1.25 mile-long road that circumscribed our island. The road was named Highway 90 because John intended to jog around the island when he turned 90. In the later years of our relationship John became more and more isolated. After his walk he would take breakfast (the equivalent of a vegetarian meal) at his desk, then swim and exercise in the water for thirty minutes. Afterward he would take a sailor's bath (a bucket of seawater taken off the stern of the boat, then a rub down with a washcloth). A second bucket followed by a brisk toweling finished off his daily ritual. He never took showers on Palm: his shower stall was packed with gardening tools and there was no way anyone could get in. John thought a sea bath was the healthiest because soap washes off the skin's protective oils. He believed a saltwater bath holds those skin oils in and keeps it acid, which was an additional repellent to bacteria and viruses. He actually thought there would be a warning on future soap bars as there is now on cigarette packs: *"Beware, overuse of soap is dangerous to your health!"*

That was John at his eccentric best.

John was also a workaholic. His personal happiness depended on long days of productive work seven days a week, year after year. Vacations were foreign to him and he never took one until we had worked nineteen years on Palm Island. I would accuse him of being "dull company" and he would readily agree. His motto was "get things done and press forward." It drove the children crazy. By today's standards he seemed bipolar—he was both an optimist and a pessimist at the same time. Simple? Hardly. John was a boatload of contradictions. In his unpublished memoirs called *"My Island and Me"* (not *Our Island and Us!*) he wrote the following and showed it to me one night:

"Life has no deep mystery for me—just a bit of confusion about what is really going on and where Planet Earth is heading as we humans overpopulate it, pollute it, defile it, and disfigure its biological communities with our own personal greed. I know just what I am and what I want. I am an accident of history, a little ball of crap, living it out till I cash in my chips and return to the crap whence I came. This is me, back in my agnostic phase again. No illusions about heaven and hell and all that baloney . . . fully convinced it's all hogwash, and that hogwash is the opium of the masses as Marx claimed, brought on by the inability of generations of mankind to face the realities of the finality of death.

"We all kick the bucket sooner or later. To me, the accidental invention of Christianity by Jesus Christ—this benevolent, itinerant, illiterate genius—and his disciples, was not unlike the aberrant forms of Christianity invented by the fateful Jim Jones of Guyana, who poisoned hundreds of his followers, and David Koresh of Waco, Texas, who burned his followers. Christianity is a necessary evil for most people: it softens the blows of life. Most people need religion to come to grips with dying; to keep themselves ethical, decent, and honest. I don't. To me death is simply a part of life, the easy way out of a tight corner; like drowning, when it is easier to give up and go under, than struggle to stay up. What I mean is this: better to let go and die than suffer deadly pain. This is the easy way out, rather than becoming the nightmare of the skeleton in shrouds with a scythe on his shoulder.

"I can stay truthful, veracious, and helpful without going to church. And if everybody had veracity and a social consciousness, that would be the best of all worlds. There would be no need to invent religion or heaven, or need to stick one's snoot endlessly into the Bible—a book filled with iniquity, incest, hate, contradictions, assassination, wars and human suffering. Some say all the crooks are in jail on Sundays. I say the majority is in church, setting up for Monday's sins. I never earned a dime in church. My first visit was when I was christened, the second, and last, was when I got married. Every church is nothing more than a business place, based on money like everything else in society. The pastor works for it. The congregation is there to expend as little of it as possible, to get as much "grace" as possible out of the turnips the parishioners contribute.

"I accept the Christian ethic as a code to live by, but the mumbo-jumbo of Immaculate Conception, Lazarus coming back from the dead, resurrection and everlasting life is for the birds: definitely not for this kid. I believe in what I can sensibly believe, see, hear, and feel in my gut. Let's face it. We are dirt and one day we will inevitably go back to dirt. That's the only practical reality this world can promise the human condition—proved by example at every funeral. Christians thump their Bible—a book that relishes war, disease, famine and pestilence as markers of the last days. Big deal. Rubbish! The earth has always been under these conditions. Any generation in history can chronicle a steady decline in the social ethic, and upturn of calamity: wars, assassinations, violent crime, and drug abuse. In recent decades of my life I have seen sharp increases in social and criminal disorder. Further decline is inevitable, spurred by overpopulation, pollution, human greed and political ineptitude. You don't have to read Nostradamus, the Bible, or watch a Mickey Mouse cartoon to predict the obvious."

"John," I said after reading this passage. "You sound positively optimistic today!" He laughed.

"It's all *true!*"

This passage was John at his most realistic. Our life with John was not always easy. He was frequently rude, threatening when things did not go his way, and angry at getting older. I think he suffered from severe, undiagnosed anxiety and depression. His sons eventually grew afraid of him and detested his impossible demands on them: demands for constant attention to Palm Island; demands for perfection; demands to be workaholics like himself. John believed that Palm Island was his destiny—his hell, heaven, and only reality. But he was not greedy and he often treated complete strangers better than his family. He had a utopian view of everyone in the world getting along together and was severely saddened by his own inabilities and those of his family.

I always believe that the child was the father to the man. John was a rebel when he was younger. He thought he was given a raw deal early in life with his ne'er-do-well drunk father. He called himself a socialist before World War II because race discrimination, poor work conditions, and workers' pay were out of line with what was decent and fair in a society in which "all men are created equal." He zeroed in on these social inequities and developed a leftist spectrum in his thinking. He was a Watts man with no ethnic biases, and he saw that during World War II, even when conditions in the workplace improved, men of color were pushed aside or held down. He hated it and even started an interracial fraternity in college (now the University of California at Santa Barbara) to promote equality between the races. The fraternity did not survive. Even during his stint as a steward in the Merchant Marines John set the interracial stage: there was to be no race discrimination.

John always ran a smooth, equitable ship. He tried to run Palm Island along lines similar to those of his shipboard operations, which were based on the concepts of mutual cooperation, respect, and sincerity. Unfortunately, he ran into human nature and discovered to his chagrin that no one was perfect, that we all had flaws—sometimes fatal ones. The result was a fraying of the Caldwell family: father against adult sons. We were all working too hard and the chasm between John and the boys became enormous. It was even physically evident back in the 70s: short-cropped graying hair against long shoulder-length hair.

A sign of the times, I suppose. John saw his young rebels gathering for fruitless nightly beer fests that wended well into the hours past midnight. The boys saw an intolerant father who demanded perfection and dedication to the task at all hours of the day and night. The old man stormed around the island constantly demanding more. In-your-face and finger-in-the-chest attacks were common. Head-on collisions between father and sons led to fierce-eyed deadlock and in the end John demanded that his "corrupt" sons clear out with their wives, kids, and baggage. I was absolutely devastated. Our dream island had in the end destroyed our family. We had been far happier as a family on the open sea, owning virtually nothing. John was sure that a few years in the Florida dog-eat-dog world would bring his sons to their senses.

After a few years Roger did phone us and asked if he could come back and skipper a charter boat for our day-sailing parties in the Beach Club. He would buy a yacht with some monetary assistance from me and the proceeds from the sale of his house in Florida. I agreed and John said to him:

"Yes, as long as you understand two things: you have to work like the rest of us; and the old man is boss."

"Okay," I heard Roger say, "I get the picture."

A few days later there was another phone call. This time it was Johnnie:

"Dad," he said," I hear you're looking for a manager for the Beach Club. Can I apply?"

"Yes," I heard John reply again, "as long as you understand two things:"

"I already heard about them," he answered, "and it's OK."

Of course I was absolutely delighted. The boys and their families returned to Palm Island and the atmosphere changed. They became very capable assistants who did first class jobs. Work began at 6:00 a.m.—without "wasteful chatting" in John's workaholic mind. John told them repeatedly "hard work is good for the pocket book, good for the economy, and good for the health, but overwork is a killer." In all the years John worked at Palm he never drew a salary, just expense money. He ploughed everything back into the island for over thirty years. He enjoyed just being an "average Joe." He was not into frills, never owned a car, and told time with an old Timex. He never purchased a tie and shunned socks ("feet can't breathe with socks," he would say). A sport shirt was "dressing-up" for John. He favored old clothes and old shoes and never cared for changing styles.

In later years, when we finally did go on vacation, we never stayed in first class hotels: it was always economy class on the plane and lodging at small inns, which arguably were more intimate and personal. Television was essentially a mystery to John. "All those channels!" he would say. We had only one on Palm and the reception rarely came in well. And after we would return from our rare vacations to Europe or the United States we would always gush about the beauty of Palm Island: No rat race syndrome (unless we created it). Or as they say in the West Indies: "Easy does it, mon." Of course, the main thrust of the West Indian way of life is to have *fun*. One of the primary edicts of the culture is to chat any time two West Indians cross paths . . . laughing is part of it too, and so is joking, drinking, and partying. Any old way of doing a job is fairly normal. To John, the work ethic of the islands was lame. But he truly loved them all.

He loved their amiability and the willing goodness of the general populace, their peacefulness and friendliness. I think he was secretly jealous that *he* could never let his hair down long enough to truly enjoy the fruits of his labor.

35

The Grenada Episode

Late in the summer of 1983, when we returned exhausted from one of our rare vacations to the ancient feuding states of Europe, Palm Island looked like a fantasyland out of a Walt Disney movie: bright and cheery, sun-soaked, and jammed with laughing humanity. But it grew abundantly clear that the Grenadine community of which we were a small part was having its own problems. Specifically, the political hierarchy of Grenada was having a serious family feud, especially with the communists.

The northern end of Grenada lies just twenty miles south of Palm Island. Rumors of general discontent riffled through the coconut radio and dribbled north to our island. It was clear: all was not right in the "commie" ranks. This all came to a head when hardliners in the People's Democratic Republic placed moderate red-leaning Prime Minister, Maurice Bishop, under house arrest.

John phoned our friend, Milan Bish, the U.S. Ambassador in Barbados, who had visited with us several times on Palm Island.

"What's the U.S. doing about that mess?" John asked in his inimitable demanding tone.

"We're watching it, John. Let us know if you hear anything."

A few days later, Bishop was released from house arrest and traveled to Fort George, overlooking Grenada's beautiful harbor area, where he was gunned down, along with some of his ministers and a host of his followers, in a burst of automatic rifle fire. Nearly a hundred people were slaughtered in this massacre. None of the bodies, including that of Bishop, was ever found. Rumor had it that they were trucked away by night to Cuban fishing boats and disposed of at sea during a gruesome five day-and-night curfew, which worked extreme hardship on the populace. This alone was enough to turn public opinion against the excesses of the Cuban and Russian leaders who were fomenting unrest in the placid Grenadines. It also amply demonstrated the ineptness and total disregard for people by the communists.

John phoned Ambassador Milan again:

"Mr. Ambassador, this is a golden opportunity for America to go in there and clean things up."

"Hold tight, John," he said. "We have options, hold tight." Milan was from Nebraska, and a close friend of President Reagan.

At that time, a U.S. task Force on its way to Lebanon changed course in mid-Atlantic and headed south. John immediately suspected that America was sending in troops. He called Ambassador Milan again:

"What about those ships?" he demanded over the phone. "Anything to do with Grenada? We've got medical students there!"

I heard a garbled response and John slammed down the phone.

"They're always playing games!" he said and walked away.

The next day, about noon, a big bristling fifty-foot sports fisherman from Barbados maneuvered under our lee and dropped its hook. Three men, casually dressed in Levis and T-shirts, came ashore and stood on our jetty with binoculars pinned on Carriacou to the south.

One of the staff ran over to John and me.

"Who dem is, John? Dem is CIA?"

John and I walked quickly down to the jetty.

"You guys CIA?" he queried demandingly.

They jumped a foot, looking around furtively. One said, "Don't say that! Don't mention the CIA!"

The reason for the secrecy was that the CIA had recently been accused of planning to assassinate Castro.

"The Ambassador sent us," one said. "He said you know these waters as well as anyone. He wants you to go with us tonight down to Grenada . . . on a mission."

I looked at John with fear that quickly enveloped my face.

"Any chance of fireworks?" he said simply, not acknowledging my concern.

"Yes. And we must go *now.*"

"*John?*" I pleaded anxiously. "Can we talk?"

"Sorry," he said, "I'm going with them. Where's my gun?"

"No time for that . . ." the leader said, "We must leave right now!"

"OK, I'm game!" John gave me a stiff hug goodbye and a moment later they all left on the boat. I clung to the voices of Radio Free Grenada all night. It was October 24, 1983, the day before the Grenada invasion. I could not glean much information from the radio but after John returned he filled in the gaps:

"By the time we got near the Grenada coast the CIA guys loosened up and I took the wheel. Our mission was to reconnoiter the Grenada shore, to pinpoint the location of the radio station, and relay its position to the aircraft carriers, the USS INDEPENDENCE and GUAM, lying with their task force south of Grenada in the open sea. We also had to locate the Ross Point Hotel (managed by our good friend and Grenada legend, Harry Hopkins. This was where the Canadian High Commissioner and his Maple Leaf entourage were housed so they couldn't be fired upon in hostilities)."

He paused to collect his thoughts.

"We had to be careful because Canadian Prime Minister Pierre Trudeau was really worried about territorial wars."

"So what did *you* do?"

"Well, we had to find out exactly where the American Medical College was located relative to the People's Revolutionary Army Headquarters—we needed to hit them hard. We also had to figure out the exact positions of the reefs in case they needed an amphibious landing."

"So you didn't engage them in battle?" I asked incredulously.

"Oh, no. We did. We would swing near shore to spook the gunboats and then scram before they spotted us. We always headed toward the American destroyer, which looked like an ominous gray shadow that lit up every time we approached. We always ducked behind her lee side."

"My, God, John! I'm glad I didn't know that before you left!"

"Oh . . . they only had three tubs they called gunboats." He chuckled. "It was nothing. Anyway, we cleared the beaches for landing. We could see the huge jet airstrip that Castro and Yuri Andropov and their commie comrades had built. Next thing, I saw butterflies drifting down as a huge air transport plane flew past. Airborne troops fell everywhere!"

"*Russians?*"

"No, Americans. It was the U.S. 82nd Airborne Division. And man, were we relieved! Right after that, C-14 jet fighters swooped down with screeching engines that deafened everyone and shook our boat. Rockets went screaming along the beaches followed by Black Hawk helicopters in clusters. We were told to vacate immediately . . . and we didn't have to be reminded twice!"

Needless to say, it was thrilling to hear the stories *afterwards.* The next day, a Black Hawk chopper landed on Palm and out stepped an alert Colonel Keith Nightingale, Deputy Commander of troops in Grenada, with his aide, Major Mike Canavan. They were attired in jungle fatigues with strips of dust-colored cloth on their helmets. Their M-16 combat rifles looked formidable to our workers, who studied them at a distance.

"Is this part of Grenada?" they asked.

"No," John said. "Want a beer?"

"Yeah!" came the chorus.

During the following months we had many Black Hawks land on Palm, bringing loads of friendly GIs for rest and relaxation. They already knew about the free beer and fresh bread, and each time we thanked them for saving the Grenadines. One day, weeks later, a Black Hawk came from the south with something large hanging down below the ship. We thought it must be something damaged. It landed near our generator station. John and I ran down and saw the pilot walking toward us.

"What happened?" John called out. "Is the chopper OK?"

"Come have a look," the pilot said smiling. He pulled a cover off a big box and inside was a brand new 60-kilowatt diesel generator unit.

"This is from the General," he said. "Don't tell anybody and don't mention my name!" With that he flew out as if he were being stalked.

With Communism mortally wounded in Grenada, our prospects for tourism suddenly perked up. We added new resort rooms, planted coconut palms by the hundreds, started new flower gardens, and extended the beaches against the ever-threatening wall of encroaching green. News of our island and its operation spread far and wide throughout the world. Over the years our internationally renowned celebrities ranged from the Queen of England to the Kennedys and from Oprah to Mick Jagger. All found a peaceful refuge on our island.

36

∞

A Hostile Takeover

In 1986, George Landeger, a multi-millionaire, with his wife and
two young daughters stepped onto our unsophisticated island.
After lunch he strode into our office and delivered a well-prepared
investment talk to us, suggesting that we might like to have a partner. He wanted fifty-one percent of our company and threw down
expansive promises. George emphasized that he wanted to keep the
island "just as it was" except for upgrading facilities and making
some improvement that he personally would fund. John would be
kept on as Managing Director and I would be John's assistant for
life. George would also advertise for a permanent manager for the
Beach Club.

It sounded too good to be true. George rattled on, describing an
Eden without an apple or a worm. Palm was to be made into an ex-
clusive retreat, with a European flavor, especially in the dining
room. We would have our own private airfield and pilot and plane,
always ready to serve our guests. George promised to pay for my
shares as soon as I could ready them for transfer to him and further
suggested that we write up a binding contract as soon as possible.
He then promised a handsome deposit and said it would be in the
mail as soon as he got back to New York. The next day he proffered
the same conditions to John: a generous deposit and early transfer
of enough of his shares to give him the fifty-one percent partnership
he desired.

But at that point he indicated to John that I must retire, contrary
to his earlier offer to me.

"I told him that Mary does the work of three women!" John muttered to me.

"What did he say to that?"

He said, "That's what I need."

Without my knowledge, John went ahead with the deal, writing up a soon-to-be infamous "kitchen contract." After twenty years of unsalaried work, John was to get a salary of $15,000 per year, have Sundays off, and a paid vacation of 30 days. That was strong medicine for an old workaholic like John. Clearly, age was beginning to fatigue him both mentally and physically.

Two days later, after returning from a jaunt to Mayreau, George literally took over, before any shares were transferred into his name and before any deposit was sent to us. *He just took over!* He took sober walks with us around the premises, pointing out a number of cosmetic jobs he wanted done immediately.

"Fix that roof. Paint that place. Put a fence there. Get rid of those steel chairs and put in rattan. Tile the men and women's bathrooms." The list of orders grew by the minute. Then he noticed a cleared area to our right, on our beautiful Casuarina Beach, the finest in the Grenadines.

"What's *that*?" he asked impetuously.

"Three choice lots," John said. "I haven't decided what to do with them."

"I'll buy them," he said. "$100,000 U.S."

"But those are valuable lots," John said chagrined.

"Yes," he answered. "Get your lawyer to draw up the transfer papers and send them up to me."

"They're worth at least $400,000!" John said forcefully. "They're the choicest lots on the island."

"Yeah, I can see that. Send the papers up," he said with stern finality.

I saw John's eyes draw to a slit. Jaws clenched. The Texas flag was rising!

In a few weeks, we got our deposit on my shares. Then came a check for $200,000. John called George:

"What's the $200,000 for?"

"Cosmetic jobs," he said.

And so it went. George always demanding and John wanting to be more businesslike. George hired a new Beach Club Manager, a flamboyant but inexperienced Dutchman who served as George's puppet. In turn, the new manager hired an eighteen-year-old young woman assistant who immediately attached herself to the Dutchman's hip in more ways than one. Together they muddled through basic operations and conspired to undermine John's authority on the island. She was a white woman who segregated herself from the other workers, the vast majority of whom were black. The West Indians were incensed at her audacity. One worker asked, "Why dis?" The thin edge of racial overtones were rising, so John demanded that the Dutchman's princess be placed in staff quarters with everyone else. The Dutchman then complained to George who demanded that she be placed in preferential hotel quarters. John was afraid of rocking the boat and deterring the sale of Palm, so he went along with George's demand.

The staff was now worried about their jobs and John was actually worried about his! Things were deteriorating quickly.

"They're trying to move me out!" John complained to me the next day.

Things got worse. George's wife spoke only Dutch and there were many long-distance phone calls from the Dutch manager to George's residence in New York. John was certain his authority would be taken away and he felt an eminent demotion. He was right. George flew down in November of 1987 and said to John:

"You'll be Resident Director and *not* Managing Director for life."

"What does that mean?" John saw his grip on the island waning.

I watched the action with my hands on my hips:

"Well," George said, "you can live on the island and be a member of the Board, and you can be skipper of OUTWARD BOUND and do the gardening and be our public relations man."

"You mean," John said icily, "every time a guest comes to the island, I'll be dragged out of the closet like a puppet to do my song-and-dance, and then hung back in the closet after my show? Not me, boy! You promised me the head guy's slot for life!"

George backed away, feeling the heat.

"Look, George," he said. "There's only one person who can effectively help you on this island—and it's not your lackey Dutchman. It's me! Pure and simple."

"I'll get back to you with my lawyers," replied George and he turned to go.

For the next month, stress on the island grew to a festering sore. The management worked in uncivil silence. The staff, unsure and uncertain of how this commotion would turn out, tried to be good with both factions. John was losing his grip and becoming more angry and adrift by the week.

Finally the showdown. George phoned John and told him he was coming down at the end of December to pay for and transfer the shares and take de facto charge of operations. John met him on Union Island and not a word was spoken all the way to Palm. The invading group sat hunched over at dinner with John and I uninvited.

"Why do you put up with this?" I demanded.

"Because I want the safe transfer of the stock and I want to ensure our survival!" he responded, irritated.

"Where's my Don't-Mess-With-Texas John?" I asked.

He just stared at me with those steely blue foreman eyes. Testosterone oozed from every pore in his body.

"OK! I've had it! Let's bounce their backsides out of here!" My eyes lit up in anticipation.

The next day John demanded a meeting with George. "OK," John said to George, "on my patio at 3:00 p.m." That way, the battle would be on his turf, at his set time, and he had all day to prepare.

John and I met George at 3:00 p.m. sharp.

"John, you need to retire." George stated firmly.

That statement lit a fuse with a rapid burn and produced a verbal explosion in John. He mixed in some creatively foul Texas slang that still falls from the Caribbean sky to this day.

"You can haul your lard-ass back to New York tomorrow! And take your losers with you!"

That was it. The next morning they packed their bags and were gone by noon. High noon. Just like in the Westerns. Peace and calm settled quickly back on our hideaway island.

These experiences had a profound effect on John. It challenged his concept of what society was all about. Although a curmudgeon by anyone's definition, John was honest and hard working. He never plotted; never undermined others. His philosophy was live and let live. John was always straight and open and avoided greed in all its human forms. He tried (and failed) to please everyone, but he could always absorb rebuffs and live with disappointments. John always felt a custodial and paternal responsibility to his workers, and the prospect of anyone coming in to interfere with their lives, so dependent on us, was abhorrent.

One day I asked him, "Why do you keep all these workers here? We have over a hundred and only need fifty."

"Honey," he said, "these are poor people. They need their jobs. We have everything we need. Our food is always there in the hotel. We have a comfortable house. This is the Third World. Let's help Union Island get on its feet. These people are helping us . . . let's help them a bit."

I was always much more practical than John, but I did understand his sentiments toward the islanders. His idea was to live modestly so others could live decent lives. He felt that if unemployment could be reduced then more goods and services could be circulated and the economy could be jump-started to vigorous growth and progress. I knew that was true. Overpopulation was and continues to be the biggest problem in these islands. But as John pointed out, "As the economy grows the birth rates decline." Unfortunately, John's message was largely wasted on the government. We had a standoff with the government of Union Island, mutual suspicion, near confrontation, and a constant state of simmering battle. John thought the islands should pattern themselves after the democracies of the Far East where government and business have a romantic embrace that fosters not new children but economic growth. On

Palm Island we kept one-hundred-and-five souls on the payroll with a living wage that brought them life's basics. John and I were not on the payroll and we lived modestly, taking unpresumptuous living expenses. Johnnie and Roger, with their young families, drew only small salaries, a pittance considering the amount of work they produced.

We, workers and managers, could pay the bills and keep the local segment of the economy fueled. In John's social worker mind, our island was an experiment in human cooperation that, if it could be spread, could help reduce the Third World morass of unemployment, overpopulation, and social decline. In our world of mounting social and ethnic conflicts, one approach that we have not tried on a large scale, is the concept that each of us consciously serve as our brother's keeper: each of us making a special effort to reach out to those less fortunate than ourselves.

That was our idea for Palm Island: to set an example of community togetherness for everyone to see. John was hopeful that his idealist do-gooder ravings would set an example. Despite our skepticism, we all pulled our share of the load on Palm. But we secretly knew it would never be the utopia John dreamed of creating. We knew that human greed and ingratitude also had the potential to raise their ugly heads and roil our calm waters into a frothy sea of discontent.

37

Workers' Unrest

We got wind of worker unrest when an anonymous caller phoned and informed us that our workers were having meetings with a labor leader at night on Union Island. We were surprised to say the least. True, our wage structure was not the best. It was an ample living wage for those who were careful, and in line with wages in the area. It was all we could afford with so many on the roll. We even gave a five percent pay increase in 1990. John made a probing round of some twenty workers and asked if they knew anything about a union in the area. The answer was "no" from all, with denials of involvement and protestations of loyalty. We believed them. We had never missed a payroll in thirty years, had never paid ourselves a salary, and had taken a vacation only three times. We plowed all our profits back into the facilities to pay bills and wages.

We could not accept that our workers would abandon us and run off to swallow the ranting of a union leader. John told them the only way we could manage a significant pay increase was to lay off twenty-five percent of the workers, and if they joined a union, we would have to do just that. On July 31, eighty-five workers came to work and sat on the wall of the jetty. Only twenty of our loyal workers continued to work the island. Our accountant was the ringleader, who demeaned his profession by stooping to the level of mindless foolishness by putting the welfare of the people at risk.

"So this is what I get for loyalty?" John said angrily that night.

"Sounds like they've been mislead by a zealot," I added.

"Yeah, and several of them are thumping their Bibles. Christians! You can't trust them. They always talk out of both sides of their mouths."

"Now, John," I admonished, but only weakly.

"It's true. They're all smug, thinking they pulled off a coup."

"But it's the wrong time of the year!" I said, laughing. "They should have done this in December!"

"I know! So much for union brains! Time for some action!" We laughed.

In the morning I watched as John approached the wall of striking workers.

"You need to leave and get to work or risk losing your jobs!" John shouted.

No answer.

"If you are not at work by 9 a.m. tomorrow, you will all be canned!"

Still no answer. John walked away and returned home.

"They're going to strike! I can't believe it!"

"Then there is nothing you can do but follow through with what you told them," I said with finality.

"Yeah, so much for loyalty!"

The next morning no one showed up for work and all eighty-five workers lost their jobs. A nasty strike was now upon us. The "union" members were regaled with rosy prospects from their union leader on Union Island (quite a coincidence at that time). They were loud and confrontational, but we played it low key. They flung up a picket line at the Anchorage Yacht Club wharf to prevent any workers from coming to Palm. They held mock-up signs on sticks and jeered and yelled as we tied the boat up to the wharf. John, Johnnie, and Roger had to step ashore each morning in their midst and shepherd our faithful workers in a close knot behind them through this line of sullen faces. The boys would walk up to the tight front of protesters and at the last moment, chest to chest, they would open a gap and we would walk through, smiling and saying thank you, which caused a ripple of merriment in the crowd.

As I watched from the transport boats the fired workers berated John and the boys as exploiters and greedy bosses. They claimed we were bringing back slavery to black people. He pointed to me in the boat:

"Mary and I are the only slaves on Palm Island! We work seven days a week, twelve hours a day! How many of you do that?" Silence. The next day was the worst. Only twelve ladies and two men showed up for work. As we started to board our launch, all the strikers jumped aboard and very nearly sank the boat. At that moment of confusion, Tony whizzed by with our seventeen-foot Boston Whaler and the fourteen workers hopped on board. With the twelve women and eight stalwart live-in staff, who did not join the mutiny, we operated Palm Island on a skeleton staff. Everyone pitched in, washing dishes, cleaning rooms.

On the third morning, we got police protection to keep unwanted passengers off our launch. People looking for work filtered in on small fishing boats from PSV, Mayreau, and Canouan, and we hired some of them. We flew others in from St. Vincent and smuggled them over to Palm when the strikers were home for lunch. Within a week things on Palm were returning to normalcy. But for an additional six weeks chaos would occasionally rear its ugly head. Then came a melee when Roger attempted to lead one of our ladies through the picket line and was butted off balance. He tumbled down some steps and broke two small bones in his left foot. That was it for John!

"We will not negotiate with any union members who practice physical violence! You people are as bad as terrorists!" John shouted at them the next day.

For the next week we kept a low-key presence. With that the union organizer packed his bags and left, allowing the scene on Palm to return to peaceful normalcy. As it turned out, the soul-crushing impact of the unnecessary and costly strike was a blessing in disguise. We closed down our construction company and offered all house repairs and new building to local contractors, meaning we no longer had to carry the expensive load of 150 workers and a heavy payroll to dig up every two weeks. With a staff

John in his later years, looking fit

permanently reduced to 60 employees, it was easier for all of us. John and the boys came and told me that I was to close the boutique on Sundays and take the day off. We also decided to pay ourselves a monthly salary. We listened to the kindly West Indian advice: "Work is good, but don't kill yourself!"

By 1993 it was obvious that time was taking its toll on both John and me. He was slowing down with great protestations and my ankles were deteriorating. Problems with walking prompted me to buy a golf cart from Florida to zip between houses, office, and boutique. John hummed along like a hardy diesel engine, with a few skips here and there. He became an addict to naturalistic medicine, taking vitamins in large quantities, especially Vitamin C, and performing daily exercise. He transformed himself from a nervous wreck with ulcers, kidney stones, and tension headaches to someone with some sense of peace. As I had told him many times before, his haphazard and stressful lifestyle was crippling him. He stopped drinking coffee and liquor, ate wholesome vegetarian foods, and cut out most fats from his diet. He also reduced his physical stress by napping twice a day for twenty minutes each period.

Nobel Prize winner Linus Pauling greatly influenced his eating behavior. A guest put him through aerobic dances, twists, turns, and shadow boxing on a four-foot by five-foot mat. He would do flex movements of his arms and legs, deep bends, sit-ups, stretching, leg raises, and deep breathing exercises. He also did aquatic exercises every morning. The boys and I were thrilled with his new attitude. John became more approachable, kinder, and peaceful. His kidney stones disappeared (he would be in such pain that when I asked him if I could help he would shout "Get the hell out!" without even looking to see who it was). Later, I would say, "My goodness, you were grumpy." His whole lifestyle changed and that changed his attitude. Maybe we *are* what we eat!

John's ambition was to carry on to 90, still hanging on as the boss of Palm, still sailing, still building dreams. "After 90," he would say, "the devil can have the rest." In his later years John lost his chip-on-shoulder pugnacity and no longer bristled up to an argument just to argue. His need to change the excesses of a world slowly growing mad began to leave him. He would have loved the opportunity to appear on international TV and simply urge that everyone be kind, gentle, unselfish, peaceful, generous, and happy. If he gained only one recruit, that was worth it. His greatest sense of achievement was the development of Palm Island with the boys and me.

Even in his later years, John still had wanderlust for the open ocean. He wanted to sail again in the South Seas or explore the remote Patagonian channels. But he had to settle for far less. The weight of years gradually foreclosed on any lengthy offshore cruising. He did decide to sail to Aves Island, however, an island just 125 miles west of the north end of Dominica, which lies between the French islands of Martinique and Guadeloupe in our Windward Islands chain. By serendipity he found a vessel. She was an ATM charter yacht that had crashed on the Howlands Reef fronting Clifton Harbor and been abandoned in deep water for six months. John claimed her, got a trawler, dragged her to Palm, and with our tractor pulled her ashore. He cleaned up the coral growth inside and out, patched the hole with layers of fiberglass mat, and rebuilt the dinette and galley with marine plywood all glassed over to add strength. *Voilà!* In three months of meticulous work John had a new boat!

We dubbed her RESURRECTION with a bottle of local-brewed Hairoun beer. As with our previous cruises, we wanted to use just a plastic sextant and navigation tables. RESURRECTION had no engine. When John salvaged her he took out the prop and shaft and plugged the hole. He had no appreciation for engines! John bought Don Street's *Cruising Guide of Eastern Caribbean Waters*, a Windward Islands bible that explored every rock and nook in the waters between Martinique to Trinidad. Don was a frequent visitor to Palm Island and a legend known and respected throughout the West Indies. He sailed his ninety-year-old yawl, IOLAIRE, a wooden-hulled boat without an engine for nearly forty flawless years. He had sailed solo across the Atlantic too many times to count and he was a close friend of John's.

We set off for Aves on Sunday, April 25, 1993, a gorgeous day in the Caribbean. We scudded along at a lively eight knots (estimated, of course; we had no speed indicators). John would calculate our speed by wadding up little squares of paper he held in his pocket and dropping them overboard, timing their movement. He did this previously as we sailed around the world on TROPIC SEAS and OUTWARD BOUND. Battery power supplied by a small solar panel on deck gave us running lights and three lights below. We mostly used flashlights, but only if absolutely necessary. We set watches as we had in the past: two hours on and two hours off. One of our workers, Ezzy, new to sailing, was a little uneasy at first:

"Me ain't see nothin' so before, mon; me 'fraid it, mon."

"Cool it mon," John called back.

It was Ezzy's first trip on the open sea. I understood his trepidation.

John kept the log up-to-date every two hours, just as he always had in the past. At seventy-five he was just as particular as ever, keeping details, constantly checking the *Nautical Almanac*. We ate like vegetarians, mostly vegetables and fruits, some fish. Every food source had its reason: raw onion for its purported natural antibiotic properties, clove of garlic for its supposed ability to clean the blood and serve as an anti-cancer agent. Everything was thought out. The next day we spotted Aves Island with its huge Venezuelan concrete living quarters for twelve marine personnel. We anchored in a hostile setting of conflicting swells on the west shore. RESURRECTION rolled gunwale to gunwale while we embarked on our inflatable to visit the bizarre-looking tower, filled with eager Spanish-speaking young men who had not had any visitors for over a month.

The Comandante greeted us warmly and John immediately showed him five coconut plants he had brought with us to plant on the sandbar. He also gave them gifts of magazines, bananas and mangoes, and some liquor, which they appreciated above all else. The island was true to its name: Aves (Bird) Island had a sky filled with mutton birds, roseate terns, laughing gulls, long-winged, and long-billed frigate birds. All around us were chicks squatting patiently in the hot sun while their parents fished. The whole view of the sea, sand, and wildlife brought back vivid memories of PAGAN, TROPIC SEAS, and OUTWARD BOUND. These were the adventures of our lifetime that could not be repeated; but here, on this small sandbar in the ocean, were remnants of those dreams.

But it was soon over, almost disappointing, as if we were leaving behind a part of our life we would never see again. At 2:00 p.m. we headed back to RESURRECTION in the inflatable and freed her from the inhospitable, coral-strewn bottom. Two anchors weighed and jib aloft, we swung to face the open sea, hoisting the mainsail on the run and waving to our new Venezuelan friends on the strange platform. I am sure they wanted to be with us. At first the wind was fresh at twenty knots and we plowed through a bouncy early evening without rain, under a beautiful half-moon with a suffused yellow halo, bright stars and castle-like clouds. The Southern Cross was right ahead and Scorpio clawed out of the sea to port; astern, the Big Dipper pointed down to Polaris.

"How many of the world's weary humanity do you think would like to be with us right now?" John asked me.

"Probably all of them," I responded, laughing quietly.

We sat there on deck with open satisfaction while Ezzy looked for sharks: he was constantly wary of sharks and had a built-in fear of them. Of course, John too never liked sharks, although he had stopped looking out for sharks years ago. Several days later we entered the clear, beautiful waters of the Grenadines. We ran briskly all day at south by east and on May 2 we arrived: Mustique on the port quarter, Canouan on the bow, and Palm Island fifteen miles to southward. Ezzy passed up bottles of ginseng offered by John-the-Almost-Vegetarian, but we all celebrated with clasping hands the return to Palm Island, our *home*.

38

Wakata Reef Revisited

Shortly after settling in from the Aves Island venture, a letter arrived from Fiji, one that brought John pains of memory and conscience. It concerned the crash of PAGAN 48 years ago and came from Jone Vale (pronounced Joanie Valley), one of Etika and Unaisie's sons, whose parents had nursed John back to health after forty-nine days adrift at sea. In the letter was a tragic sentence that stood out above all the others:

"Fren John, you mus come Loma Loma. Ole people who help save you want see you before them die."

I saw a wave of sickness descend over John's face. I have never seen him look lonelier than at that moment. John realized that not only had the years ticked away, but that he had forgotten the deep ties his tragic arrival on Tuvutha had welded with those remote and kind people.

"I've got to go back," he said.

"Yes, you must," I replied.

Etikia and Unaisie had passed away years ago; John knew this from previous correspondence. But he also realized that he had some unfinished emotional business to settle in Tuvutha. He had become a local legend and the people had an emotional deed title to John's life. He left with several friends from St. Louis on June 15, 1993, with a single suitcase and a carry-on full of gifts. When he returned he was a changed man:

"It's still a lush island . . . I couldn't believe the views from the mountains . . . the same silvery beaches and foaming reefs."

"Oh, I'm so happy for you."

"But you know, things have changed. I'm now known in Fiji as Jone Kai Papalagi—the white man from the sea!"

"How funny!"

"It seems my wrecking PAGAN at Wakata Reef played into ancient sea lore and everywhere I heard people whispering Jone Kai Papalagi. I was also known as Coci."

"*KoChee?*"

"They pronounced it *thothee*. It's a monster from one of the outlying islands. When things are good on the island Coci gets blamed; when things are bad on the island, he is also blamed. On Tuvutha, Coci is supposed to eat little children if they are naughty or venture near his three caves, which amazingly enough are located exactly where I was shipwrecked at Wakata Reef!"

"So you are a living *legend!*"

"Yes, I am a legend. When the children first found me dying on the beach they thought it was Coci incarnate poised to swoop down on them. They thought because they were naughty that Coci was alive and ready to gobble them up!"

"Oh, how *bizarre!*"

"Even better, I got to sail with a skipper who wouldn't let me do anything except sit back and relax. We went right by the little islet of Nukulau . . . remember that?"

"Of course . . . that's where we had the earthquake and the tidal wave!"

"Brings back great memories, doesn't it?"

"Beautiful memories. We were so free then!"

"And so were the villagers. But now there are earphones, discos, and instead of woven pandanus strips for village homes they have corrugated galvanized walls . . . the romance of the South Seas is gone . . . gone forever. We were so lucky to have seen it then before civilization reached out with its homogenizing claws of mediocrity."

"That is very disappointing," I remarked.

"The old ways are going fast. Remember how a whole village would construct a home for a new family? Not any more. It's more like every man for himself, like the rest of the world. But at least the kava is the same!" He laughed and patted my stomach.

"Kava is *awful!*" I said disgustedly.

"At one ceremony they recounted my adventures and they would clap their cupped hands together so loud it sounded like thunder. Then they made me tell my story again for the archives and I ended up teary eyed and they broke into a rousing island song. I've rarely been touched like that in life."

"Maybe you're softening in your old age," I replied giving him a squeeze.

"Maybe . . . I also revisited the exact site where I clawed my way out of the sea. I forgot how spiky and slippery the rocks were. From there I could see the hardwood keel with broken bronze keelbolts pointing at crazy angles to the sky. It was the grave of PAGAN."

"I remember the place . . . it gave me the shakes!"

"It was a beautiful but hard week there. When I left the men shook my hand and slapped me on the back and I had all these lovely ladies wrap me in their chubby arms to choke away the tears in my eyes. I felt so loved there. And they sang out 'farewell dear friend, safe passage, we will never forget, come back to Loma Loma again, we will remember you always, take our love with you and re-member our sadness!' It was just a remarkable experience. I had no idea I meant so much to those people!"

"I think you'd be surprised how much you mean to people around here too. I know it isn't always obvious and that we've had our hard times, but we do love you."

With that, John C. ("all alone" John C.) wiped a tear or two from his eyes and gave me a big hug, rocking me slowly back and forth in his arms. Then he stopped.

"You know, Mary, if I could live my life over I would change few things: I would change all the insulting remarks I have made, my frequent bouts with loss of temper, ungrateful responses, arro-gance, and things like that. But I wouldn't change anything else. I am happy here on Palm Island. I do know that the main thing hold-ing us back is ourselves. That's why I was so hard on the boys, to push harder, work harder, discipline themselves, make sacrifices, learn and all that. I just overdid it and was too stubborn to back up. I should have listened a lot more to you and worked more like a team member than a commander."

"Well, I think we know you realize that now. It's never too late . . ."

"No. But you know I've never cared about money for money's sake. I never cared if I were a millionaire or not. That's not a sign of achievement in my book. I prided high ideals more than money, certainly anyone who knows me understands that."

"Absolutely . . . there can be no mistaking that!"

"The problem is this: I am an anachronism now. I don't fit in anywhere. There are too many rules, regulations, and signs these days. I liked good old friendly relations, and agreements with a handshake. That's all gone. We're still destroying ourselves with greed and the need for power and domination. I am thankful that we live on this peaceful island. At seventy-six, I still feel young and I want to live to be ninety . . . and still bossing people around!"

I laughed and choked back the tears, dabbing my runny nose.

"I still want adventure. I want to see the other side of every hill, strive for new experiences, whet my appetite for challenge. I don't want to follow the crowd! And I don't want to be *in* the crowd. I want to be flexible, easy-going, helpful, and able to change. I want to be faithful to myself."

"And I want you to as well."

39

Farewell Johnny Coconut
Farewell Palm

On the morning of October 28, 1998, a worker rushed into the Palm Island Boutique and screamed, "John, he fall down!" With a pounding heart I jumped into my golf cart and sped to the house. Johnnie and wife Margaret had already arrived and the island doctor was there conferring in hushed tones with another doctor who happened to be a guest in the hotel. John sat quietly on a couch, looking like a defeated little man, hunched over, in a daze, rubbing his right hand over and over again with his left hand. I pulled him close to me and whispered anxiously, "John, John . . . can you hear me?" There was no response. He just stared at me blankly with that a quizzical look of detachment. Minutes seemed eternal, but it soon became clear to all that John was confused, physically weak, and rapidly getting worse.

Months earlier, in the middle of the night, John had suffered a bite to his leg from a feral cat. The crazed cat would not release its grip and John had to beat it off with a boot. The wound never healed properly and despite hospitalization, John in his typical fashion eschewed continuing his doctor-mandated antibiotic treatment. Now he had suffered a stroke, apparently induced by latent toxemia from the cat bite. The doctors told us there likely was anticoagulant medication in Barbados, medication that if administered as soon as possible could mitigate the long-term effects of the stroke. The medical personnel in Barbados promised to rush it by plane to the hospital.

Johnnie arranged for a small two-seater private plane to take John to the hospital in St. Vincent. Justin, Johnnie's pilot son, met the plane at the St. Vincent airport and helped John into an ambulance. They rushed to the hospital where the doctors administered the anticoagulant medication. We arrived shortly afterward and things seemed to calm down. Several hours later, with John resting peacefully, we returned to Palm, leaving Justin to stay for the remainder of the day. At seven-thirty, Justin called:

"Grandma," he started, "when I was taking Grandpa to the hospital he kept looking around Kingstown, and he seemed really bewildered. He'd glance at me nervously with a confused stare as if this was the last time he'd see home. It was really sad!"

"Yes, I know. He looked so small and pathetic. Is he still resting?" I asked.

"Yes, he seems to be comfortable."

"That's a relief," I said. "We'll be back shortly."

John passed away in his sleep just moments before we arrived. We never had a chance to say goodbye and he went into the night alone. We were all devastated, but particularly Johnnie, who realized at that moment how much both of them had lost as two headstrong men vying for years to govern a 130-acre island. Johnnie lamented openly at not being able to turn the clock back to rekindle the love he had as a child for his father.

Prior to John's burial, grandson Justin flew the casket over the surrounding peacefulness of the Caribbean, the ocean John loved above all others. Justin approached and circled Palm, banking steeply to give John one last view of his beloved island. The family and staff went out into the middle of the old airfield during the flight and watched the plane circle as John made his last farewell. While the plane droned overhead, Johnnie understood for the first time, perhaps, the love that John had for Palm Island and what it had meant to him. Johnnie later confided in me that he wanted to stay on Palm for the rest of his life and finish his father's work.

John's burial day was November 1, 1998. He was 81 years of age. There was a viewing of John's body at the church prior to the service. The heads of seven different denominations were there that day, officiating in the service, and one of them commented that this was the first time it had ever happened. A massive funeral procession of hundreds of people from around the world followed the casket down to the gravesite overlooking Palm Island. Heavy rains had fallen for days prior to his burial and the ground was saturated to the point that standing water covered the bottom of John's grave. When they laid the coffin to rest it began to float around and almost instantly the good people of Palm Island smiled at each other as a mourner pointed to the bobbing coffin and said:

"John he takin' his last sail!" Instant smiles and muted laughter mixed oddly with the communal tears still on the mourners' faces. Moments later, we sang joyously from a hymnal:

Now the labourer's task is o'er
Now the battle-day is past
Now upon the farthest shore
Lands the voyager at last.

We had endured many family difficulties over the years on Palm Island, but John's death seemed so extraordinary, so unbelievable. John was not supposed to die (people often joked that he was too ornery to die). The entire family had a great deal of difficulty adjusting to a world without John on the island. He always seemed to be in such good health and indeed called the road around the island Highway 90—he intended to walk or run around this road on his ninetieth birthday! That was his competitive nature, even with his own death.

We all knew that John's death marked the end of an era in the Grenadines. Our staff later celebrated his burial site by planting coconut trees around it, just as John surely would have done.

A few years later Palm Island was taken over by a developer who promised much and delivered little. With broken promises of payment for the sale of Palm Island, Johnnie, his family, and I were forced to move from our island to Inverness, Florida. Here we settled down on a small parcel of property we had owned for years and where Roger currently lived. Johnnie was the most affected by the move. He would never be able to fulfill his dream of taking over for his father and finishing what his father never had a chance to do.

Johnnie would move back to Palm Island in a heartbeat if it were ever possible, and likely, a large part of the family, including me, would join him. The people of Union and St. Vincent were always very supportive, compassionate, and generous to our family. I miss their politeness, their fun-loving nature, and their great sense of humor. They are always family oriented, and always made my family feel welcome. And the people of St. Vincent obviously had a tremendous love for John. We still recall fondly that people from all over the West Indies had come to John's funeral, by plane, by boat, by bicycle. People went to such great lengths to see that our emotional needs were met. They always treated us like family.

I still talk to John, perhaps out of habit, perhaps out of knowing that somewhere in time and space he is still there, selling his beliefs to some celestial audience. Age has set in and I find it difficult to get around as I used to. I frequently look at old pictures of my early life's voyage and question aloud whether we actually did everything portrayed in the pictures. Those times on the open ocean with children were certainly our best. We miss them deeply. But we have so many incredible and indelible memories. Roger even carved accurate replicas of our boats TROPIC SEAS and OUT-WARD BOUND now displayed on a shelf in an old barn that he converted into a facsimile of a West Indian rum shop. Here, in a sadly reminiscent way, we can relive our sailing adventures and the building of Palm Island.

It often feels like we live in a time warp: Pictures of our life adventures clutter the walls of the rum shop and all our adventures seem so fresh, but each night we go to bed without seeing the brilliance of the stars over an open ocean, without smelling the ocean air, and without hearing the constancy of the Caribbean surf. A great deal of our souls has perished along the way. We are stranded now just as John was stranded with his crippled PAGAN on the open ocean, hopeful of rescue.

No matter, we have remained a united family throughout it all, and that fact is our ultimate solace.

Other books of interest from Sheridan House

DESPERATE VOYAGE
by John Caldwell

John Caldwell's harrowing account of finding himself stranded in Panama after World War II and setting out single-handed on a 9,000-mile journey aboard the 29-foot PAGAN to rejoin Mary in Sydney.

"An astounding tale of courage and adventure."   *Sailing Today*

"Some have called [Caldwell's] desperate voyage foolhardy, claiming that despite his mission, his lack of preparation had stacked the odds against him. No matter; the fact that he made it and wrote about it is our luck."   *SAIL*

"Could rank alongside the best thrillers for sheer irrepressibility of its hero . . . You'll find it hard to put this one down."   *Motor Boats Monthly*

THE LONG WAY
by Bernard Moitessier

"Moitessier was the original mystical mariner and inventor of the charismatic French boat-bum persona: French cruisers have pretty much had a bad reputation ever since, but there's no denying Moitessier's impact on bluewater sailing. This account of his most legendary exploit, in which he blew off winning the 1969 singlehanded non stop Golden Globe round-the-world race so he could 'save his soul' in high southern latitudes, is a bible to ocean sailors with a metaphysical bent. His decision to quit the race and keep on sailing, in more ways than one, marks the point at which ocean racing and ocean cruising went their separate ways."   *Cruising World*

SURVIVE THE SAVAGE SEA
by Dougal Robertson

In June 1972, when killer whales attacked the Robertson family's 43-foot schooner LUCETTE, it sank within 60 seconds.

"For stark excitement, marine natural history, practical lessons, and human love and stresses, few records, if any, of hazard and survival have ever bettered it."   *Washington Post*

"Well-written . . . an unexpectedly personal view of a man's physical and a woman's emotional courage that, when bonded, produced the strength to survive."   *Sailing*

WANDERER
by Sterling Hayden

The controversial autobiography of Sterling Hayden. Just as he approached the peak of his career as a movie star, Hayden suddenly abandoned Hollywood, walked out on his marriage, defied the courts, and set sail with his four children aboard the schooner WANDERER.

"An impressive writer. Like Fitzgerald, Hayden is a romantic. His writing about the sea evokes echoes of Conrad and McFee, of London and Galsworthy . . . Beautifully done."   *Los Angeles Times*

"A superb piece of writing . . . Echoes from Poe and Melville to Steinbeck and Mailer. A work of fascination on every level."   *New York Post*

America's Favorite Sailing Books
www.sheridanhouse.com